An Introduction to Family Social Work

An Introduction to Family Social Work

Donald Collins
University of Calgary

Catheleen Jordan
University of Texas at Arlington

Heather Coleman
University of Calgary

THOMSON

BROOKS/COLE

Australia • Canada • Mexico • Singapore • Spain • United Kingdom • United States

Edited by Janet Tilden
Production supervision by Kim Vander Steen
Designed by Lucy Lesiak Design
Composition by Point West, Inc.
Printed and bound by Courier, Westford

ISBN: 0-87581-424-7
Library of Congress Catalog Card Number: 98-68668

Wadsworth/Thomson Learning
10 Davis Drive
Belmont CA 94002-3098
USA

For information about our products, contact us:
Thomson Learning Academic Resource Center
1-800-423-0563
http://www.wadsworth.com

For permission to use material from this text, contact us by
Web: http://www.thomsonrights.com
Fax: 1-800-730-2215
Phone: 1-800-730-2214

Printed in the United States of America
10 9 8 7 6 5 4

Contents

6 THE BEGINNING PHASE *100*

7 THE ASSESSMENT PHASE *122*

8 THE INTERVENTION PHASE   *143*

9 PROMOTING BEHAVIORAL CHANGE   *163*

14 SPECIAL SITUATIONS IN FAMILY SOCIAL WORK   *247*

It is a sobering thought that the social worker's power of influence may extend, through his daily acts, to many whom he has never seen and never, even for a moment, had in mind. This is particularly true of all the members who are unknown to him in the family group of his clients. For better or worse, he influences them and they, in turn, help or hinder the achievements of the ends that he has in view.

Mary Richmond, 1917

Preface

The *family* has been a focus of social work practice since the beginnings of the profession. Social work pioneers such as Mary Richmond argued for a family focus five decades before the modern family therapy movement, yet social work often has been humble in acknowledging its contributions to families. The profession needs to reclaim its heritage.

Many current textbooks on the family emphasize family therapy, a highly specialized activity that is usually practiced at the graduate social work level. Although nearly 400 accredited baccalaureate social work programs in the United States and Canada train students to work with families, few courses and textbooks specifically target the role that BSWs will play in assisting families after graduation. Thus, the primary goal of this book is to provide undergraduate social work students with sufficient beginning knowledge and skills to work with families in a variety of settings outside the traditional office environment.

Undergraduate social workers often are employed in agencies that do not provide office-based family therapy, and few BSW student field placements are offered in traditional family therapy (office-based) settings. Rather, many beginning social workers are employed in agencies that provide support, teaching, and concrete services to families with a variety of needs and problems. Settings for family intervention include child welfare, family support, women's shelters, schools, and correctional facilities, to name a few. Similarly, many families experience multiple problems within the family as well as within the community. Social work students and new graduates may be overwhelmed by the number and types of problems experienced by the families they encounter. Difficulties for many overburdened families come from many directions and are not exclusively in the domain of relationship dysfunction or disrupted homeostasis, which are the focal points of traditional family therapy approaches. Families require a wide range of services to deal with different types of problems.

New social workers may find it difficult to anticipate what it will be like to see an overburdened family for the first time. They may have basic questions about what they need to know to prepare to see a family for the first, second, or third time. In addition, they may wonder how to engage families, earn their trust, and encourage meaningful and lasting changes. Social workers need access to practical information and skills to help families deal with a particular issue or set of issues.

This book is intended for undergraduate social work students and new social work graduates who are (or will soon be) working with families for the first time. In it, we provide a framework for thinking about "family," as well as practical suggestions to guide family social work practice.

Most social work programs offer interviewing courses that focus on one-to-one interviews, often with adult clients. Family social work courses often rely on theoretical texts explicating family therapy models. This focus is an important aspect of social work education, but it is often too abstract and office-specific to assist students to learn about the basics of family social work. The instructor is challenged to be comprehensive enough to equip learners with sufficient knowledge and skills to work with families and also be specific enough to address concrete situations that students may encounter.

In this book, we attempt to present in a clear, succinct manner the knowledge and practical skills needed to engage in family social work. This book can be used in a beginning interview course or a family course as an introductory text on basic family social work theory and practice. It can also be used as a preparatory text before exposing students to the range of theoretical models offered in family therapy texts.

The structure of the book orients the reader to the step-by-step process of family social work (FSW). Chapters 1 and 2 offer a philosophical perspective of family social work and an understanding of family functioning. Students in family social work need to have a context in which to place their practice and framework for action. In Chapters 3 and 4, we describe the assessment process. In Chapters 5 through 10, we discuss fundamental issues such as protecting clients' confidentiality, and we describe the various phases of social work with families: beginning, assessment, intervention, and termination. In Chapters 11 and 12, we explore gender-sensitive and culturally sensitive family social work practice. In Chapter 13, we consider special situations that family social workers are likely to encounter in family social work with children. Finally, in Chapter 14 we discuss situations that family social workers often encounter when working with adult clients.

This book is designed to assist students and other new family social workers to understand general dynamics and principles of family social work. It can be used in a family social work course with each chapter providing the structure for a weekly class. Throughout each chapter a number of exercises are suggested to give students an opportunity to apply the concepts presented in the chapter. Finally, this text can serve as a primer to a family therapy text.

The authors are indebted to the support given by Ted Peacock, who has generously welcomed us into his "family" of authors. Without Dick Welna's commitment, guidance, and leadership, this project would not have come to fruition. It was a pleasure to work with our exceptional editor, Janet Tilden. We also want to thank Kim Vander Steen, who handled the production of the book, and Carey Scott, our secretary at the University of Calgary. Finally, we are indebted to our children, Tara, Michael, Ryan, Kate, and Chris, who have taught us the meaning of family.

1

The Field
of Family
Social Work

When students begin their first placements in family social work, the following questions are often uppermost in their minds:

- What is the purpose of family social work?
- How does family social work differ from family therapy?
- What is my role as a family social worker?
- Will I be able to work effectively with families that are different from my own?
- How can I work with an entire family, all at the same time?
- How will I know what questions to ask family members?
- How can I encourage family members to participate if they are resistant?
- What should I do if family members get angry?
- How do I prioritize a family's problems?
- What do I need to know when making a home visit?
- How can I protect my own safety when making home visits in dangerous neighborhoods?
- Do I know enough to really help families?
- What do I need to keep in mind when interviewing children?
- How can I help a family deal with a crisis?
- Is family social work different with families of diverse ethnic or racial backgrounds?

In this book, we will address these and other questions about family social work. Our goal is to help you be as effective as possible in assisting families.

WHAT IS FAMILY SOCIAL WORK?

The primary purpose of family social work is to help families learn to function more competently while meeting the developmental and emotional needs of *all* members. Family social work is not the same as family therapy, which uses office-based intervention to help families make systemic changes.

Family social work targets the following objectives:

1. Reinforce family strengths to get families ready for change (or intervention);

2. Provide additional support following family therapy so families maintain effective family functioning;

3. Create concrete changes in family functioning to sustain effective and satisfying daily routines.

Family social work is often both home-based and community-based, occurring within the daily routine and natural environment of families. Although the family social worker (FSW) may sometimes interview a family in an office, much of the work is carried out in the family's home. Home-based intervention allows the FSW to become familiar with daily aspects of family functioning. This knowledge is particularly helpful when crises occur. The FSW often concentrates on concrete needs and daily functioning of client families as targets for change, a focus matching the needs and expectations of many high-risk families (Wood & Geismar, 1986).

There are many ways in which a family social worker can provide on-the-spot, concrete assistance. For example, when a teenager and a parent become involved in a conflict, the FSW has an opportunity to identify the problem and intervene. A FSW can help the parent and child discover what led up to the argument and identify ongoing repetitive and problematic interaction patterns that keep arguments going. Once these tasks have been achieved, the FSW can work with the parent and teenager to replace dysfunctional behavior with more rewarding behavior. When a young child throws a temper tantrum, the FSW can teach the parent more effective methods of dealing with problematic behavior on the spot. Additionally, a FSW may be available when a family member threatens suicide and can thus intervene at a point of crisis. When a parent loses a job or the lease is not renewed, the family shares this experience with the FSW. While office-based family therapy deals with family scenarios after they have happened, regular family events are not easily reproduced in the office. Ultimately, the FSW supports and teaches the family when and where problems emerge.

Since the home is where problems often develop, it is also a setting where solutions can be designed and carried out. Because the family social worker operates primarily within the family home or community, he or she can make an *immediate* difference in the lives of troubled families within their *natural environment*.

Although family social work addresses a range of individual and family problems in the home, including challenges facing the frail elderly and adult psychiatric patients, our focus in this book is on family social work involving children. We approach family work from a child-valuing perspective, and our guiding philosophy is to promote the well-being of children. We believe that children have the right to live in healthy, supportive, and growth-promoting environments. We also believe that parents have the right to receive assistance to raise children. Consequently, the foundation of family social work is the principle that "Children are helped when their families function well." Parenting is difficult and requires a range of skills together with a strong social support system. Parenting skills are neither instinctive nor intuitive; these skills must be taught and nurtured. In a nutshell, "The problem with being a parent is that by the time you're experienced, you're unemployed" (Efron & Rowe, 1987). A FSW can speed up the learning process for parents.

Historically, society has assumed that parenting is instinctive, adding to the myth that parents should function without the need for outside assistance. In other words, society expects every parent to raise children with the least amount of input from the state or other external agencies. This unfortunate assumption contributes to the belief that support is necessary only for "bad," "failing," or "incompetent" parents.

It is puzzling that, while failing to ensure that parents receive necessary support, society holds high expectations for them. When parents have difficulties, social institutions are often punitive or intrusive. For example, child welfare systems may remove at-risk children from their homes, rather than provide adequate resources in the home to resolve family problems and keep families intact (Fraser, Pecora, & Haapala, 1991).

Society waits until parents fail, instead of providing timely assistance to parents. Interventions that are punitive fail to change parent or child problems. Thus, the function of many agencies is to monitor, correct, or evaluate families *after* a problem has been identified. At worst, agencies may remove a child from a home without first providing support and aid proactively to *prevent* the child's removal. Rather than "lend a hand," the motto often seems to have been "point a finger."

Family social work, as a profession, is built on the idea that parents, children, and the family as a unit deserve support to avoid later (and often more severe) "correction." Families need support from peers, neighbors, communities, and agencies. They have a right to receive aid from family agencies that provide a family-centered approach. In keeping with a holistic philosophy, family social work departs from traditional approaches that counsel family members individually, separated from the family unit and isolated from the social context.

Based on these assumptions, a family-centered approach toward family social work is both necessary and practical. Family social workers may work with families who have experienced longstanding problems and multiple interventions from diverse helping systems. Because of previous experiences, vulnerable families frequently have become either "treatment shy" or "treatment sophisticated." They may be hesitant to discuss family problems with a professional who, in their view, operates from within the detached environment of an office, removed from the family's natural life experiences.

SOCIETAL ATTITUDES TOWARD FAMILIES

1. Do you believe that today's families live in a profamily or an antifamily society? Back up your opinion with specific examples.

2. How is life different for today's families, as compared to family life ten years ago? What are some positive and negative changes?

The family social worker is in an advantageous position to assist families who are hard to reach or reluctant to accept help. Families usually feel more secure in their own environment and may be more willing to interact with a social worker in their home. Receiving help on their own turf eases engagement in a working partnership and allows families to participate actively in the helping process. Meeting families on their own ground also demystifies intervention and empowers clients to bring about changes that shape their lives.

Helping families to identify and nurture both informal and formal support networks in communities is important for maintaining improved family functioning. The ultimate goal of family social work is to develop a healthy and satisfying environment for family members through support, education, and development of new skills. Family social work is complex, however, and no individual member's needs should take precedence over the needs of other members (Johnson, 1986). This difficult balancing act challenges all FSWs. The family social worker fulfills many valuable functions while working with families and ensuring that the rights and needs of all family members are met.

The tasks of family social workers culminate in support of families to allow children to remain at home safely and to ensure that the family is a functional unit within the community. Sometimes family social work may involve reuniting a child with a family after foster care. Alternatively, families may be assisted before or during foster or adoptive placement.

HISTORICAL BACKGROUND OF FAMILY SOCIAL WORK

The social work profession emerged in the late nineteenth century as part of a movement toward improving the lot of the poor and underprivileged (Nichols & Schwartz, 1998). The practice of family social work dates from the days of the "friendly visitor" and the beginnings of the social work profession (Richmond, 1917). From the beginning, Mary Richmond argued for a family perspective. Social work emerged to address problems associated with the industrial revolution such as poverty, crime, and mental and physical disability. By the early 1800s, the first social welfare agencies became part of the landscape of an industrialized society. These agencies, often initiated by clergymen and religious organizations, were privately run and funded by charities and philanthropists. Until the early 1900s, helpers and affluent "do-gooders" functioned with little training and operated without a theoretical understanding of human behavior. The science of helping people was underdeveloped. Early private services first focused on addressing basic physical needs by providing necessities such as food and shelter. Emotional and personal difficulties were thought to be dealt with best through religious counsel because social problems were considered moral problems. Families were expected to develop a "moral" life-style modeled after that of the friendly visitors.

Early social workers struggled to eliminate problems related to poverty, illiteracy, disease, exploited labor, slum housing and overcrowding, unemployment, and poverty. Paralleling the development of social reform was the establishment of Charity Organization Societies (COS). The COS evolved from the desire to elevate almsgiving (now known as Welfare) to scientific, efficient, and preventive levels. The COS movement was the precursor to modern clinical social work (Ledbetter Hancock & Pelton, 1989). COS workers believed that poverty was more effectively alleviated through personal rehabilitation of the poor than through providing relief. The guiding purpose of the COS movement was to eliminate poverty by investigating the character of poor families and educating them. Case conferences and "friendly visiting" illuminated problems of the poor and clarified methods of rehabilitation. In fact, early caseworkers knew something that it took psychiatry fifty years to understand—families must be considered as whole units (Nichols & Schwartz, 1998; Richmond, 1917).

From its inception in 1877, the COS movement proliferated across the country. Private agencies united forces to form Charity Organization Societies. They were designed to fulfill the following functions:

- Providing direct services to individuals and families (forerunners of social casework and family counseling);
- Coordinating private agency attempts to ameliorate social problems (precursors to community organization and social planning).

Charity organizations investigated applicants for services and financial aid, maintained a central client registry to avoid duplication of services, and used "friendly visitor" volunteers to work intensively with needy families (Ledbetter Hancock & Pelton, 1989). Friendly visitors gave sympathy, not money, and encouraged the poor to live frugally and to seek employment. Friendly visitors, most of whom were women, perceived poverty as evidence of personal shortcomings and moral deficits.

In the 1950s and 1960s, the social work profession focused again on multiproblem families. Work by Geismar and his colleagues was influential in helping social workers understand families by examining the social competence of members (parents in particular) to accomplish tasks related to socially expected functions. How effectively family members performed certain tasks was thought to determine the well-being of individual family members (Wood & Geismar, 1986).

FAMILY SOCIAL WORK AND FAMILY THERAPY

Modern family social work is rooted in the early "friendly visitor" movement and work with the multiproblem family (Wood & Geismar, 1986). Today, trained professionals "visit" families to offer concrete support and instructional assistance. Sometimes social work is initiated when a family first enters the helping network, and social work interventions may eventually lead to family therapy. In other situations, family social work is introduced during or after family therapy.

Family social work differs from family therapy in several ways. The broad focus of family social work emphasizes the complex interrelationships of individual personalities and social systems. Family social work also focuses upon clearly defined, concrete events and interactions in the daily routine of a family, whereas family therapy is more formal, conducted in an office setting, and is often concerned with abstract patterns and structures of relationships and family functioning.

The family therapist restructures roles and relationships in the family based on the assumption that altered roles and relationships will result in more effective family functioning and eventually the elimination of presenting problems. Family therapists believe that individual problems often arise from dysfunction of a family unit. For family therapists, the family unit is the target of change, and they seldom concentrate on individual family members. By comparison, FSWs are free to concentrate on specific problematic issues such as parent-child conflicts or school-related problems. Thus, the FSW can respond to an assortment of family member needs and relationships. Often their responses involve concrete problem solving, rendering support, and teaching skills and competencies to individuals, dyads, or the entire family. The FSW also helps the family access concrete services and resources available within the community, such as job training or substance abuse programs.

Family therapy and family social work fulfill roles that are both important and distinct. Therefore, it is critical that the roles of the family social worker and the family therapist be clearly understood to avoid causing role confusion and working at cross-purposes. Clarity of roles is especially important when a family therapist and a family social worker are involved simultaneously with the same family. In such instances, family therapists and FSWs must work together to provide focused and mutually reinforcing interventions for the family.

FAMILY SOCIAL WORK AND FAMILY THERAPY

Differentiating between family therapy and family social work is important. They play equally important but different roles in helping families. List four of the goals and worker's roles of each discipline.

REALITIES OF FAMILY SOCIAL WORK PRACTICE

Family social work differs from the traditional family therapy model of the fifty-minute, once-a-week interview with the family in a therapist's office in that FSWs often work in the home and become attuned to the fabric of the family's home environment and daily interactions. Work is done with the family when the need for help is most acute and when the family is most receptive to intervention and change. This often means that the FSW becomes directly involved in the home beyond the once-a-week session that a family therapist traditionally provides. It is not unusual for the FSW to be available to families (around the clock) during crises. Meeting these time demands can be stressful for the family social worker.

The nature of their involvement acquaints FSWs with life experiences of families through directly witnessing the impact of daily events. The FSW provides support, knowledge, and skills in the "here-and-now." Because FSWs are familiar with daily family events and functioning, families do not need to wait for a weekly appointment to work on family problems. When FSWs are not on-site, they can be a phone call away, enabling them to be available during critical family incidents. Thus, family social work is "hands-on," practical, and action-oriented.

Not surprisingly, families often see family social work as more informal and less intimidating than family therapy, in part because of the emphasis on developing a worker-family coalition. FSWs use engagement and relationship skills to create a problem-solving, growth-oriented partnership with families. Since the family social worker joins with the family and participates in daily events for several hours at a time, opportunities for developing a partnership with the family are available. Yet, the partnership between worker and family must extend beyond engagement. One of the strengths of family social work lies in the fact that FSWs encourage family members to try new or different problem-solving skills and develop alternative daily living skills that can be applied during and after the helping process.

Thus, a worker can offer emotional support to an isolated and overwhelmed mother; teach a misunderstood ten-year-old to express his needs and feelings more appropriately; or help a disorganized family structure dinner, homework, and bedtime routines so they can function more harmoniously, while eliminating routines that create stress and unpleasantness. At agency and community levels, family social workers can also advocate for families in accessing other helping systems in the community. The overriding purpose of family social work within the community is to develop fulfilling environments for family members while concurrently meeting the expectations and standards of communities.

During work with the family, the family social worker addresses concrete issues related to family problem areas. Families, especially impoverished and overburdened families, are most concerned about meeting concrete needs and are responsive to an honest and straightforward approach (Wood & Geismar, 1986). Essentially, family social workers construct the building blocks of a family system, one block at a time. Underlying family social work is the assumption that if enough areas of dysfunction can be changed, the family's future ability to meet the needs of its members will be strengthened. Such an emphasis results in stronger families and healthier individual family members. This enhanced competence enhances the immediate environment of the family and equips children to learn to be more effective parents later. Effective family social work therefore can have a multigenerational impact.

ROLES AND OBJECTIVES OF THE FAMILY SOCIAL WORKER

Historically, professional helpers have approached families and individual clients from the vantage point of the "expert." With presumably more knowledge and experience than clients, professionals worked with families to solve problems, make decisions, and show families the route to effective parenting. As an expert, the helping professional carried out this role as an authority external to the family. Families were not considered partners in a change process. Power and knowledge were in the hands of the professional helper. In the process, the helper gave and the family received.

Changes in social workers' professional roles and expectations emerged from shifts in how the family and effective helping were perceived. The family is no longer considered a passive recipient of help, but an active partner and participant throughout the change process. Nor does the family social worker know better than the family (Wood & Geismar, 1986). The family, within parameters determined by society, must define its own needs, setting priorities and stating preferences for services. Consequently, the family social worker acts as a collaborator, facilitator, and negotiator. These multiple roles demand that workers be well trained. Indeed, to fulfill these roles, family social workers must use multiple helping skills and be competent in a range of domains pertinent to their program and profession. The role of family collaborator and partner demands that workers reject canned "expert" solutions to predefined problems. Families have the right and the responsibility to identify their special concerns and goals in relation to their family situation and to play an active role in their resolution.

To better help families, family social workers must examine their own family and interpersonal interactions in the process of understanding mutual respect and partnership with the particular families. Broadening the focus beyond the individual to encompass the entire family is a profound shift for many professionals whose training and inclination motivate them to advocate for children, sometimes in an *adversarial* role to the family. The shift from an individual to a family perspective requires incorporating the belief of family competence into the decision-making and problem-solving process.

As partners with families, family social workers use seven roles as a springboard from which to stimulate change: empathic supporter, teacher/trainer, consultant, enabler, mobilizer, mediator, and advocate.

1. In the role of *empathic supporter*, the guiding philosophy of a family social worker is to identify and reinforce family strengths while recognizing family limitations or lack of resources. Acknowledging strengths enables the FSW to join with the family and develop a bond that will create motivation and optimism to work toward change. Every family has strengths, and often social workers have been preoccupied with dysfunction and pathology, possibly even reinforcing dysfunction by focusing primarily on a family's problems. For example, despite negative parenting practices, most parents care deeply about their children. Such caring should be emphasized and used as the foundation for dealing with targeted problems.

2. The *teacher/trainer* role allows the FSW to cultivate areas where the family is deficient or lacking in skills or knowledge. Viewing family problems as the result of skill deficits (or even more palatably, as new skills to be learned), rather than as evidence of pathology, makes families more open to working on problems nondefensively. Problem areas may include deficits in communication, parenting skills, problem solving, anger management, conflict resolution, values clarification, money management, and skills of daily living.

Sometimes the teaching role involves helping parents replace verbal reprimands with positive and constructive parent-child interactions. Other times, the family social worker teaches parents to work more effectively with difficult child behavior by reinforcing positive behavior and discouraging negative and annoying behavior. Through such teaching activities, parents can become their children's best therapists.

3. The family social worker as *consultant* acts as an advisor to the family for specific problems that arise. For instance, the family generally may function well but find adolescence a particularly difficult time for which they need specialized help. The FSW, acting as a consultant, can provide valuable information to parents on typical or "normal" teenage behavior. In the process, parents gain deeper insight into their adolescent's needs and will be less inclined to consider their child a problem in future interaction. The family social worker can also provide ongoing feedback to parents and children who may lack mechanisms to obtain this feedback from other sources.

4. The *enabler* role allows the family social worker to expand opportunities for the family that might not otherwise be accessible. For instance, an immigrant family may not be familiar with the various services appropriate for their special needs. Informing a family about available services and helping them to use these services will empower families. The empowerment that family members experience when accomplishing a task can pave the way for future successes.

5. The family social worker as *mobilizer* captures the worker's unique position in the social network of helping resources. A social worker, knowledgeable about helping systems and support networks, activates and manages the involvement of various community groups and resources to serve families. The FSW can mobilize community agencies to work with a family. When school poses problems for children, for example, the FSW can coordinate with both the school and the family to establish additional opportunities for a struggling student.

6. In the ***mediator*** role, the family social worker addresses stress and conflict between conflicting parties. Mediation can occur at any level of the system. The FSW can mediate solutions when the family faces conflict with the community, or at a narrower level, mediate between family members in conflict. When a family member has an antagonistic relationship with a landlord or neighbor, the FSW can also attempt to resolve the conflict.

7. The family social worker acts as an ***advocate***, a role that requires activism on behalf of client families. The FSW is in the unique position to understand how family problems may be rooted in conditions within the broader societal context. Consequently, community activism and political action give family social workers the means with which to work for social and legislative reform benefiting clients.

ROLES OF FAMILY SOCIAL WORKERS

There are many circumstances in which family social workers can assist families. Consider each of the seven roles that a family social worker might assume. Give an example of a situation where each role might be used and provide an example of what the family social worker can do to fill the role.

Incorporated into the performance of a family social worker's roles are seven primary intervention objectives. The roles discussed previously are the means through which these objectives are achieved. Objectives and their usefulness vary from family to family and must be considered within the context of individual family needs, but they include the following goals:

1. To help family members manage daily living activities and interactions more effectively, thereby decreasing stress and increasing family harmony;

2. To help families learn more effective problem-solving skills, reduce the number or crises, and manage unavoidable crises more capably;

3. To help parents develop child management skills pertinent to the unique needs of each child and to contribute to the improvement of parent-child and parent-parent relationships;

4. To help family members learn effective conflict resolution skills, thereby assisting the family to deal with inevitable moments of stress and disagreement in a constructive and growth-promoting manner;

5. To help family members communicate individual wants, needs, and desires as well as feelings of pain, hurt, and disappointment clearly, directly, and honestly, thus increasing the likelihood of supportive rather than destructive family interactions;

6. To help families access concrete and social resources during periods of stress through promotion of individual, family, and community networking and to develop skills for solving problems;

7. To help families appreciate the unique worth and potential of each family member, thereby expanding opportunities for growth and development.

The role of the family social worker, then, is to help families achieve improved social functioning. Much of the work performed is direct and concrete. The FSW works with families to eliminate obstacles and extinguish negative and dysfunctional behaviors. The family social worker, in partnership with the family, promotes healthier social functioning, ongoing relationships with the family's social environment, and the ability to utilize resources when necessary.

ASSUMPTIONS OF FAMILY SOCIAL WORK

Family social work is guided by fundamental assumptions concerning effective work with families. These assumptions include placing a high value on *family-centered* and *home-based* practice coupled with recognition of the utility of *crisis intervention*. Another strong emphasis is on *teaching* families and children technical skills that promote new behaviors and create more effective methods of managing family relationships. Finally, family social work recognizes that families are embedded in a set of nested social systems that provide both risks and opportunities to families. This recognition is known as the *ecological* approach. These assumptions of family social work are discussed below.

Home-Based Support for Families

Interest in home-based family work has grown over the past decade, particularly in the field of child protection. The fact that family social work is practiced in the home provides some unique advantages. For example, home-based assessments might provide more accurate evaluations of families than office-based assessments of family functioning (Ledbetter Hancock & Pelton, 1989). In the home, family social workers can obtain direct information on family functioning and map out the relationships between family members as they interact within a familiar environment. Parents like the home-based focus of intervention. In one program a parent stated, for example, "I liked the home-based services so my child could be observed in a normal atmosphere" (Coleman & Collins, 1997).

Advantages of family social work in the home do not stop with assessment. Therapy in an office is governed by the assumption that the changes made by clients during an office interview are readily transferred to settings and occasions outside the office, particularly in the home and community. Yet, we now know that changes do not consistently or easily transfer from office settings to the home (Sanders & James, 1983). Abusive parents in a parent training program, for example, did not transfer skills easily from the classroom to the home (Isaacs, 1982). In another program, mothers and adolescents recounted less improvement at home after an office-based intervention than did a similar group who had received home-based services (Foster, Prinz, & O'Leary, 1983). It is more productive to intervene in the setting where problems spontaneously appear. When most client contact is in clients' homes, the problem of office-to-home generalization is eliminated.

Home-based services overcome treatment obstacles such as lack of transportation and other causes of missed appointments. Providing services in the home offers several additional advantages: (1) service becomes accessible to a wider range of clients, particularly those who are disadvantaged or disabled; (2) dropouts from counseling and appointment no-shows are reduced; (3) *all* family members are more readily engaged; and (4) the home is a natural setting in which to make interventions (Fraser, Pecora, & Haapala, 1991; Kinney, Haapala, & Booth, 1991).

Home and family have been recognized as "training grounds" for children's later adjustment problems (Patterson, DeBaryshe, & Ramsey, 1989). Providing family social work in the home, within a flexible service schedule, engages reticent family members more readily in treatment, a pivotal issue for family social workers. Additionally, entrance into clients' worlds where problems naturally emerge provides opportunities to capitalize on "teachable moments" and allows the FSW to respond immediately to client problems (Kinney, Haapala, & Booth, 1991). Families also value receiving services in the home. In some programs, for example, parents rate the importance of therapists coming to the home highly, illustrating the receptiveness of clients to home-based services (Fraser, Pecora, & Haapala, 1991).

With the FSW working in the home, face-to-face contact with all family members is optimized, an especially important concern when participation of all family members, including both parents, is critical to success. Total family involvement does not always occur when families must travel to appointments at remote locations, often at their inconvenience. Home-based family social work may also be particularly effective in maintaining contact with isolated or impoverished families and families who are resistant to professional intervention or suspicious of service. Although home-based family work gives the social worker a better chance to meet all family members, it still may happen that a family member will avoid meeting with family workers by not being present when a social worker visits the home. In a later chapter we will discuss practical strategies for involving family members in the helping process.

Unfortunately, the issue of portability and transferability of changes is a "double-edged sword," since behavioral changes made at home encounter similar obstacles when applied in settings outside the home, such as school (Forehand, Sturgis, McMahon, Aguar, Green, Wells, & Breiner, 1979). High placement rates for adolescents with problem behavior attest to the complexity of setting generalization. Delinquent adolescents, in particular, are often influenced by peers and settings outside the family and become insulated from family and therapeutic influence as they grow older and become more independent. Thus, family social workers must also become involved in settings where family members work and play, such as schools and recreational organizations. Additionally, early intervention when problems are less entrenched could prevent the development of more severe problems later.

Family-Centered Philosophy

A central belief of family social work is the idea that the family is the springboard from which treatment originates. In this sense, the family is pivotal to children's well-being. Family social work is bolstered by the belief that it is every child's right to develop in a nurturing and protective environment. Further, family-centered work stresses the importance of understanding people's behavior within its natural context.

Considering the family as the focal point of treatment offers many benefits. Parents may experience problems with several children in the same family or have concerns about other children once a targeted child receives treatment. A family-based intervention can address problems beyond those presented by the target child. Through work with the entire family, parents learn to apply what they have learned with the target child and not repeat the same mistakes with other children, thus giving family social work a preventitive role. Many families value the family-centered philosophy of family social work, as exemplified by the following comments from parents: "Worker put the whole family on a contract," and "[Worker] directed attention to the entire family. It was useful to keep the whole family perspective and value the family as a unit" (Coleman & Collins, 1997).

PERSPECTIVES OF INDIVIDUALS AND FAMILIES

Select a problem you are currently facing, and describe the problem in terms of its effect on you and upon other people. Try to understand that problem first from an individual perspective and then from a family perspective. Compare how the perspective changes when viewed from these two different understandings.

Changes beyond the target child are an important aspect of family work. "Sibling generalization" involves bringing about changes in the behavior of siblings who are not the specific focus of intervention. Given that parent training in child management techniques is a core ingredient of family social work, it is reasonable to expect an impact on siblings. Logically, skills learned by parents can be used with all of the children in the family. Teaching parents to manage most child behavior problems more effectively produces changes in the entire family that can make it less likely that problems will reappear. For example, one program found that when mothers decreased punishment for inappropriate child behaviors, fathers stepped into the disciplinary role (Patterson & Fleischman, 1979). This suggests that family structure adapts to incorporate new behaviors learned at home.

Working with the entire family unit has been useful in interventions with delinquents. Programs have shown generalization of treatment effects to siblings of socially aggressive boys in treatment (Arnold, Levine, & Patterson, 1975; Baum & Forehand, 1981; Klein, Alexander, & Parsons, 1977). Family interventions are premised on the belief that parents are effective and preferred therapists for their children and that a change in the family system will also change sibling behavior. Such programs have seen a decrease in deviant behavior of siblings by more than two-thirds, compared with behavior before treatment, and positive changes can continue for several years after services end. Declines in problematic sibling behavior beyond target child improvement also testify to the importance of family-based social work.

The Importance of Crisis Intervention

Family social work provides crisis intervention during stressful family events. This is particularly important when interventions are triggered by the endangerment of a family member, as by abuse or suicidal threats. Accordingly, the prompt and on-site presence of the FSW is often necessary to reduce risk to vulnerable family members, lasting at least until healthy family functioning and individual safety have been restored.

Time-limited crisis intervention is an important ingredient of family social work and requires provision of "on-the-spot" assistance in emergencies. During a crisis, the worker's intervention with the family focuses on problem solving and decision making, with the goal of resolving the crisis and helping the family to develop adaptive coping skills. Through crisis intervention, family social work helps members move beyond their collective pain to a point of renewed growth and better coping. To achieve these results, interventions can target concrete and practical problems experienced by the family.

Crisis intervention is effective in working with families that have a variety of problems, and under some circumstances it can be as effective as traditional long-term therapies (Powers, 1990). The dual aims of crisis intervention include immediate resolution of problems and adaptation to abrupt life events, and long-term skill building to reduce failure and maximize adaptation to future crises. Often changes made during crisis intervention remain intact long after services end. Family crisis intervention has been effective in preventing hospitalization for some children and contributing to shorter psychiatric hospital stays for others (Langsley, Pittman, Machotka, & Flomenhaft, 1968).

Unfortunately, social workers often believe that "more is better" in terms of hours devoted to a particular problem. This is not always the case, as some interventions have a "threshold effect." For example, spending fewer hours on a problem does not consistently result in less success. Results of a thirty-five-hour traditional family therapy were comparable to those achieved by a four-hour crisis intervention (Ewing, 1978), with both producing a reduction in children's symptoms, increased adjustment by children, and improvement in the family's coping abilities. While there are unanswered questions about the effectiveness of crisis intervention for clients with chronic difficulties (Ewing, 1978), a family social worker can expect to encounter several family crises throughout work with a particular family. The family social worker not only deals with family crises but also looks at what led up to a particular crisis in addition to the long-term impact of a crisis on family functioning.

"Teachability" of Families

Family social workers often work with family members to increase skills that promote family harmony. Parenting and child management techniques are necessary skills that family social workers can help parents develop. These skills may involve a variety of methods, including (1) reinforcing effective behaviors; (2) helping family members deal with anger; (3) teaching parents how to track children's behavior; (4) using time-outs when family conflict or child behaviors become unmanageable or too stressful; (5) practicing positive behaviors by using techniques such as role-playing; (6) developing social skills for parents and children; (7) teaching relaxation techniques to help parents cope with stress and learn to self-nurture more effectively; and, finally, (8) developing parenting skills and child management techniques.

Studies support the effectiveness of teaching parenting skills to eliminate abuse and change children's behaviors in a positive way (Baum & Forehand, 1981; Foster, Prinz, & O'Leary, 1983; Wolfe, Sandler, & Kaufman, 1981). Notably, abuse and behavior problems are two primary reasons for family social work involvement with families. Behavioral training for parents has also been effective in teaching self-control techniques (Isaacs, 1982) and changing behaviors of delinquent children (Webster-Stratton & Hammond, 1990).

Parent training to eliminate abuse and child behavior problems is built on observations of family interactions on a moment-by-moment basis. Family social workers need to pay close attention to patterns of parent-child interaction and help the family to change these patterns in tangible ways. It is noteworthy that families with abuse and conduct-disordered children show similar types of minute-by-minute interactions. Observations of parent-child interaction reveal ongoing interaction patterns within families, particularly repetitive behavior patterns between parent and child. In these patterns, abusive parents and parents of children with behavior problems communicate less frequently than other parents and use more negative and aversive parenting styles, ignoring prosocial child behavior (Patterson, DeBaryshe, & Ramsey, 1989). One component of parent skills training involves changing dysfunctional "molecular patterns" by teaching parents to respond positively to children's prosocial behavior, first within short time frames, and later extending into longer periods.

Ecological Approach

Social workers and other professionals have begun to recognize the importance of understanding behavior within a social context. The ecological approach is especially relevant when working with families who are marginalized in a society (Okun, 1996). A family's social context can offer both risk and opportunity. For example, living in a high-crime area where families do not know one another represents an ecological risk. In such a neighborhood, neighbors cannot watch out for one another and offer support during stressful times. By contrast, ecological opportunity is present in a close-knit neighborhood. When neighbors know and support one another, they are more likely to provide assistance to a family in need. To develop a comprehensive understanding of families, social workers need to be able to identify potential sources of ecological risk and opportunity. They also need to be aware that the roles performed by family members within the family tend to parallel the roles they play outside the family (Geismar & Ayres, 1959).

A common error of social workers has been to focus solely on a family's internal functioning or its social environment, a split that oversimplifies a complex problem (Wood & Geismar, 1986). In fact, some work with families has met with limited success because all of the family's problems are attributed to patterns of family interaction. This leads to the limiting idea that only family interaction needs to be changed. Conversely, effective family social work involves identifying strengths and resources within both the family and the social environment, as well as assessing the match between the two. Family social work accounts for factors beyond family boundaries and focuses on multiple dimensions of family functioning that go beyond relationships and communication. For example, parental effectiveness is closely linked with the quality of the social environment in which parents raise their children (Garbarino, 1982).

■ BARRIERS ENCOUNTERED BY FAMILIES

No family lives in isolation from the rest of society. At times, society makes survival difficult for some families. List some barriers in our society that impede families from reaching their fullest potential.

Family social work advocates working with families in neighborhoods, communities, and the larger society to broaden the scope of material and social supports for families. Viewing families as isolated, disjointed social units is inaccurate. To intervene effectively, social workers need to recognize that every family is a system embedded within a series of overlapping systems and thus families are affected by interactions with the workplace, the school, and larger systems at any given time. Family social environments are complex, interactive, and influential. Recognizing the complexity of the interactions between families and their social contexts offers social workers a new set of conceptual lenses to use as they describe, analyze, and intervene. Family social workers must be comfortable with assessing and interviewing in the social environment of each family member. This assessment balances the strengths and resources of the family with the strengths and resources of the environment, examining mismatches between the two. The family social worker assesses family coping and recognizes the ways in which the environment impinges upon family functioning.

Even healthy families, living in oppressive or nonsupportive environments, will eventually show symptoms of strain, despite their abilities and strengths. The needs for intervention to span home, school, and the community and to promote give-and-take between systems is fundamental to the family social work approach. Building bridges between families and appropriate social support systems in the environment is therefore an essential ingredient of family social work.

Many resources are available within the social environment. These resources can include material or monetary supports (Berry, 1997) as well as social resources. The social environment can be understood by looking at the availability of social support. Social support has mistakenly been identified as a source of dependence. An absence of social support might imply independence to some, but more often it reflects vulnerability and isolation. Family privacy and geographical mobility in our society has isolated families from sources of valuable social support.

Significant persons in the family's environment can provide support and feedback to family members and to the family as a whole. When social resources are adequate, crises can be averted (Berry, 1997), and when resources such as social support are inadequate, family members are more apt to display emotional distress or physical illness. For example, women with little social support are more likely to experience complications during pregnancy than are women who receive a wider range of support, and women who receive sufficient emotional and physical support during pregnancy are likely to give birth to a healthier baby. Thus, social support benefits not only women but also their unborn children. Helping a family nurture new support networks will not only optimize competencies but also help the family avoid becoming dependent upon the worker. By the time the social worker terminates with a particular family, the family members should have established skills and resources from which to draw later.

SOCIAL ENVIRONMENTS OF FAMILIES

To prepare for work with families, we need to think about how families function within their social environments or communities. To complete this exercise, think about your own family and other families you know. List four social environments in which family members live, work, and play. Next, write down the roles and responsibilities of family members that might be associated with each of these social environments. An example is provided to help you get started.

Social Environment	Roles of Family Members	Responsibilities
Neighborhood	Parents:	
	• Adult	To look out for the safety and well-being of neighborhood children
	• Coach	To coach baseball team of 9- and 10-year-old children
	• Neighbor	To reach out to neighbors and provide support if necessary
	Children:	
	• Family member and playmate	To let parents know who their friends are and where they are going
	• Team member	To follow the rules and help teammates

Considering the environment of the family has direct practice implications for family social workers. Traditionally, family services consisted of interventions restricted to externally predefined needs of children and families. Outside authorities, such as public health, school, or child protection officials, decided what the family was missing and implemented remedial interventions to "fix the problem." These interventions frequently resulted in failure because workers did not consider the context within which problems were occurring.

Working within a comprehensive framework permits a thorough response to the needs of everyone. Families receiving services are often families under stress. Responding to stressors requires resources (Berry, 1997). An effective partnership between a social worker and a family addresses the family's concerns when identifying needs, priorities, and options for service. Developing individualized services tailored to the unique situation of each family replaces standardized interventions to which the family must conform. This approach respects the self-responsibility that family members should assume to obtain the services they need. Conversely, dictating a course of action does not encourage self-sufficiency, nor does prescribing a standard package of services for all families. *One size does not fit all.*

Although there is a trend toward providing more comprehensive services, the family's right to negotiate services and to individualize interventions implies that not all families will desire or require a broad-based approach. Often, the FSW and the family negotiate a contract, specifying services to be provided. Social workers should be aware that some families might want help only with one specific issue (such as remedial educational assistance with a learning disadvantaged young person) rather than broader interventions. Broader services are not better services if they do not fit the unique needs and expectations of the family. The importance of formulating a mutually acceptable contract with specific goals cannot be overemphasized. The process of negotiating a contract is a key aspect of family social work and will be discussed in more detail in Chapter 5.

There is growing interest in providing early interventions for problems, before concerns become full-blown or unmanageable, instead of intervening only after the situation has become explosive or destructive. Prevention is preferable to picking up pieces later. Helping people learn parenting skills is more effective if done before, rather than after, and adult has abused a child. Interest in prevention is also reflected in the increased attention to early childhood stimulation programs as opposed to later remedial programs for school-aged children. Early intervention assumes two forms: intervention early in the life cycle and early intervention in the problem cycle. Family social workers do both types of intervention.

Another changing direction in family social work is the belief in building family strengths rather than responding only to deficits and problems. For example, programs for children with special needs are focusing not only upon the medical needs of the child but also upon helping families include members with social and developmental disabilities in the family's ongoing activities. These principles promote growth and recognize the need to consider the family as part of a larger community of extended resources.

The broad focus of the family social worker does not make decisions easier when he or she must set priorities for services or address conflicting demands within the family. Rather, a broad focus forces the FSW to consider the needs of all family members, not just the child whose problems may provoke the initiation of services. Based on these considerations, the family social worker must identify the needs of family members, decide how to best address specific problems, and locate available internal and external resources. Whenever possible, these considerations should be made in collaboration with the family.

CHAPTER SUMMARY

Family social work offers numerous advantages for working with families. It can reduce barriers to available services, diminish the need for later and more intrusive interventions, and improve the social functioning of families. Family social workers strive to develop growth-promoting competencies with families and to help each family and its members attain their fullest potential. Family social work encourages connections, support, resource development, and the integration of families as contributing members of their social environments.

2 Diverse Family Structures

A single definition of *family* does not exist, yet family social workers must develop a clear concept of "family" that encompasses a variety of structures, roles, and functions. For many beginning family social workers, their only real experience with family functioning has been in their own family of origin (Munson, 1993). This singular experience can hinder family workers' awareness of the diversity of family types and styles.

In this chapter we describe different family structures and offer several ways to visualize family structures and functions, using genograms and other mapping techniques. We conclude the chapter by listing key assumptions about families and beliefs about family social work.

WHAT IS A FAMILY?

One of the most perplexing issues in a book about families stems from the deceptively simple question: "What is a family?" Asking this question is similar to seeking a universal definition of femininity, fatherhood, or love. Everyone has a personal definition of each of these terms, but a universally agreed-upon definition is difficult, if not impossible, to arrive at. Despite this fact, social workers must be able to understand what constitutes a family if they are to determine eligibility for services. How family membership is defined can help identify who should be included in an intervention (Hartman & Laird, 1983). On a broader scale, a clear definition of "family" will decide who is covered by a family social policy and eligible to receive benefits such as maternity leave, day care subsidies, public assistance, or health care.

PURPOSES OF FAMILIES

> What purposes (benefits) do families serve? Identify five purposes a family serves for its members and five purposes a family serves for society.

What kind of grouping qualifies as a family, as compared to friends or roommates? Where do extended family members fit in? What about common-law relationships? How do gay and lesbian relationships fit into definitions of family? Similarly, how do communal relationships or polygamous relationships fit into the category of family?

Defining the family is a complex task, yet a working definition of family is crucial for family social work. If the family is not defined and conceptualized, social workers are forced to rely on personal assumptions, beliefs, and stereotypes. One must be able to define the client group in order to devise appropriate interventions. Our first task in this chapter, then, is to examine common biases and beliefs about families.

MYTHS ABOUT THE NUCLEAR FAMILY

Throughout history and across different cultures, the family has assumed diverse forms; nevertheless all people come from a nuclear family. The nuclear family is any kinship group of more than one person residing in the same household and related by marriage, blood, societal or self-sanction. This definition is so broad that one could easily ask, "What grouping does not qualify as a family?" The definition is broad enough to include all who have been or are currently members of a nuclear family. Indeed, being a member of more than one nuclear family in a lifetime is both possible and likely.

Generally people think of the "traditional family" when referring to the nuclear family. Rigid definitions of the family are limited to members related by blood (i.e., biological parents and children) or legally sanctioned marriages. Clearly such a rigid view of family could exclude more people than it includes. The idea of a traditional family conjures an image of the mother at home, father at work, and 2.2 children. Distress about the current state of the family has been accompanied by the belief that the best way to resolve serious social problems is to return to this "traditional" form.

In reality, the traditional nuclear family existed more in fiction than fact. North American family structures have always been diverse. The family with a male breadwinner and female full-time homemaker was prevalent only for a brief period, most commonly in white, middle-class households (Coontz, 1996). During the 1920s, a small majority of children grew up in a family where the male was the breadwinner and the female was the homemaker. Today, this type of family comprises only 7 percent of all households (Gavin & Bramble, 1996). The current idealized "traditional nuclear family" espoused by the conservative politicians existed primarily in the 1950s (Coontz, 1996).

In colonial times, wealthier settlers established independent households by exploiting the services of poor immigrant workers and slaves. African Americans were denied the legal protection of marriage and parenthood and consequently developed extensive kinship networks (Coontz, 1996). Middle-class, white women were able to enjoy the luxury of domesticity because working-class women liberated them from household tasks that formerly fell to them.

Throughout history, death, desertion, divorce, and separation have made blended families a regular feature of family life, contrary to current proselytizing. In a blended family, divorced or widowed parents remarry, bringing with them children from the previous marriage. Blended families may have been even more common in the past because of high mortality rates for women during childbirth. Historically, disease and wars claimed many lives, leaving some adults single several times during adulthood. Remarriages were common. Poor women and their children worked outside the home even before the Industrial Revolution. Thus, the traditional nuclear family existed primarily in middle and upper classes of European lineage.

Those who now blame social problems on changing family structures are placing "the cart before the horse." Social problems such as economic inequity and the ravages of race, gender, and class discrimination all contribute to the breakdown of the family. As proposed by Coontz:

> These inequities are *not* driven by changes in family forms, contrary to ideologues that persist in confusing correlation with causes; but they certainly exacerbate such changes, and they tend to bring out the worst in *all* families. The result has been an accumulation of stresses on families, alongside some important expansions of personal options. Working couples with children try to balance three full-time jobs, as employers and schools cling to policies that assume every employee has a "wife" at home to take care of family matters. Divorce and remarriage have allowed many adults and children to escape from toxic family environments, yet our lack of social support networks and failure to forge new values for sustaining intergenerational obligations have let many children fall through the cracks in the process (1996, p. 47).

Our historical overview of the family in Western society reveals a variety of family forms that diverge from the popular notion of the family as a single, monolithic form. Looking past structure is necessary to accurately understand unique family experiences as well as the common needs of all family units within society. A childless couple, a couple with two (or ten) biological, adopted, or foster children, a single mother with children, or a gay couple with children are all examples of different family structures, but families nonetheless.

Family structure in the United States and Canada is especially diverse. Families differ in terms of lifestyle and racial heritage. In the United States, for example, distinct ethnic neighborhoods exist in some cities. Additionally, various racial groups have experienced discrimination and lack of service. In Canada and in the United States, indigenous or native peoples remain an underserved group.

Family social workers must recognize and accept a wide range of family forms. Unfortunately, many people believe that they grew up in abnormal or dysfunctional families because their family of origin did not conform to the rigid mold of the traditional family. This is particularly true for families who are neither middle-class nor white. For example, many people of non-American descent believe in selfless loyalty to their families. Members of other cultures, however, may label such loyalty as overinvolvement (Nichols & Schwartz, 1998).

Many people, children in particular, have felt stigmatized or ashamed because they consider their family different from the mainstream. Definitions of family contribute to practice norms, and if family social work rigidly adheres to an "ideal" family, those who do not resemble the ideal become marginalized (Hartman & Laird, 1983). Even the notion of what is normal is vague and difficult to define clearly. Armed with knowledge that many forms of family exist and are widespread, the family social worker can overcome barriers and attitudes so that people who were raised in households that do not adhere to the stereotype feel neither abnormal nor dysfunctional.

FAMILY VARIATIONS IN THE 1990s AND BEYOND

As mentioned previously, less than 10 percent of today's families conform to the traditional nuclear family. In fact, more than 60 percent of all children will have spent at least part of their childhood in a single-parent household by the age of eighteen, and the majority of these single parents are mothers (Gavin & Bramble, 1996). Of all current families with children, one-fourth are single-parent households, with many of these parents employed outside the home. However, single-parent families have a greater probability of being poor. On average, today's families have fewer children than in the past, and people are marrying later in life. The divorce rate is approximately 50 percent, and about 70 percent of divorced individuals will eventually remarry.

Cultural diversity in society is also growing rapidly, and whites are slowly becoming a minority of the population (McGoldrick, Giordano, & Pearce, 1996). Minority family values may differ from the dominant culture (Lum, 1992) and sometimes bear little resemblance to beliefs and assumptions that guide mainstream family work.

Regardless of cultural group or socioeconomic status, families include a range of structures. The most common family structures that include children are presented below. The same family can fit into two or more categories.

Family of Orientation   Most individuals belong to at least two family systems over a lifetime. All have belonged to families of orientation, commonly referred to as the family of origin. This is the family in which a person is born or raised. It is possible for some people to come from two or more families of orientation. For example, a child who is adopted during infancy was, at least briefly, part of a family of orientation with the birth mother. To the child, however, the family of orientation is more likely to be that of the adoptive parents.

Family of Procreation   A family of procreation consists of a couple who, through self or state sanction, have developed a relationship and have children. The couple in a family of procreation may be of opposite sexes or the same sex, and procreation may occur through heterosexual intercourse or through one of the assisted reproductive technologies such as artificial insemination or surrogate parenthood.

Extended Family   An extended family includes two or more family units. For example, an extended family may consist of a household in which a grandmother lives with her married son, daughter-in-law, and grandchildren. While grandparents are the most common extension, an extended family may also include aunts, uncles, or cousins. For members of some ethnic groups, the extended family plays an especially important role (Lum, 1992). Grandparenting is discussed in more detail in Chapter 7.

Blended Family   A blended family, or stepfamily, consists of two people living with at least one child from a previous relationship. The parents may also have biological children together.

Adoptive Family   Adoption involves a legal commitment to raise children who have been born to others.

Foster Family   In a foster family, parents temporarily nurture children born to others. The length of time in which a foster child is in the home can vary from several days to most of childhood. Although most foster families have a formal arrangement with child welfare authorities, other fostering arrangements are made informally with friends or relatives.

Single-Parent Family   A single-parent family consists of one parent and one or more children. The parent can be either male or female and can be single as a result of the death of a partner, divorce, desertion, or never having been married. A growing number of single parents are single by choice (Okun, 1996).

AN INCLUSIVE DEFINITION OF FAMILY

Eichler's (1988) definition of family provides a foundation on which to build:

A family is a social group that may or may not include one or more children (e.g., childless couples), who may or may not have been born in their wedlock (e.g., adopted children, or children by one adult partner of a previous union). The relationship of the adults may or may not have its origin in marriage (e.g., common-law couples); they may or may not occupy the same residence (e.g., commuting couples). The adults may or may not cohabit sexually, and the relationship may or may not involve such socially patterned feelings as love, attraction, piety, and awe (p. 4).

Cultures also differ in how "family" is defined. The definition of the majority culture focuses on the nuclear family, whereas African American families include an expanded kin network, Chinese focus on ancestors, and Italians look at several generations of extended kin (McGoldrick, Giordano, & Pearce, 1996). In minority families, relationships with extended family and kin networks are based on principles of interdependence, group orientation, and reliance on others (Lum, 1992). Cultural values about family practices that someone from another culture may label as "strange" or "unhealthy" also guide people. Family activities may diverge dramatically from mainstream culture. For example, some Puerto Ricans believe so strongly in family obligation that they find it acceptable to use public office to benefit family members (Lum, 1992).

Finally, minority families are often structured according to a "vertical hierarchy of authority" (Lum, 1992). Thus, authority in these families often is assumed by males or elders as heads of households. Cultural clashes can occur when children or females from a minority family encounter differences in the dominant culture. Culturally sensitive practice is discussed in more detail in Chapter 12.

DEFINITION OF FAMILY

Develop a definition of a family, based on your own family of orientation. How has your family changed over the years, and when, if ever, has your family fit the description of a traditional nuclear family?

Lack of awareness can lead family social workers to be less objective about families whose backgrounds are either very different from or very much like their own families. In either case, social workers may work less intensely, understand parents poorly, or be unable to overcome communication and cultural barriers, such as language barriers, religious differences, or varying styles of parenting. Another danger is that social workers may make inaccurate assessments about parental strengths and weaknesses. Thus, FSWs must be honest with themselves about their own motivations, prejudices, and blind spots. Only then will they be able to work empathetically with parents from different backgrounds.

Contemporary family lifestyles and structures are fluid and evolving. Therefore, a broad definition of family is needed. Despite the difficulty of developing a clear and simple definition of family, most people can construct an unambiguous description to fit their own particular family, and working definitions of the family can be established for most situations. The family, in its most basic conceptualization, is what a person in a family says it is. The experienced "family" reality, rather than strict adherence to a static and rigid definition, is crucial to family social work and determines the nature of the work conducted with a family. Social judgments about family structures play an important role in determining what resources and barriers a family will encounter in getting their needs met.

■ WORKING WITH DIVERSE FAMILY STRUCTURES

Consider the following families who have been assigned to your caseload at your FSW field placement. How is each family like or not like your own family of origin? What special challenges, if any, will you face in working with the family?

- The Sims family was referred to you by the high school due to the children's poor attendance and grades. Jeanne Sims is forty-two years old, Caucasian, and a housewife. Jeanne's husband Dick is forty-three years old, Native American, and works as a mechanic at a gas station. During your initial interview with Jeanne and her teenage daughter, Lisa, Lisa tells you that many of the family's problems stem from her father's drinking, bad temper, and physical abuse of his wife. Jeanne says she stays with her husband because of her religious beliefs, which require that wives submit to their husbands.

- The Thompson family was referred to you by the local mental health clinic at which Diane Thompson receives medication for schizophrenia. Diane, an African American single female in her twenties, lives with her parents Jim and Stella. The parents are concerned because Diane takes her medication sporadically and disappears for weeks at a time when off her medications. The Thompsons have been informed that Diane has been living on the streets during these periods. They are afraid for Diane's safety.

- Liz Frank, a twenty-three-year-old Caucasian female, and her four-year-old daughter Tina were referred to you by Child Protective Services. Tina's day care teacher reported the family to CPS when Liz recently divorced Tina's father and moved herself and Tina in with her new partner Sylvia. The teacher reports that Tina frequently appears at school hungry, unbathed, and with clothes that appear "slept in."

- Joy Jimenez, a thirty-nine-year-old Hispanic female, referred herself and her family to your agency. Joy is the recently divorced mother of six children, sixteen-year-old Alicia, thirteen-year-old Joe, eleven-year-old Maria, seven-year-old twins Carlos and Juan, and four-year-old Dora. Joy, her boyfriend Tom, and the children moved in with Joy's mother and stepfather last week. Joy's parents have volunteered to help out with the children, as Joy's job takes her away from home for many hours each day.

GRAPHING FAMILY COMPOSITION: THE GENOGRAM

Because family structures and family problems can be complex, diagrams are useful tools with which to summarize detailed data. Visual recording techniques help the family social worker to organize information efficiently and to develop a coherent plan for intervention. Social workers often find graphic tools useful for recording important details in complex cases. Because of the detail of graphic instruments, many problems and issues stand out. This does not mean that every identified problem becomes the target of intervention, but diagrams provide a backdrop against which other problems can be understood. Family social workers and their clients will be challenged to select interventions that have the greatest potential for positive effects.

The amount of material included in a single graphic depiction of a family depends on the worker's defined role. A chart should include enough detail to capture the family's complexity but remain simple enough that it can be easily understood.

A genogram is a "tree" diagram that can help the family social worker become aware of who is included in a family and the nature of family relationships. This family diagram can be utilized to depict the structure and nature of relationships across several generations. Family members who assist with genogram construction may find the process informative, as both the social worker and clients gain insight into family patterns and interactions.

Genograms display family information to permit a quick overview of complex family patterns. They provide a detailed picture of significant family events such as births, marriages, separations, and deaths. Genograms can also convey social information such as racial group, social class, and religion (Holman, 1983). Finally, genograms help the social worker to understand past and present family patterns and to reframe and detoxify family issues (Kaslow & Celano, 1995).

Genograms are appealing to family social workers because they represent a family concretely. They permit family social workers to map family structure clearly and update the family picture as it develops. A family's genogram might change as the social worker and family members learn new information. As a clinical record, the genogram provides an efficient family summary, allowing those unfamiliar with a family to quickly obtain a vast amount of information about the family, including important issues and concerns.

Genograms help ensure that all significant people are included before an intervention is planned. They are especially useful when detailed family information is needed (Hartman & Laird, 1983). Through genograms, family social workers can identify repetitive patterns experienced by a family. Information in a genogram is easy to find, in contrast to volumes of case files in which information may be lost or overlooked. A single genogram condenses the contents of pages of narrative information to fit on a single page.

The process of genogram construction creates opportunities to establish rapport between the FSW and the family, rapidly engaging the family in the work to be done. Working together in genogram construction sets the stage for the worker-family partnership and draws families into a participatory style of problem identification and problem solving.

How to Draw a Genogram

No standard method of genogram construction exists, despite the widespread use of this tool. (See, for example, Hartman & Laird, 1983; McGoldrick & Gerson, 1985; Wright & Leahey, 1994.) There is some degree of consensus about what specific information to include, how to record information, and how to interpret it. Fortunately, the general structure of the genogram follows conventional genealogical charts. It is standard practice to include at least three generations in a genogram (i.e., grandparents, parents, and children). Many symbols are used, because the core information of genograms is conveyed in shorthand. Typical symbols used in a genogram include the following:

☐   = Male

○   = Female

–M:–   = Married

| = Offspring

D| = Divorced

S: = Separated

X   = Deceased

The genogram shows family members in relation to each other. A sample genogram is shown in Figure 2.1. Every family member is represented either by a rectangle or circle, based on gender. Double outlines surround the rectangle or circle denoting the individual client (or identified patient) for whom the genogram was constructed. Family members of the same generation are identified in horizontal rows that signify generational lines. For example, a horizontal line denotes marital or common-law relationships. Children of a union are named on a different horizontal line underneath the parents and joined to the line of the parents by a vertical line. Children are ordered from left to right by age, from oldest to youngest. Each individual in the family must be represented at a specific, strategic point on the genogram, regardless of whether the person is currently alive or living in the household. If a family member has ever existed, he or she is included in the genogram. Depending on the number of people and relationships involved, genogram construction can become quite involved.

Each family member's name and age should be placed inside a square or circle. Outside each symbol, significant data (for example, "travels a lot" or "school dropout") should be recorded. If a family member has died, the year of death, the person's age at death, and the cause of death should be recorded.

Lines between people on the genogram describe the nature and quality of relationships. For example, the social worker may write a descriptive word or phrase next to a line, such as "conflictual." Questions such as "What was the nature of your parents' relationship?" or "To whom did you feel closest in your family?" can help to capture the quality of family relationships. The social worker is advised to work with one family of

FIGURE 2.1 Genogram of the Bonita Taylor Family

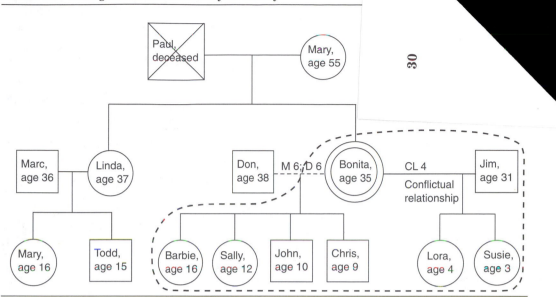

origin at a time. At a later time, the social worker can ask the parents to interpret how their own families of origin affect the current family unit, particularly their marriage (Brock & Barnard, 1992). In doing family-of-origin work with the couple, the worker should identify themes and repetitive patterns that may be re-created in the present family. An example of a theme might be, "Males have the final say in major decisions affecting the family."

CHARTING A FAMILY'S RELATIONSHIPS WITH THE ECOSYSTEM: THE ECOMAP

While the genogram exposes the family's internal dynamics, the family's external dynamics and relationships can be represented on an ecomap. This chart depicts family relationships with the outside world (ecosystem) and captures the strength and quality of external connections and areas of conflict between the family and the ecosystem. Ecomaps demonstrate the flow of resources from the environment to the family, as well as deprivations and unmet needs (Holman, 1983). Since ecomaps account for client transactions with the environment, they are useful for assessing and conceptualizing families holistically and contextually. Important observations concerning family-community connections can be catalogued on an ecomap. As with the genogram, the primary advantage of an ecomap is the visual and conceptual impact of inserting an extensive amount of information on a single page. The map is an easy-to-read depiction of family support systems. Family social work relies heavily on the information portrayed on an ecomap because needs and community resources are central to family work.

The process of creating a family's ecomap can occur during assessment and planning, concentrating on crucial information such as boundary issues and mutuality of social relationships. Preparing an ecomap should reduce the amount of narrative needed for case files, but there may be tradeoffs between the level of detail required and the time it takes to complete the diagram. Ecomaps are now a standard part of agency recording, especially in agencies with high staff turnover and clients having many unmet social needs.

As with the genogram, participating in constructing an ecomap can be beneficial to the family, particularly during the early stages of engagement. It is important to note that families of color have experienced societal discrimination and that the effects of this discrimination should be recorded on the ecomap.

Ecomaps capture transactions with systems outside the family, while genograms identify exchanges within the family. If the focus is on the interaction between an entire family and its social environment, the ecomap will include a family genogram. An ecomap may revolve around just one individual if the focus is on the individual's interaction with the social environment. Both workers and clients find these tools useful. By providing concrete and diagrammatic depictions of abstract concepts, genograms and ecomaps produce greater understanding and retention of material.

How to Draw an Ecomap

The ecomap comprises a series of interconnected circles representing various systems outside the family. The first step in creating an ecomap is to place the previously constructed genogram in a center circle labeled as the family or household. Circles placed outside this center circle represent significant people, agencies, or organizations in the lives of the members of the family. The size of the circles is not important. Lines drawn between the inner and outer circles indicate the nature of the existing connections. Straight lines (—) show strong connections, dotted lines (.......) denote tenuous connections, and slashed lines (-/-/-) represent stressful or conflictual connections.

YOUR FAMILY'S GENOGRAM AND ECOMAP

Describe your family of origin. Complete a genogram and illustrate patterns within your family that became evident as you were completing this exercise. Include the following information about each family member (if known): age; occupation; living/dead (cause of death); health; personality type/description. Next, create an ecomap of your family; identify systems outside your family that were significant in the life of your family as you were growing up.

FIGURE 2.2   Ecomap of the Bonita Taylor Family

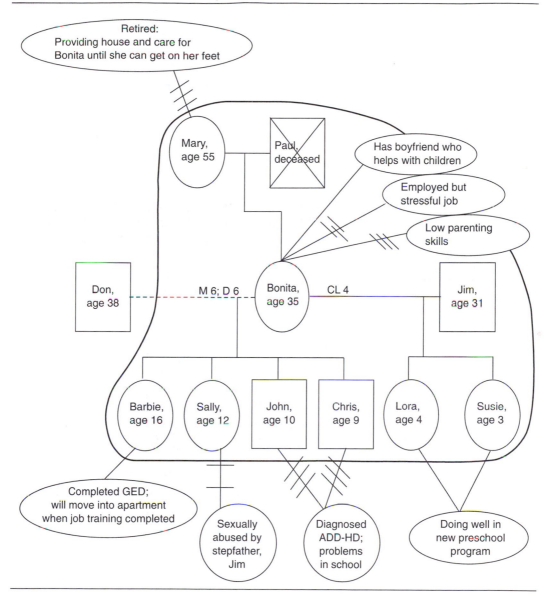

The thicker the line, the stronger the connection. Additional circles can be drawn as necessary, depending upon the number of significant contacts. The ecomap may be modified as the family changes or as the family shares additional information with the family social worker. An example of an ecomap is shown in Figure 2.2.

OTHER VISUAL TECHNIQUES

Another related technique for depicting family relationships is to have the family draw a picture showing all its members. Family members can also draw their family separately, and the portraits of individual family members can later be discussed and compared. Alternatively, a family member can be asked to "sculpt" their family (Satir & Baldwin, 1983)—that is, have family members stand in a room posed in ways that depict the nature of their relationships. Members take turns arranging family members in relationship with one another; body gestures, distance, and physical actions convey the meaning of the sculpture. Each family member takes charge of their particular sculpture, instructing family members what position to assume. Essentially, the sculptor treats family members as if they were made of clay (Holman, 1983). Sculptures of the same family will differ, depending on the perceptions of the one directing the sculpture. Sculpting is especially useful for nonverbal families, as it offers a means of understanding one another's viewpoints without words (Holman, 1983).

Another similar technique is to have families pose for a family photograph. How people position themselves will generate information about family relationships.

BELIEFS ABOUT FAMILIES

Beliefs about family life form the foundation of worker attitudes about the family. Viewpoints that are sensitive to realities of family life will guide ethical and humane practice with families and offer a road map for worker-family relationships. Conversely, negative attitudes about families interfere with the partnership that workers must develop in family work.

The following beliefs guide family social work:

> **Belief I: Families want to be healthy.**   Typically, people who are committed to an intimate relationship intend to remain together, and when people have children they expect to be competent parents. Unfortunately, marriages terminate and children grow up in less than optimal environments. This does not mean that the family made no attempt to resolve its difficulties. It probably means that they considered their problems to be insurmountable. Family social workers believe that early, timely intervention creates a potent opportunity for change, assuming the inherent motivation of people to try to be healthy.

> **Belief II: Families want to stay together and overcome their differences.**   Contrary to popular notions, most people prefer to remain in relationships rather than to be alone, and most are motivated to remain together to work out their differences. People do not suddenly decide to break up but instead try, using available resources, to resolve differences and overcome pain. However, many families have difficulty handling problems and require

assistance to resolve them in constructive and mutually satisfying ways. Family social workers can provide practical, supportive, concrete help. Early interventions are important to help the family deal with difficulties in a way that promotes lasting change.

Belief III: Parents need understanding and support for the challenges of maintaining relationships and raising children.   People receive little, if any, training on how to be effective partners and parents. These important social roles require knowledge, patience, consistency, and unselfishness. People need all of the understanding and support they can get! Often individuals are blamed when a marriage fails or when parents are inconsistent or ineffective; observers may be quick to judge results without appreciating a family's pain at the dissolution of a relationship. Blaming creates defensiveness and anger, but understanding and support can generate opportunities for new learning, constructive change, and possible reunification of families.

Belief IV: Parents can learn positive, effective ways of responding to their children if they are provided with support, knowledge, and skills.   All parents can benefit from the support of friends, relatives, and the community. In fact, these supports are necessary for adequate social functioning. However, some parents have had little access to parenting role models and knowledge. Helping parents acquire appropriate knowledge and skills benefits everyone. This assumption asserts that all people want to be their best and can improve their skills when they are taught positive parenting techniques.

Belief V: Parents' basic needs must be met before they can respond effectively and positively to the needs of their children.   Unemployed parents, parents distressed about housing or food, or those who are experiencing other forms of anguish often find it difficult to meet the needs of others despite how much they care. Thus, even when the goal of family social work is to help parents develop more effective ways of enhancing their children's development, attention must also be directed toward helping parents meet their own needs. Helping parents to eliminate stress can free them to manage their children in more positive ways.

Belief VI: Every family member needs nurturing.   People need to feel loved and connected to other people. Sometimes becoming angry and blaming others seems easier than sharing love and caring. Every family needs to be a sanctuary in which each member can experience nurturing and love. If only one person is getting his or her needs met at the expense of others, then the family is not functioning properly.

Belief VII: Family members, regardless of gender or age, deserve respect from each other.   Within the context of different cultural groups, the family social worker should examine existing power structures in a family rather than assuming that one person is "head" of a household. This means respecting differences and unique contributions to the marriage, parenting, and family. Children should be respected and accorded due rights as people. Gender differences also should be respected. Equal opportunities for growth and participation must therefore be guaranteed to all family members, regardless of age or gender. At the same time, social workers should understand that roles related to gender and age may vary in different cultures.

Belief VIII: A child's emotional and behavioral difficulties cannot be viewed outside the context of the family. To understand children, one needs to understand families. Further, to work effectively with children, one must work effectively with their families. Problems experienced by families generally do not reside either within the parents or within the child, but instead are an intimate part of the daily pattern of family interactions.

Belief IX: All people need a family. All children need to feel connected with someone who cares for them. This unconditional positive regard and acceptance from another person is critical for a young person's development.

Belief X: Most problems in families do not appear overnight but have developed gradually over the years. Although a situational crisis frequently is the catalyst for families to seek help, most problems in families develop over a protracted period. Consequently, change is unlikely to occur overnight. Families need to have an understanding of the need for long-term support during the process of change.

Belief XI: A difference exists between thoughts and actions in parenting. At times, parents may feel overwhelming levels of frustration when managing children; they may even consider leaving their children or escaping from the family. Parents' escape fantasies may lead the family social worker to believe that the parent is unloving or uncaring, but this is probably not the reality. Saying something or thinking something is different from doing it.

Belief XII: A difference exists between being a perfect parent and a "good enough" parent. Parents do not consistently do the right thing at the right time. Parents may yell at their children, or they may sometimes fail to meet their needs. These actions will seldom destroy a child. Rather than being a perfect parent, the goal is to meet *enough*, rather than *all*, of the needs of the young person. The definition of "enough" will be modified over time, paralleling the child's evolving developmental needs.

Belief XIII: Families require fair and equal treatment from environmental systems.   Many minority families have not been treated justly by society. Historically, members of different groups have not had equal access to the same resources and systems of helping. Thus, we describe certain populations as "underserved." Social workers seek to equalize the imbalance between groups and to promote social justice for all families. Similarly, single-parent families or families who do not conform to the prescribed norms suffer when resources and support fall short of their needs.

CONFLICTING NEEDS OF FAMILY MEMBERS

Sometimes families experience stress when one member has needs that must be met. For example, a physically challenged child requires special attention. Make a list of the types of needs that a family member might have and beside each one, determine how meeting these needs might conflict with meeting the needs of other members and of the family as a whole.

PRINCIPLES THAT GUIDE FAMILY SOCIAL WORK

The following principles equip social workers to emphasize family strengths and positive options in family work. They ensure that the foundation of the work conveys a belief in the family's capacity to evoke positive change.

Principle I: The best place to help families is in their home. The home is the natural environment for the family. Through in-home observation of family interactions, the family social worker is best able to assess the family. Interventions based on accurate knowledge of the family in their social context provide optimal opportunities for success. Family needs may require the FSW to be in the home for many hours a week, focusing on the family's daily issues and interactions. The FSW in the home can provide immediate feedback regarding alternative methods of interaction and problem solving.

Principle II: Family social work empowers families to solve their own problems.   One goal of family social work is to help families become more competent. Providing immediate solutions may alleviate current stresses, but imposed solutions will not leave the family better equipped to deal with future issues. Families change by learning and practicing new skills. It is critical for the family social worker to be aware that a major goal of intervention is to promote family participation in change in a way that facilitates increased self-reliance and independence.

Families vary in their ability to cope with stress. Some families have strong coping skills but require extra assistance during a particularly stressful time, while other families require continuing assistance, perhaps from more than one agency. All families have unique strengths and weaknesses, and no family is completely lacking in abilities or strengths. An accurate assessment of the specific capacities of families should precede the design of the intervention.

Principle III: Intervention should be individualized and based upon an assessment of the social, psychological, cultural, educational, economic, and physical characteristics of the particular family.   Family social work begins "where the particular family is." This principle is true whether it is the social worker's first or the twenty-first visit. Family strengths and issues must be continually assessed and evaluated to ensure appropriate and timely intervention. What is effective for one family may not work for another family with similar problems.

Interventions based on predetermined formulas do not permit modifications tailored to the special needs of a particular family. One of the advantages of family social work is its capacity to plan interventions that reflect the uniqueness of families. In fact, in the 1980s family workers were challenged to become more culturally sensitive because characteristics of ethnic families such as extended kin networks had been considered dysfunctional by conventional family therapy standards (Nichols & Schwartz, 1998).

Principle IV: Family social workers must respond first to the immediate needs of families and then to their long-term goals.   Hungry children need food; they cannot grow and develop on promises of future food while their parents learn a trade or seek employment. The family social worker must assess a family's immediate needs and see that these needs are met.

Maslow's hierarchy of needs is a useful road map for assessing and meeting the needs of children and families. Maslow (1967) outlined a hierarchy of needs, starting with basic physical needs such as the need for food and shelter. The second level of needs involves safety. Satisfying these needs involves protection from physical harm, including living in a safe neighborhood. The third level includes needs related to belonging. Belonging needs are met when one is accepted and valued by a group, the family being the first social grouping. The next level involves esteem needs, and the final level is the need for self-actualization. The family social worker first ensures that family members' basic physical and safety needs are met, then works with the family on its other needs.

HIERARCHY OF NEEDS

Using Maslow's (1967) hierarchy of needs, as described in this chapter, provide examples of these needs for individuals within a family, ways of meeting these needs, and ways in which the needs might remain unfulfilled.

Individual	Needs	How to Meet Needs	Threats to Meeting Needs
Example:			
Infant/Toddler	1. Physical	Parents feed child and change diapers.	Lack of money for food or diapers.

Families' changing needs should guide the priorities and focus of helping. A family worker's inability to respond flexibly to shifting priorities may interfere with the working relationship. For example, a family social worker who continues to talk about infant development to a parent who has just received an eviction notice will have difficulty maintaining the confidence of the parent, because infant development is the last thing on the parent's mind. If the social worker persists in imposing an inappropriate agenda, the parent may be less motivated in future visits. The FSW may alienate the family by not tracking its immediate needs.

Principle V: The family is a social system. Thus, intervention efforts directed at one member could influence the whole family. Families are like mobiles; one member's behavior influences the behavior of the others. This means that the family social worker must constantly evaluate the probable consequences of proposed changes for each family member. Questions such as who will benefit from a particular change and who will suffer are important issues to address. Will the benefits outweigh the costs to individual members and to the family as a unit? Anticipating possible adverse consequences can help the FSW and the family deal with them.

Principle VI: A collaborative helping relationship should exist between the family social worker and the family. This collaborative relationship emphasizes benefits gained through cooperation and interdependency. The family is part of the treatment team throughout the change process. Although the FSW contributes expertise in planning ways to resolve family problems, the FSW and the family collaborate on defining problems and solutions. This collaborative partnership can identify common problems, set goals, and devise solutions.

Principle VII: A goal of family social work is to promote social justice for all groups, regardless of race, creed, or country of origin. Problems of historically underserved families have been neglected because of bias, prejudice, and lack of accommodation for special circumstances (e.g., lack of transportation to the social service agency). Cultural norms, values, and expectations contribute to family problems, and it is important to understand how these impinge on social functioning (Okun, 1996). A goal of family social work is to provide effective services to family groups. This may require that the FSW assume the role of advocate, educator, or social change agent. A family social worker must be committed to pluralism in all its forms. The profession cannot be bound by narrow family structures, nor can it rely on values appropriate only for a single family form. The FSW must avoid imposing one cultural viewpoint on another, striving instead to capitalize on strengths from a family's cultural heritage (Garbarino, 1982).

CHAPTER SUMMARY

Families are social groupings that grow and contract to reflect changing membership. No family remains static. Family dynamics are shaped by members' definitions rather than by a rigid, predetermined formula. Genograms and ecomaps assist the family social worker to understand family dynamics and provide a visual overview of family membership, relationships, and environmental connections.

Effective family social work is contingent upon the application of a set of core beliefs and assumptions that affirm the value of families and family social work. These beliefs assist the worker to develop competency-based, respectful interventions designed to promote collaborative relationships with the family. Through such teamwork, family social workers can help families capitalize upon their own particular strengths.

3
Family Systems

The family systems approach is the bedrock upon which most family work is built. Adapted from biology, systems theory proposes that common organizing and operating principles govern living organisms. Because systems concepts provide a useful framework for working with families, these concepts have gained prominence in family social work in recent years. Systems theory helps us understand how a family functions and how it relates to its environment.

Systemic family work is based on three main ideas:

1. Problems occur as the result of ongoing patterns of communication within the family;
2. Family crises produce both instability and opportunities for change; and
3. Families operate according to established rules that must be changed before problems can be resolved.

Family systems theory is useful for understanding family dynamics, but it has limitations in explaining serious problems such as wife battering or sexual abuse. In addition, feminists have criticized family systems theory for its inherent gender bias. These issues will be addressed in later chapters.

WHAT IS A FAMILY SYSTEM?

Family systems theory is based on the idea that all families are social systems. This viewpoint removes problems from being attributed to individuals and locates them in the arena of relationships and social interaction. When FSWs provide services to families, they become immersed in a family context where problems are created and maintained by ongoing communication patterns and rules. Family systems theory provides a conceptual framework for assessing family members within a context of family relationships.

A system is a complex set of elements in mutual interaction. When a family is viewed as a system, the social worker looks at it as a set of interconnected units. The focus of intervention is on how family members influence one another, rather than on each individual's behavior.

The key to working with families as systems is to understand that family interactions and relationships are reciprocal, patterned, and repetitive. Family interactions are woven together to create a complex but patterned family fabric. Social workers need to understand how family life provides the backdrop for individual behavior, especially how each member interacts with the others. The focus on family interactions means that the FSW looks first for *what* is happening, rather than *why*.

The following passage from *The Lost World* is applicable to the family as a system (Crichton, 1995, p. 2).

> It did not take long before the scientists began to notice that complex systems showed certain common behaviors. They started to think of these behaviors as characteristic of all complex systems. They realized that these behaviors could not be explained by analyzing single components of the systems. The time-honored scientific approach of reductionism—taking the watch apart to see how it worked—didn't get you anywhere with complex systems, because the interesting behavior seemed to arise from the spontaneous interaction of the components. The behavior wasn't planned or directed; it just happened. Such behavior was therefore called "self-organizing."

This quotation highlights the limitations of observing one family member in isolation from the others. Behavior within a family is interdependent, and one person cannot be understood by looking at his or her behavior alone. The actions of each family member influence the actions of the other members.

KEY ASSUMPTIONS ABOUT FAMILY SYSTEMS

It is important to understand several key ingredients of family systems concepts:

- The family as a whole is more than the sum of its parts.
- Families try to balance change and stability.
- A change in one family member affects all of the family members.
- Family members' behaviors are best explained by circular causality.
- A family belongs to a larger social system and encompasses many subsystems.
- A family operates according to established rules.

The Family As a Whole Is More than the Sum of Its Parts

Using a systems approach, we consider the family to be a social system that is more than the sum of the individual characteristics of each family member. Von Bertalanffy, the biologist who first formulated general systems theory, suggested that when the component parts of a system are organized into a pattern, the outcome of that organization is an entity greater than the individual parts. No matter how well acquainted we become with individual personalities, we can understand a person's behavior only by observing his or her interactions with others. Families have a tremendous influence on who people are and how they behave. When the focus is on children, FSWs can best understand them by observing how they interact with other family members. Through this focus, the FSW develops an appreciation of the patterns of family relationships. Thus, a child who is noncompliant with parental and family rules is not viewed as a "bad" child. The child is acting out because of how family members interact both before and after the noncompliant episode.

Assessing a family involves identifying its strengths and problems, and trying to understand how the interactions of individual members detract from or contribute to effective family functioning. Many kinds of individual problems either originate or are expressed through family interaction. Consequently, family work is designed to transform dysfunction into mutually supportive family relationships. Changed family interaction is both an end in itself and a vehicle with which to understand and address individual difficulties. The overarching goal of family intervention is to improve overall family functioning by promoting better interpersonal relationships and interactions.

One way to understand how a system can be more than the sum of its parts is to think of how musical notes are organized in such a way as to make a tune. Separately, the notes mean nothing, but together, the notes are organized into a melody. The combination of single notes creates a sound that has characteristics completely different from the individual notes alone or from a different combination of notes. Despite how much the FSW knows about individual family members, their behavior is best understood through observations of family interaction. In conclusion, the interaction of family members creates an entity that is more than the sum of the individual personalities.

Families Try to Balance Change and Stability

To survive, all systems need stability, order, and consistency. The struggle to maintain the status quo is called *homeostasis*. Homeostasis is ensured through family rules that determine which behaviors are allowed. Just as a thermostat in a house keeps the furnace or air conditioner operating to maintain a stable temperature, homeostasis works to keep a constant balance in the family. In families, the "thermostat" represents family rules through which families strive to function consistently and predictably.

Often families struggle with maintaining the status quo. Families face continuous pressure to grow and develop in response to the changing external environment and evolving needs of family members. In the process, they try to find a balance between opposing demands for consistency and change. Families in different stages of the life cycle will vary according to what activities are required to maintain stability and what activities are required to promote development. Paradoxically, families must continually adapt and change in order to remain stable. Destabilizing crises disrupt family patterns, making life both unpredictable and stressful.

Family social workers should not assume that stability and health are interchangeable. Stability merely frees up family members from constantly having to respond to unpredictable demands, enabling members to function adequately in daily routines.

At different stages in a family's life cycle and in certain situations, family functioning seems more or less set. After a crisis, the family reverts to precrisis functioning. For example, if a parent becomes temporarily unemployed and remains at home, the initial stage of adjustment might be marked by crisis while family members adapt to living with an unemployed parent who may also be depressed. However, after a temporary disruption, the family creates new routines and functioning based upon the new set of circumstances. When the parent returns to work, the family may slowly revert to previous patterns of functioning. That is, the family returns to its "normal" state.

A family's initial reaction is usually to deny and resist impending change, striving to maintain balance and stability. Family resistance to change can be quite strong, as social workers who have attempted to challenge rigidly maintained behavior can attest. This is one reason why family work can be so taxing. Changes in family functioning may be difficult to sustain unless treatment ensures that families will incorporate the changes permanently. Families can experience distress or discomfort with new behaviors even when changes are positive, as when an alcoholic member stops drinking.

Resistance involves avoiding or opposing something (Brock & Barnard, 1992). Resistance to change by families is normal and should be expected. People may seek relief from anxiety, guilt, and shame. In addition, the behavior of the social worker might play a role in resistance. The most important skill for preventing resistance is recognizing the right amount of pressure to apply and to avoid pushing family members too hard. Countering resistance requires disarming and neutralizing behavior. Even when a social worker uses an appropriate intervention, it may be ineffective because the social worker has asked the family to do something that makes no sense to them. Resistance can be diminished when the family becomes more comfortable with the social worker (Lum, 1992).

When change is desirable, the family social worker's goal is to help the family decide how to achieve a new point of homeostasis. This shift requires that the family reorganize and devise new patterns. For example, when a child is removed from the home, the family might reorganize to deal with the loss, with members assuming various roles and functions of the absent member. Failure to find a new balance means that some, if not all, of the family members might not get their needs met, perhaps leading to family chaos or even disintegration. Once a family has reorganized into a state of new family homeostasis organized around the absence of the child, reintegration of the child back into the home may be more difficult. If the family does revert to older, more familiar patterns, the reasons for the child's removal in the first place may not be addressed. The thrust to reestablish stability and equilibrium ("normal family functioning") during periods of change is a powerful force that should not be overlooked by social workers who are trying to create change that endures after the social worker is no longer seeing the family.

Although it appears that families prefer equilibrium, in fact families are never static. According to Michael Crichton (1995), complex systems seem to strike a balance between the need for order and the imperative for change: "Complex systems tend to locate themselves at a place we call 'the edge of chaos'" (p. 2). The survival of a social system necessitates that it remain on the edge of chaos where there is enough vibrancy to keep the system alive. On the other hand, the system needs sufficient stability to keep it from falling into chaos. In the same way, families are always changing. They may be unbalanced and stable at the same time. When pressure to change or adapt is placed on families through an extended crisis, a new pattern of family functioning evolves, creating an altered state of family balance. This is a very important point for family social workers to keep in mind, as much family work is started because of a family crisis. The hope is that parents who have adopted new parenting strategies for an extended period will incorporate these strategies into their "natural" and "normal" parenting style after the social worker leaves.

The coexistence of change and stability is one of the most difficult concepts of systems theory to understand in terms of social work practice. Often, social workers will view families either as stuck or as being in total disequilibrium (i.e., chaotic). It is important for the FSW to realize that families try to maintain a balance between stability and change.

Experienced family social workers appreciate the complexity of families and recognize that when families seem stuck or appear to be moving from one crisis to another, they may be maintaining either rigid equilibrium or chaotic change. Eventually, the family will need to adopt solutions that include a balance of stability and change.

Some family theorists suggest that presenting problems (often child-related problems) are primarily an attempt for the family to maintain homeostasis. However, caution should be exercised in seeing the homeostatic mechanism in families in this way, since it has been used to rationalize and justify a range of problem behaviors in the family such as sexual abuse and domestic violence. These concerns are explored in more detail in Chapter 11.

Two types of change can occur within a family: *first-order* and *second-order* change (Watzlawick, Beavin, & Jackson, 1967). First-order change occurs when the behavior of one family member changes, but *rules* that govern the family remain the same. In second-order change, the rules are altered. Consequently, first-order change is likely to result in families reverting to their "normal" precrisis patterns. Second-order change, on the other hand, is likely to represent more enduring family changes.

Family homeostasis has implications for crisis theory. Family social workers often encounter families who have undergone a destabilizing crisis such as a report of child abuse. Recognizing the tendency to revert to "normal" functioning after a crisis can help the family social worker capitalize on destabilizing periods by helping a family create second-order, long-lasting changes. The task of FSWs then, is to challenge families to move to a new state of balance by reorganizing patterns of interaction and creating new rules to regulate these patterns (Goldenberg & Goldenberg, 1996). In this way, the family will abandon past preferred states of balance in favor of new ones.

FAMILY HOMEOSTASIS

Reflect on your family of origin and try to recall a couple of crisis situations that occurred as you were growing up. Describe one situation in which the family reestablished homeostasis quickly. Describe another crisis after which the family did not revert to homeostasis as quickly. Compare the two situations.

A Change in One Family Member Affects All of the Family Members

To understand families as social systems, we need to realize that a change in one member of a family affects every other family member. Recognizing this tendency can explain a family's response to a member's attempts at change, as well as its response to the FSW's attempts to create change. If one family member begins to behave differently, other members may resist this change in an effort to keep the family in balance. Some authors have suggested, for example, that when one family member's symptoms improve, another may develop symptoms. Further, if the member changes successfully, the family will be unable to revert to its previous behavior patterns because of the changes. In other words, change in one part of the system forces change in other parts of the system.

For example, if a parent yells at the children to complete their homework but eventually does the work for them, children may learn to rely upon the parent's efforts every evening. However, should the parent stop doing the children's homework, the children must then finish their own homework, get someone else to do it, do the homework themselves, or suffer the consequences of not doing it at all. We see, then, that the family system adapts in response to one member's altered behavior.

Family Members' Behaviors Are Best Explained by Circular Causality

The way that families function is often both predictable and patterned. Thus, the family social worker needs to pay attention to the patterns of communication between family members. Communication patterns in a family are reciprocal and mutually reinforcing.

Linear causality describes the process whereby one event is thought to *cause* another event. For example, when an alarm clock rings at 7:00 A.M., a child wakes up. Event A (ringing of the alarm clock) causes event B (child waking up), but event B does not cause event A. That is, the sleeping child does not cause the alarm to go off!

Often temper tantrums are viewed in families as linear events. Parents observe that when they say "no," the child protests. Such a conceptualization of the problem allows the parent to label the child as "bad" or "spoiled." Family members are detached from the role that they play in the development and continuation of the problem. Linear explanations for behavior problems fail to account for relationships, history, and ongoing communication patterns. Linear explanations of individual problems attribute the problem to personality factors.

Conversely, circular causality places ongoing interaction patterns within a context of patterned family relationships. In working with a family, the social worker should look for circular patterns of interaction between family members. Circular causality accounts for how the behaviors are perceived and how members feel about the interaction. Circular causality disputes the belief that events simply move in one direction, with each event being caused by a single previous event (Goldenberg & Goldenberg, 1996).

Circular causality, then, describes a situation in which event B influences event A, which in turn contributes to event B. For example, a parent shows interest in her child's homework, and the child then explains the assignment to the parent. This is likely to result in an ongoing circular and reciprocal pattern of interaction. The parent continues to take an interest and offer support regarding her child's homework, the child feels supported and may make an extra effort when doing homework, asking the parent for help, thus reinforcing the pattern. The circular pattern is characteristic of ongoing family relationships. Rather than one event causing another, events become entangled in a series of causal chains.

Family social workers will often need to become involved in altering maladaptive patterns within the family. Consider another homework example. A parent yells at a child to do her homework. The child interprets the yelling as a message that she is bad and a failure, leading her to feel anxious, to have difficulty concentrating, and to do poorly on the homework. The parent, observing that the child is not concentrating or doing the work, interprets the child's behavior as laziness and defiance. In response, the parent scolds the child about her poor attitude and performance and the circular maladaptive pattern becomes entrenched after several repetitions of the cycle.

Figure 3.1 illustrates examples of some common patterns of circular causality.

Over time, patterns of interaction among family members can become highly repetitive. In conceptualizing circular causality, however, we must be careful to incorporate power into the analysis. Until recently, power was con-

FIGURE 3.1   Examples of Circular Causality

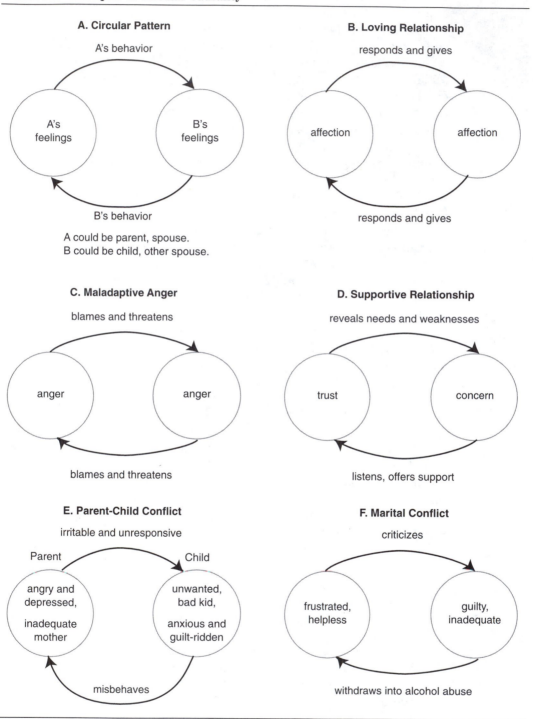

A. Circular Pattern

A's behavior

A's feelings   B's feelings

B's behavior

A could be parent, spouse.
B could be child, other spouse.

B. Loving Relationship

responds and gives

affection   affection

responds and gives

C. Maladaptive Anger

blames and threatens

anger   anger

blames and threatens

D. Supportive Relationship

reveals needs and weaknesses

trust   concern

listens, offers support

E. Parent-Child Conflict

irritable and unresponsive

Parent   Child

angry and depressed, inadequate mother   unwanted, bad kid, anxious and guilt-ridden

misbehaves

F. Marital Conflict

criticizes

frustrated, helpless   guilty, inadequate

withdraws into alcohol abuse

sidered too linear to be applied to patterns of family interactions. However, just as certain components of a mobile are heavier than others, different family members exert more influence over others. As feminists have argued, power imbalances must be taken into account in understanding family relationships.

CIRCULAR CAUSALITY

Reflect upon a well-established relationship in which you are currently participating, or a relationship from your childhood. Try to identify an ongoing circular pattern of interaction between you and the other person. Label your own thoughts, feelings, and behaviors, then try to do the same for the other person. How does circular causality work when there seems to be a power imbalance?

A Family Belongs to a Larger Social System and Encompasses Many Subsystems

An important systems concept concerns the relationship between systems, subsystems, and larger-scale systems (suprasystems). All living systems are made up of subsystems in relationship with other subsystems. The family consists of a group of individuals within a wider family system. The marital subsystem, parental subsystem, and child subsystem are all examples of family subsystems. Subsystems also can be identified within individuals—for example, physical, cognitive, and emotional subsystems. Family subsystems may be organized around gender, age, and power, to name a few variables. Commonly, the marital subsystem (the parents) is considered the "architect of the family" because it is (or should be) the most influential subsystem with the family (Satir, 1967). The success of the family is largely dependent upon the parental subsystem (Goldenberg & Goldenberg, 1994), whether it is a single-parent unit or two parents.

Larger systems to which families may belong include the extended family, the city, the neighborhood, recreational organizations, the church, and so on. These in turn are part of even larger systems, such as nations or groups of nations. The FSW will focus on the family, its subsystems, and the larger systems to which the family belongs.

Environmental support is necessary for family and individual well being (Garbarino, 1982). Informal support from friends and family is particularly important. Yet, for many families formal sources of support predominate their support networks, and unfortunately, many have a pattern of negative interactions with the social service system (Kaplan, 1986).

A rich and diverse network of social relationships is a sign of maturation and health. For example, young children start out in a relationship with one significant person (often the mother), gradually relating to other children and adults in the family. Eventually, children incorporate children and adults outside the family circle into their support networks. This occurs through school and exposure to others through family activities. Children are disadvantaged when their parents have a limited support network.

Individuals who consider themselves part of a family do so within the context of family boundaries. A *boundary* determines who is included in the family and who is not (Nichols & Schwartz, 1998). Family boundaries may vary according to definitions based on culture and lifestyle. In Native American communities, for example, the extended family plays a central role in raising children (Pimento, 1985) and in-laws are considered part of the primary family unit (Sutton & Broken Nose, 1996). A boundary related to lifestyle could include a family where both parents have demanding jobs and have hired a live-in nanny. Live-in nannies are often considered members of a family.

Boundaries also determine who belongs to subsystems within the family. Some families have very definite boundaries, whereas in others the boundary between the family and the outside world is unclear. The FSW needs to identify family boundaries in order to decide who belongs within the family system and who interacts with whom. Services most often target individuals within family boundaries.

Healthy families have clear, flexible boundaries that are open enough to assimilate new thoughts, ideas, and resources when needed, but sufficiently closed so the family maintains a sense of identity and purpose. Ideally, closeness is neither overbearing nor intrusive to family members. Family environment boundaries should ideally be permeable and allow information and resources to enter and leave the family freely. In rigid families, these boundaries are closed, and no information enters or leaves the family.

When family members are cut off from one another emotionally, they are *disengaged* or underinvolved (Kaplan, 1986). In disengaged families, members share few activities and are poorly connected. Disengagement is often signaled by neglect (Kaplan, 1986). Conversely, interpersonal boundaries that are too open or *enmeshed* weaken individual integrity and prevent family members from acting as autonomous individuals. Enmeshed relationships occur when family members are too involved with one another. Both disengaged and enmeshed relationships are signs of poor functioning in families.

Boundaries between subsystems and individuals serve similar functions. Boundaries between generations are particularly important in family work (Brock & Barnard, 1992; Nichols & Schwartz, 1998). Boundaries between parental and sibling subsystems should be clear and allow for role differentiation based on appropriate development and socially sanctioned functions.

Families with boundaries that are too closed or too open expose members to greater risk than do families with more balanced boundaries. For example, families with incest perpetrators often have limited involvement with the outside world, allowing offenders to control family members, while communicating to the victim that disclosure is a betrayal of family loyalty. Friendships, particularly for the victim, are tightly controlled. At the same time, incest is a profound breach of intergenerational boundaries.

Conversely, children in loose-knit, disengaged families may be at risk of sexual abuse by perpetrators external to the family because these offenders are able to move in and out of the family freely, and children may lack adequate supervision. Gender also has an influence on whether the abuse will be intrafamilial or extrafamilial. Male children are given more independence in Western culture, making it more likely that they will encounter sexual abuse from people outside the family.

Most theories about families suggest that families should not only have flexible, clear boundaries with the outside world, but they must also have well-established intergenerational boundaries. In other words, the parents should be partners in parenting the children. A dysfunctional intergenerational boundary exists when one or more children form a coalition or alliance with one parent against the other. Similarly, families experience intergenerational boundary problems when a parent abandons his or her role and a child assumes the parental role. These children are described as "parentified" because the child assumes an adult role, and the parent becomes a child. For example, often in families with an alcoholic parent, one child steps into a parental role. If a child becomes primarily responsible for household chores or child care, or for meeting the emotional needs of family members, intergenerational boundaries are breached.

Families with rigid or overly closed external boundaries restrict involvement of members with the outside world, creating difficulty in accessing external resources. To the detriment of families, Western culture values autonomy and devalues interdependence (Garbarino, 1982). "Self-sufficient" families may come close to imploding before being able to request and accept external assistance. In addition, social isolation hides abuse within the family and protects perpetrators from detection, placing victims at risk of ongoing abuse. Alternatively, families with loose boundaries fail to regulate involvement with the outside world. Individuals may slip in and out of the family indiscriminately, based not upon family needs but upon individual needs, regardless of the consequences to family members. Garbarino (1982) has noted that a positive orientation toward relationships beyond the family and even beyond the larger kinship group is important to complement or counteract the idiosyncrasies of individual family patterns.

Consider the following example illustrating a family's problems with boundaries.

> Gloria and Robert Hatfield, a Caucasian couple in their mid-thirties, were referred to you by Family Court Mediation Services. The couple was seeing the court mediator as required during their divorce proceedings for the purpose of establishing child custody, visitation, and support payments for their only child, Elliott, aged three. The mediator noted that Elliott seemed to be having difficulties adjusting to his parents' divorce, showing aggression toward his classmates and his parents. The boy had been expelled from two day care centers for hitting and biting the other children. The parents reported that Elliott's behavior ranged from angry rages to clinging when making transitions between his parents' separate homes.

Mr. Hatfield initiated the divorce proceedings against his wife's wishes, though both report marital problems during most of their fifteen-year marriage. Mr. Hatfield reported that the relationship had been tolerable until the birth of their son. Prior to Elliott's arrival, Mr. Hatfield described the marriage as "two people going our separate ways." He said he and his wife had little in common, few mutual friends, and different life goals. After Elliott was born, his wife became very attached to the baby and Mr. Hatfield reported having felt excluded by his wife. She wouldn't let him hold or care for the baby unless he insisted. Also, she breastfed Elliott until he was two years old, against her husband's wishes. Mr. Hatfield now believes his ex-wife to be angry about the divorce and especially upset that he initiated it. He describes her as "unable to move on with her life" and to be using Elliott to "get revenge" on him and "trying to turn Elliott against him." He reported that his ex-wife is overinvolved and overprotective of Elliott and that consequently Elliott is a "Mommy's boy, afraid of his own shadow."

Gloria Hatfield denies her ex-husband's allegations, though she does report that they "could have tried harder" to stay together. She reports that they did go to marital counseling for a few months, but that Mr. Hatfield felt it was not helping and dropped out. She said that this kind of behavior was typical of her ex-husband; that he withdraws emotionally at any sign of conflict and that he was "unable to establish a truly intimate relationship." She believes that now she is teaching Elliott how to have a close relationship. She is fearful that Mr. Hatfield cannot provide an appropriate male role model for her son.

In sum, Gloria Hatfield feels her son's problems stem from her ex-husband's inability to establish an intimate relationship, while Robert Hatfield feels the problems originate from the mother's overinvolvement with Elliott.

Relationships with significant others outside the family constitute an important source of emotional support (Wahler, 1980). Mothers who have little positive daily contact with supportive persons outside the family apparently behave more negatively with their children than those with more frequent positive interactions outside the family. In assessing the quality of a family's social supports, it is useful to look at *reciprocity, density, complexity, sufficiency, emotional climate,* and, finally, *feedback characteristics* (Rothery, 1993).

- *Reciprocity* involves the extent to which social support is exchanged with others. Many relationships with formal helpers are based on a one-way relationship in which the helper gives and the family takes. A more useful relationship occurs when the family both gives and receives support.

- *Density* involves the number of relationships that family members have with others. Ideally, each family member will have multiple relationships outside the family with supportive individuals. Family members should also be free, depending on their developmental abilities, to form relationships with significant others outside the family.

- *Complexity* refers to the capacity of a social support network to meet a variety of individual and family needs.

- Social support networks are *sufficient* when social supports are adequate to meet family and individual demands and needs.
- *Emotional climate* refers to the quality of relationships with others outside the family. Relationships that are mostly caring and supportive are preferable to aversive relationships.
- *Feedback characteristics* involve the type of information that is provided by those in the support networks. Ideally, feedback needs to be clear, direct, and honest. It also needs to be corrective or supportive when needed.

Family social workers need to observe the social functioning of the family. Social functioning is best understood by looking at the social roles that family members perform. Individual behavior and adjustment reflects how well family members perform their social roles. Geismar and Ayres (1959) proposed four areas of role performance within the family and four outside the family.

Internal roles include:

- Family relationships and family unity.
- Child care and training.
- Health practices.
- Household practices.

External family roles include:

- Use of community resources.
- Social activities.
- Economic practices.
- Relationship of the family to the social worker.

It is important to consider multiple aspects of family functioning. Originally, work with families was considered a "maverick" intervention because it emphasized understanding the individual within the context of the family. Over the past decade, however, family interventions have been criticized for not considering the impact of a family's social environment. To paraphrase the words of one observer, "to do so is like watching a parade through a keyhole" (Goldner, 1985).

A Family Operates According to Established Rules

Family rules determine what is allowed and what is forbidden in the family. They also regulate family members' behavior toward one another (Goldenberg & Goldenberg, 1994). Most family rules are unwritten, and understanding patterns of interaction within a family allows observers to understand implicit family rules. Family rules may guide what is allowed in the family, describing patterns of behavior that are acceptable or unacceptable.

Family rules act as a family "thermostat," keeping the family environment comfortable. Roles become established based on family rules, such as how children will be cared for, who does the laundry, who makes wages, and how the money is spent. Division of family labor evolves over time, and children might assume distinct roles. Understanding family rules allows workers to see how family members view their relationships with one another.

Family rules are established through diverse mechanisms related to gender, age, culturally linked expectations, and so on. It is possible to change the rules once they become clear and explicit. However, family social workers should also be aware that there are *rules about rules* that dictate how members interpret rules as well as how they change them.

FAMILY RULES

All families are governed by unspoken rules. Identify the rules of the family in which you grew up. Describe how the rules differ according to age and gender of family members.

CRITERIA FOR ASSESSING FAMILY FUNCTIONING

A helpful way to understand and assess family functioning is to use the Family Categories Schema based on the work of Epstein, Bishop, and Levin (1978). These authors designed an instrument for FSWs to complete after their initial meetings with families. This instrument and other valuable family assessment scales are presented in *Measure for Clinical Practice* (Fischer & Corcoran, 1994). The instrument is a sixty-item self-report questionnaire containing eight categories: (1) problem solving, (2) affective responsiveness, (3) affective involvement, (4) communication, (5) role behavior, (6) autonomy, (7) modes of behavioral control, and (8) general functioning. After describing each category, we will present a sample item from the instrument.

Problem Solving

Problem solving is concerned with how a family copes with threats to emotional or physical well-being or to the family's survival as a functioning unit. Threats can be either instrumental or affective. Instrumental threats involve "mechanical" or concrete aspects of living, such as economic, physical, or health concerns. Thus, parental unemployment or the physical abuse of a child are examples of instrumental threats to the family. Affective threats threaten the emotional well-being of family life, examples include a depressed child, an overwhelmed parent, or a maladaptive circular interaction. Frequently, instrumental and affective problems overlap. A parent feeling depressed because of unemployment is one such example.

An example of a self-report statement related to problem solving is "We resolve most everyday problems around the house."

Affective Responsiveness

Family members should be able to express a variety of emotions within a supportive family environment. The range of emotions can be divided into two major categories: *welfare emotions*, such as happiness, joy, tenderness, love, and sympathy, and *emergency emotions*, such as rage, fear, anger, and depression.

The FSW should assess the family's ability to respond with the appropriate quality and quantity of feelings to affect-provoking stimuli. Family social workers are concerned with the welfare and emergency emotions expressed in the family, as well as the pattern of their expression. This involves whether the expressions of emotion are clear, direct, open, and honest or indirect, masked, and dishonest. The degree to which individual family members participate in the affective interchange is also important.

An example of a statement related to affective responsiveness is "Some of us just don't respond emotionally" (Fischer & Corcoran, 1994).

Affective Involvement

To what extent do family members become emotionally involved with one another in activities and interests that go beyond those needed for instrumental family functions? Involvement transcends mere expression of affect and captures the amount and quality of the emotional involvement that family members have with each other. It is one thing to praise a child for doing homework, and it is something else to actually sit down with the child and discuss homework. We strongly endorse the need for parents to support children; thus, parents need to be actively involved in their children's interests and activities.

One example of a statement related to affective involvement is "It is difficult to talk to each other about tender feelings" (Fischer & Corcoran, 1994).

Communication

Communication can be quite complex. An adage of communication theory is: *You cannot not communicate*. Hence, the verbal and nonverbal communication within a family are both important. Communication serves two functions: to communicate content, and to define the nature of the relationship between the speaker and listener. The second function is called *metacommunication*. Listening carefully to how family members communicate with one another will give the FSW important clues about a family's relationships. A message conveyed out of care will come across differently from a message conveyed out of anger, even if the content of the messages is the same.

Healthy family communication is clear, direct, open, and honest. As with problem solving, communication can be categorized into affective and instrumental areas. Affective communication is defined as that in which the communicated message is mostly emotional in nature, whereas instrumental communication occurs when the message is primarily "mechanical." An instrumental message is related to the mechanics of "getting things done" and involves the regular, ongoing tasks of family living.

Communication occurs both verbally and nonverbally, through posture, voice tone, gestures, and facial expressions. If a person says, "I'm listening" while making eye contact and smiling, the words are interpreted differently from how they would be perceived if the speaker were hiding behind a newspaper. Ideally, verbal and nonverbal communication should be congruent. Additionally, information that is exchanged should be reciprocal and positive (Brock & Barnard, 1992).

An example of a statement related to communication is "When someone is upset the others know why" (Fischer & Corcoran, 1994).

Role Behavior

A family is confronted with daily pressures, tasks, and obligations. To cope, each family member plays roles that develop into established and predictable patterns of behavior. Roles are repetitive patterns of behavior that serve a function in day-to-day family life (Brock & Barnard, 1992). They can take many forms, such as those that follow traditional role definitions (such as gender roles) and roles that deviate from traditional roles, known as idiosyncratic roles.

Traditional roles involve those of mother, father, husband, wife, son, or daughter, as traditionally defined and accepted by a culture. Roles based on gender are much less clear today than they used to be, as are spousal and parental roles. However, most people still regard children as more the mother's responsibility than the father's (Eichler, 1997). Roles that are not always clearly agreed upon include the parental role to socialize children and be responsible for their emotional and physical well-being. Idiosyncratic roles fall outside the traditional social prescriptions. For example, a mother may assume the role of primary financial provider (traditionally the male role) while the father cares for the children and takes care of household tasks. Some idiosyncratic roles are related to the family's presenting problem, as when one child takes the role of scapegoat. Other idiosyncratic roles, such as the clown and the hero, are seen in alcoholic families.

Optimal family roles include:

- Clearly differentiated roles of parents and children;
- Flexibility of roles when the situation demands;
- Roles that are performed competently (Brock & Barnard, 1992).

An example of a statement related to role behavior is "Each of us has particular duties and responsibilities."

Autonomy

Autonomy concerns the ability of family members to act independently and to make individual, responsible choices. Autonomy is demonstrated when each member has a sense of identity as a separate person rather than an extension of others, is able to make choices in selecting or rejecting outside influences, and is willing to take responsibility for making personal choices. Autonomy should be assessed in light of each member's age, developmental abilities, and potential. Also of importance is the degree of individuation that occurs in the sphere of the family unit and in the individual members' life beyond the family unit. Individuation refers to the sense of being a unique individual, distinct from others.

An example of a statement related to autonomy is "Mom is always telling me what clothes I should wear."

Modes of Behavioral Control

Behavioral control involves the family's way of dealing with impulses, maintaining standards of behavior, and coping with threatening situations. Four modes of behavioral control are described below.

- *Rigid:* a fixed pattern of familial behavior that is intolerant of individual variation (e.g., children are never allowed to sleep over at a friend's home).

- *Flexible:* a familial pattern of behavior that is firmly and clearly defined but at the same time involves a flexible style allowing for individual variation (e.g., agreed-upon family rules are present but may be bent in the case of special circumstances; i.e., children usually are not allowed to have sleepovers on weeknights, but the rule is bent to celebrate a birthday).

- *Laissez-faire:* no effective or established patterns of behavioral control exist (e.g., the rule might be that no sleepovers are allowed on a school night, but the rule is altered inconsistently, such as when a child pleads).

- *Chaotic:* a pattern of complete inconsistency in modes of behavioral control within the family (e.g., there is no rule about sleepovers during a school night and on one occasion, the child is permitted to sleep over, but on other similar occasions, the child is denied a sleepover; thus, the child is not aware what rules regulate sleepovers).

These four modes of behavioral control can be evaluated with regard to whether they are consistent or inconsistent—that is, whether the mode of behavioral control is predictable or unpredictable.

An example of a statement related to behavioral control is "We have rules about hitting people."

FAMILY FUNCTIONING

> Develop at least two questions from each of the eight areas of family functioning identified in this chapter. Be especially alert to any sexist, ageist, or cultural biases that enter into your questions.

General Functioning: Integrative Skills Assessment Protocol

Figure 3.2 illustrates an example of a structured protocol for assessing an individual and his or her family (Jordan & Franklin, 1995).

FIGURE 3.2   Integrative Skills Assessment Protocol

I. Identifying information
1. Name
2. Address
3. Home phone number
4. Work phone number
5. Date of birth
6. Family members living at home
   a. Name
   b. Age
   c. Relationship
7. Occupation
8. Income
9. Gender
10. Race
11. Religious affiliation
12. Briefly describe the presenting problem or symptom(s).

II. Nature of presenting problem
13. List all the problems identified by the client and/or practitioner.
14. Specification of problem(s)
   a. History
      (i) When did the problem first occur?
      (ii) Is this a long-standing, unresolved problem? A recently established one?
   b. Duration
      (i) How long has the problem been going on?
   c. Frequency
      (i) How often does the problem occur?
   d. Magnitude
      (i) What is the intensity of the problem?
   e. Antecedents
      (i) What happens immediately before the problem occurs?

      f. Consequences
- (i)   What happens immediately after the problem occurs?

      g. Reasons for seeking help
- (i)   What made them seek help now and not before?

      h. Prior efforts to solve problem
- (i)   How has the client sought to solve the problem previously, including other therapy?
- (ii)   With what results?

      i. Client motivation
- (i)   What is the level of motivation for solving the problem?

      j. Client resources
- (i)   What are the client resources available for solving the problem?

      k. Other
- (i)   Are there other difficulties associated with or in addition to the problem?

15. Prioritize problems.
      a. Through negotiations with client, prioritize problems in terms of severity.

III. Client

16. Intrapersonal issues

      a. Cognitive functioning
- (i)   What is the client's perception of the problem?
- (ii)   Is there evidence of problem-solving capacity?
- (iii) Is there evidence of rational vs. irrational thoughts?

      b. Emotional functioning
- (i)   Describe the client's affect.
- (ii)   Is there evidence of appropriate vs. inappropriate affect?

      c. Behavioral functioning
- (i)   What is the client's physical appearance?
- (ii)   Mannerisms?
- (iii) Disabilities?

      d. Physiological functioning
- (i)   Has the client been seen medically during the past year?
- (ii)   If so, with what results?
- (iii) Is there any evidence of drug and alcohol usage?
- (iv) Any medications taken?
- (v)   Describe diet, caffeine usage, etc.

      e. Client mental status
- (i)   Note disturbances in appearance, dress, posture, etc.
- (ii)   Note disturbances in thoughts (e.g., hallucinations, delusions, etc.).
- (iii) Note disturbances in level of awareness (e.g., memory, attention, etc.).
- (iv) Note disturbances in thought processes (e.g., logic, intelligibility, coherence).
- (v)   Note disturbances in emotional tone (either deviations in affect or discrepancies in verbal reports of mood and client affect).
- (vi) Note the degree to which the client seems aware of the nature of the problem and the need for treatment.

      f. Ethnic/cultural considerations
- (i)   What is the client's ethnic group?
- (ii)   What is the degree of acculturation?

         (iii) What is the client's perception of how ethnic/cultural group identifi-
             cation has helped or not helped?
         (iv) Are the sources of conflict related to ethnic/cultural issues?

  g. Motivation
        (i) Does the client want to change the problem?
        (ii) What are factors that may contribute to client motivation, either caus-
             ing client discomfort or causing client to have hope for thefuture?

  h. Client roles and role performance
        (i) What roles does the client perform (e.g., wife, mother, etc.)?
        (ii) What are client issues related to role performance?
        (iii) What are client issues related to satisfaction or
             dissatisfaction?
        (iv) What are gender issues?

  i. Developmental considerations
        (i) Trace the birth, developmental history of the client (e.g., the mother's
             pregnancy, developmental milestones, illness, trauma, etc.).

17. Interpersonal: Family
  a. Is there an "identified patient"? If so, who?
  b. What is each family member's perspective of the problem(s)?
  c. Marital status
        (i) What is the client's sexual, dating, and/or marital history?
        (ii) What is the quality of the client's intimate relationship?
        (iii) How long has the client been married?
        (iv) How many times?
  d. Family structure
        (i) What is the quality of the client's family interactions?
        (ii) Describe the family boundaries, family alliances, family power struc-
             ture, and family communication patterns.

18. Interpersonal: Work or school
  a. Occupation or grade in school
  b. Satisfaction with work/school
        (i) Are there indicators of successful achievement in this
             setting?
        (ii) What are issues related to grades, pay, promotions, etc.?
        (iii) Describe relationships with colleagues/peers.
  c. Effect of problem(s) on work/school
        (i) Does the problem(s) occur in this setting also? If so,
             describe how the client gets along with peers, teachers, boss, other
             authority figures.
        (ii) What is the academic/work history?
        (iii) Any evidence of antisocial behavior?

19. Interpersonal: Peers
  a. Satisfaction with number of peers/friends.
        (i) Who are the client's friends and what is the quality of these
             relationships?

IV. Context and social support networks

20. Agency considerations
  a. Does the agency setting have an effect on the problem/client (i.e., does the
     client have negative feelings about seeking
     services at this agency? Is the agency located too far away to be accessible
     to the client? Does the agency have the resources to deal with the client's
     problem in terms of worker time, interest, etc.?)

      b. Suitability for referral
         (i)   Would referral be best for the client, and if so, what is the best refer-
ral source?

21. Client's environmental context
      a. What environmental resources does client have (e.g., does the client have
adequate housing, transportation, food/clothing, recreation, social supports, educational opportunities, etc.)?
      b. What environmental resources exist that the client is not
currently utilizing (e.g., access to family or peer support or support from
agencies in the neighborhood)?
      c. What environmental resources do not exist and need to be
developed? What are the gaps in resources that exist for this client?

V. Measurement (use either global assessment measures or rapid assessment instruments)
  22. Family functioning
  23. Marital (or significant other) functioning
  24. Individual functioning
  25. Social supports

VI. Summary
  26. Practitioner impressions
      a. Summarize problem areas for presentation to client. Obtain client feed-
back.
  27. DSM diagnosis
  28. Problem for intervention
      a. To be negotiated with client and prioritized.
  29. Progress indicators
      a. What are the goals for client change?
  30. Baseline
      a. Results of either pretest or repeated measurement of targeted problem.

SYSTEMS CONCEPTS

Use the integrative skills assessment protocol in Figure 3.2 to learn more
about yourself and your family. Select a partner and review each other's
findings. What new insights resulted?

CHAPTER SUMMARY

The family systems approach allows the FSW to assess a family within the
context of interactions and relationships. The systems approach is com-
plementary to the developmental approach, which will be described in the
next chapter. The developmental approach considers stages in the family's
life cycle. With a systems perspective, relationships at each stage of the
family life cycle are the focus of assessment.

From a systems view, the social worker focuses on the family as a
whole, rather than individual family members. The family is seen as trying
to achieve a balance between change and stability. Change that affects one

member affects the whole family. Causality is "circular" rather than linear. The family system includes many subsystems and also is part of larger suprasystems.

This chapter includes tools for gathering information about families, based on a systems perspective. Finally, an integrative skills assessment protocol is offered for assessing families from a systems perspective.

4 Family Developmental Perspective

Family social workers must be able to assess how a family is functioning and identify what it needs. In this chapter we will build upon family systems theory by discussing the developmental perspective, an important theoretical framework with which to understand the predictable crises of family life. Most people are familiar with stages of child and adult development, but fewer are aware of family developmental stages. The family life cycle perspective helps us identify problems that may arise at specific stages (Duvall, 1957; Carter & McGoldrick, 1988). Assessing a family from a developmental perspective can help the FSW understand whether a family is meeting social expectations for child rearing (Holman, 1983). Few families progress smoothly from one stage to another, and problems are particularly likely to develop during critical family stages, such as adolescence.

We will begin by presenting the developmental stages that are typical for middle-class families. This model presumes that families will remain intact, and it fails to account for diverse family forms that include never-married or divorced parents. Variations of family development under these divergent themes are discussed later.

DEVELOPMENTAL STAGES

Since families grow and change in relatively predictable ways, one useful way to understand them is to examine each developmental stage. It is difficult to predict how a specific event will affect a family, but it is easier to identify the types of crises families may experience over a lifespan. Each family reacts uniquely to life events, yet most families encounter a similar range of developmental crises, such as the death of a member. All families must cope with loss at times. Families generally progress through similar developmental processes, marked by an identifiable beginning or transition event such as a wedding, the birth of the first child, or the retirement of parents. Each stage challenges the family with unique developmental issues, tasks, and potential crises to be resolved. Knowledge about the family life cycle can help social workers identify ways in which a family has become "stuck" and identify changes that will help the family to move on.

Social workers need to understand how a family must shift attitudes and modify relationships to adapt to evolving family life stages (Holman, 1983). Family crises can be anticipated, and no family can sidestep them. Life cycle transitions intensify family stress, and family problems that arise at certain points suggest that a family is having difficulty functioning at a particular developmental stage. Every family responds to crises in a distinct way. Some families have evolved excellent problem-solving skills and strategies, in addition to strongly developed support systems. Others have not. Family social workers who are aware of developmental issues facing the family are in a better postition to assess the family's issues, the crises that occur as a result, and the coping tools used by families to address these issues. During developmental crises, family social workers can provide much-needed knowledge, skills, strategies, and support to families who are overwhelmed by difficulties associated with developmental crises (see Chapter 8).

Geismar and Krisberg (1996) have suggested a direct relationship between social functioning and the family life cycle. Families with limited economic and social resources become more disorganized as the family progresses through the family cycle. Family disorganization suggests a bad fit between the family's *need* for service and resources and the *availability* of services and resources as well as the family's ability to use them. The growing need for economic and social resources strains the family's economic, social, and emotional resources.

Certain tasks accompany each family stage. Transition to a new stage is usually accompanied by some kind of crisis, whether large or small (Petro & Travis, 1985). While transitions between stages are not discrete, each transition point places demands upon the family system to adapt. For example, roles of family members change as children mature. Additionally, family boundaries need to be adjusted throughout the family life cycle to fit the changing needs of family members. For example, as children enter adolescence family boundaries should become more flexible to adapt to the changing developmental needs of teenagers. If family boundaries are too rigid during adolescence, parent-child conflict is likely to result. Conversely, if the boundaries are too loose during adolescence, the child may lack adequate monitoring of activities and become prematurely disengaged from the family.

The stages of family development presented in Figure 4.1 below are adapted from three models: Carter and McGoldrick (1988), Becvar and Becvar (1993), and Duvall (1957). Description of stages of family development include marriage/partnering, birth of the first child, families with preschool children, families with school-aged children, families with teenagers, and families with young people leaving home. Later family stages are relevant to this text inasmuch as grandparents are an important part of family life for some families.

This model of the stages of family development is helpful, but it has some shortcomings. First, each family is unique, and developmental stages may vary greatly from one family to another. Second, developmental models tend to focus only on the milestones of one individual, usually the eldest child (Becvar & Becvar, 1993). How would we classify a family that included a newborn child as well as a teenager who was ready to leave home? Where would a never-married single parent fit into the family developmental life cycle? There are many variations of the family life cycle, some of which are quite complex (Breunlin, 1988; Eichler, 1997). Breunlin, for example, depicts family transitions as oscillations between stages rather than an inevitable progression from one stage to the next.

FIGURE 4.1   **Stages of the Family Life Cycle**

Stage	*Family tasks*
1. Marriage	• Committing to the relationship • Formulating roles and rules • Differentiating as a couple while separating from families of origin • Making compromises and negotiating around concrete and personal needs
2. Families with young children	• Restabilizing the marital unit with a triangle • Accepting the child and integrating that child into the family • Reconsidering relationship with one another and with work
3. Families with school-aged children	• Allowing greater independence • Opening family boundaries to accommodate new social institutions • Understanding and accepting role changes
4. Families with teenagers	• Dealing with teen independence through boundary adjustments • Adjusting to a new definition of personal autonomy • Rule changes, limit setting, role negotiation
5. Families with young people leaving home	• Preparing teen for independent living through schooling and job skills • Accepting youth's independence
6. Middle-aged parents	• Adjusting to the "empty nest"
7. Aging family members	• Involvement with grandchildren and partners of the children • Dealing with problems of aging

Source: Adapted from Becvar & Becvar, 1993; Carter & McGoldrick, 1988; Duvall, 1957.

The number of alternative family forms has been increasing in recent years. There has been a growing number of births to unmarried women. Additionally, many families undergo changes initiated by separation, divorce, and remarriage. Between 38 and 50 percent of children born in the United States during the 1980s will experience the divorce of their parents. Most often, the mother retains custody and the father is given visitation status (Curtner-Smith, 1995). In many families both parents work and child care must be arranged. Some couples prefer to remain childless, while others delay having children beyond age 40. Spousal roles are often no longer premised on traditional gender arrangements, and social changes have led to altered family structures that at one point in our history were excluded from the mainstream, such as parenting by gay or lesbian couples. Finally, issues inherent in the changing family life cycle include grandparents' involvement as primary caretakers, parenting later in life, and intergenerational family configurations (Helton & Jackson, 1997). Diversity in family development is discussed later in this chapter.

Families in different ethnic groups show cultural variations not seen in the "typical" family life cycle. For example, the African American family may consist of an extensive kin network, often including more than one household. Several families may live under the same roof, and children may reside in a kinship household different from the one in which they were born. Recent immigrants to North America often show cultural variations in which the previous generation exerts control over the new family, and families function as collective units (Lum, 1992). Lum also suggests that the collective interdependence of the minority family requires that the social worker thoroughly assess intergenerational linkages between parents, children, grandparents, and other members of the extended family since family members often base decisions on how they will affect the complete family unit.

The following case example illustrates some of the crises a family may face during a time of transition.

> The Lee family consists of Sam and Lark, both in their early forties, and their three daughters, ages seven, nine, and fourteen. Problems with Mary, age fourteen, have brought the couple to the family social work agency.
>
> Sam and Lark were both born in mainland China, and they met while studying at the University of California. The Lees describe enjoying a "traditional Chinese lifestyle." Both Sam and Lark are devoted parents who want their children to know and respect their Chinese background and culture.
>
> The family's problems had begun when Mary entered junior high school. Although Mary continued to receive high grades at her new school, her behavior had undergone a radical transition. Their previously compliant daughter had become defiant. She had cut school to be with her friends on several occasions, and she had been absent from several family celebrations against her parents' wishes. When her parents had tried to correct Mary's misbehavior, she had become agitated and started yelling at them.
>
> The event that had brought the family to the agency was Mary's reaction to an argument with her parents during the previous week. She had left home during the night, apparently climbing through an upstairs window. Mary had

stayed at the homes of various friends for five days, and her parents had been frantic.

Mary, who has accompanied her parents to the FSW's office, tells the social worker that she needs some freedom from her parents' autocratic parenting. She feels that her parents are old-fashioned and unfair in comparison to her friends' parents. She explains that although she loves her parents very much, she does not share their attachment to traditional Chinese culture. She wants to be like her friends.

The family social worker, assessing the Lee's situation from a developmental perspective, sees a family with intergenerational values conflicts as well as developmental issues that frequently arise when children enter adolescence.

Marriage/Partnering

Before a new relationship can occur, young people usually leave their families of origin. At this stage of life, members must separate from their parents, develop intimate peer relationships, and become established in work (Holman, 1983). Today, however, young people in middle-class families are inclined to live with their parents longer because of greater educational demands, lack of employment opportunities, and overall economic difficulties. In other families, young people are leaving prematurely, running away from home, leaving school early, and working in low-paying, unskilled jobs. How individuals leave their families of origin will greatly affect the rest of their lives. Although people can return to school later in life, this becomes more difficult when they are responsible for a family. Thus, there are wide variations in how and when young people leave home and what educational and career skills they bring into relationships. They will also differ in the degree to which they have separated from their families of origin.

Each new stage in a family's life cycle is a critical transition point requiring an adaptation in roles and tasks. Change creates stresses and conflicts that must be resolved in order for the family to reach fulfillment and satisfaction. Three major tasks of the newly partnered couple are establishing a mutually satisfying relationship, realigning relationships with extended families (who must accept the new partner), and making decisions about parenthood. People bring to a new relationship ways of living that they learned while growing up. Upon entering a new relationship, they are confronted with different ways of living that may contrast sharply with what is familiar to them in all areas of family life. Most aspects of life will need to be negotiated between the two, including financial arrangements, housekeeping, social and leisure activities, and relationships with in-laws.

Forming a relationship with another person, whether in marriage or by mutual agreement, requires adjustment, compromise, and hard work. They also must adjust to the behaviors, feelings, habits, and values of another person. The realities of adjustment to extended family, shared finances, conflicting wants, desires, and living patterns mean that the couple will experience pressures that must be resolved in order for the marriage to succeed. The FSW must assess the couple's satisfaction with their own relationship, their relationships with extended family, and agreement concerning decisions about parenthood. In assessing the marital relationship, the FSW will find a marital satisfaction scale to be helpful. (See Hudson, 1982.)

Problems may appear on several fronts during the first phase of the family life cycle. A partner who has not successfully negotiated independence from his or her family of origin may experience divided loyalties that threaten the fragile, new relationship. Similarly, a partner who wishes to continue the social life of a single person also creates stress on the relationship. Also, they may have children so soon that there is little time to sort out crucial agreements about the relationship.

Birth of the First Child

Parenthood is a major life upheaval, requiring changes in lifestyle. Why people have children is a puzzle for many parents, but Satir (1967) suggests that there are many reasons, including fulfilling social expectations, obtaining a feeling of immortality, and addressing issues from the parents' past. It can be helpful for the FSW to explore with the parents the reasons and expectations associated with having children.

For some people, the birth of the first child is a crisis that initiates a critical (although usually temporary) family adjustment period (LeMasters, 1957). Once people accept responsibility for a child, they must continue to accept that responsibility for many years, maintaining a joint commitment to their child as well as to each other. The arrival of a child complicates family life and can create upheaval for the couple. For example, studies show an initial decrease in marital satisfaction after the arrival of the first child (Spanier, Lewis, & Cole, 1975). The first crisis of this stage, then, is preparing for and adapting to the birth of the child and resolving conflicts regarding commitment and fears associated with becoming a parent.

Satir (1967) points out the trap of having a child to fulfill one's emotional needs, only to discover that the child's needs are more pressing than one's own. New parents may experience conflict about caretaking roles that may threaten the existence of the marriage. Research indicates that a couple who have negotiated a successful relationship adapt more easily to having children (Lewis, 1988).

With the birth of the first child, a variety of unique parental roles are suddenly needed. Having children is a difficult adjustment, contributing to grief about lost freedom in lifestyle, recreation, and career choices. Previously, parents had the opportunity for self-indulgence, career development, and couple bonding. With the birth of the child, former lifestyles change. Suddenly the couple has less time for themselves or each other, less money, and more responsibility. Parenting a newborn child takes time and energy, and it requires new levels of self-sacrifice and self-denial. Needs of children must take precedence over the needs of the parents, a difficult adjustment for many new parents. People who have difficulty getting their own needs met have a hard time meeting the needs of others, particularly those of young children. The stress a newborn causes is enormous, and the threat to family stability is high.

A lot of attention has been given to the concept of "bonding" or "attachment." Most hospitals now encourage ongoing contact between parents and the child immediately after birth to encourage parent-child bonding. Hospitals also encourage the father to be present during childbirth. Yet, in the early phases of a child's life, mothers typically assume most of the child care responsibilities (Garbarino, 1982; Mackie, 1991).

Being reasonable, patient, consistent, and cheerful is difficult when night feedings, colic, and diaper changing disrupt sleep patterns. The arrival of the child requires adjustment by both parents, and the strain on the couple's relationship may result in one or both parents feeling neglected or misunderstood by the other. Meeting the needs of one's child as well as one's partner requires much effort even when the child is wanted.

Adjusting to parenthood is complicated by the fact that society expects parents to be equipped automatically with knowledge and skills to meet the needs of children without having received any education on parenting skills or child development. Many new parents rely on their own parents for advice at a time when they are still trying to redefine that relationship in "adult to adult" terms. More than likely, the grandparents also have had little preparation for parenthood.

During this stage, parents must develop a mutually satisfactory, reciprocal parent-child relationship. To help the child learn to trust others, they must be dependable in meeting the child's needs. It is necessary for both to feel good about the relationship, but reciprocity is difficult when the newborn does not reward the parents by smiling, laughing, or talking. It is easy for new parents, especially parents who are needy themselves, to become frustrated by the one-sided nature of the early relationship with a child.

Again, our description of this stage in the family life cycle was based on typical situations. Children born with disabilities stress most families, and families may not have adequate resources and skills to care for children with special needs. Alternatively, one of the partners may be faced with infertility, requiring the couple to decide whether to undergo infertility treatments, adopt a child, or remain childless. If both parents are working, the couple must decide whether one person will remain at home to care for the child. Usually, the decision has a greater impact on the woman, regardless of whether or not she returns to work. If she returns to work, she often assumes responsibilities related to the child. If she stays at home, her earning power is diminished and career advancement is placed on hold. A child born to an impoverished family or a family with many social problems may exacerbate the stress that the family already feels.

At first, a newborn interacts with only one person at a time, most often the mother. As the child matures, his or her relationships gradually encompass more people and more situations (Garbarino, 1982). A child benefits from a varied family life that includes diversity of relationships. That is, the "social riches" of a child's life are augmented when relationships are multifaceted, reciprocal, and lasting (Garbarino, 1982).

Families with Preschool Children

The child who was formerly totally dependent soon becomes more active and strives for independence. As motor skills improve, nothing may be too risky for the child to try, including hopping off the stairs or climbing into the toilet. Superman pajamas may transform the youngster into a superhero recklessly jumping off furniture. The child's energy seems inexhaustible. At the same time, the parents' energy may be depleted and their relationship strained by lack of privacy. A young child greets each new experience—the moon, a dog, or another child—with glee. The toddler absorbs stimuli that adults take for granted, and new experiences contribute to the growing cognitive abilities of the child. Unfortunately the exploratory skills of the child are a mismatch with awareness of safety, making parents tense and on guard for disaster. Inadequate parental supervision during this time creates risk for the child. So does the failure of a parent to provide sufficient cognitive stimulation.

Parents should be concerned about the safety of their children during this stage and provide an acceptable amount of stimulation while at the same time ensuring safety. It may be difficult for parents to encourage independence and at the same time protect the child. Parents either allow too much independence, placing the child at risk, or become too protective, thereby, discouraging development.

Parental energy levels can also be an issue. Sometimes parents become careless or rigid because they run out of energy. The energy drain of the parents can be compounded if a second child arrives while the first is still a preschooler. Such a change in family dynamics might not be appreciated by the older child, resulting in sibling rivalry and added parental stress. The increased cognitive ability of the firstborn can intensify the stress as the first child strives to attract the parents' attention. For example, a three-year-old may try to distract the parents' attention from the newborn by using creative strategies. This can include filling the kitchen sink to take a bath or urinating on a rug during the infant's feeding. These attempts to recapture the center stage of the parents' attention create added stress for the parents.

At this stage of family development, children need to develop increasingly complex social relationships that emphasize work, play, and love (Garbarino, 1982). Optimal development requires that children have access to a variety of significant others, gradually expanding relationships from parents and siblings to a peer group.

Families with School-Aged Children

Family patterns are altered again when the oldest child reaches school age, because family members must begin to plan schedules around school and extracurricular activities. The daily process of separating from and reuniting with the parents usually is established by the time the child reaches school age, and most kindergartners are ready to take their first major step away from home. Family tasks in this stage involve supporting the child's adjustment to a formal learning situation in which he or she interacts cooperatively with peers and authority figures other than parents. During this period, children must also learn to adjust to a regulated routine.

Some parents believe that having school-aged children resembles running a taxi service. Baseball practices, swimming lessons, school meetings, and numerous other activities are very time-consuming for all of the family members. Skills required to negotiate this phase include organizing, cooperating, and supporting family members. At this stage, differences in family income levels become strikingly apparent, and some children notice that their schoolmates have more possessions and are involved in more activities. Classmates may have more clothes, toys, access to recreational services, and spending money even if they attend the same school. Another difference that has an impact on families is in the amount and type of food available to children from different socioeconomic backgrounds. Children who have not had a nourishing breakfast or who do not have enough to eat for lunch are disadvantaged in the classroom. Parents who cannot afford to provide children with the basics, let alone the luxuries, often feel inadequate when their children enter school.

The effort involved in getting children to school makes this endeavor overwhelming for some parents. Just getting children ready for school each morning is a major task that includes organizing lunches and books and choosing clothes. Getting the children out of the door on time can be exhausting. It becomes even more complicated if the parents also are trying to get themselves ready for work, particularly if they must leave before the children do.

When children reach school age, working parents face the need to make arrangements for adequate out-of-school care. Arrangements should include care and supervision before and after school hours, during school vacations and holidays, and other school closures. Meeting this requirement can be difficult. If arrangements are inadequate, the children become vulnerable to potential danger at home and on the street. Low-income parents may find out-of-school care too expensive and may be unable to make safe after-school arrangements because of inadequate income for child care or no extended family support. Although a responsible adult should be with children when they are not in school, too many children come home to an empty house after school. These young people, often seen wearing a house key on a string around their neck, are called latchkey children.

The increase in the number of women, and consequently parents, in the workforce is well documented and might even be described as a revolution that has taken place since the end of the Second World War. More than half of new mothers work. The number has grown steadily over the past ten years. Younger new mothers are more likely to stay home with their children than women over the age of thirty. Mothers with college educations are more likely to return to work as are single parents. Finally, African American new mothers are more likely to return to work within the first year of a child's birth than are Hispanic mothers (Hunter College Women's Studies Collective, 1995).

The growing participation of both parents in the workforce has affected family life enormously. Parents face tremendous challenges as they try to juggle work responsibilities, child-rearing tasks, and household chores while attempting to meet their own personal needs. The demands are even more difficult for single parents, as they often have fewer economic resources and assume all household and child care responsibilities alone.

In single-parent or two-career families, children may be left at home unsupervised. Children are more likely to be injured when they are home alone (Peterson, 1989). They may be vulnerable to increased anxiety and fear. Ideally, young children should not be unsupervised. When this is not possible, children should be given explicit instructions on safety including rules concerning cooking, answering the telephone and doorbell, and what to do in case of an emergency. The length of time a child can remain unsupervised depends on the age and competence of the child, as well as the risks that the child is likely to encounter.

Another task of parenting during this stage is to assist children to acquire necessary skills and attitudes for survival in a school environment. In today's society, school success is equated with life success. To help children succeed in school, parents must adopt an "academic culture" and communicate a positive regard for schooling (Garbarino, 1982). Parents can help children interpret the new world of school, and when children have accomplished something, the parents should reinforce the accomplishments. At other times they can provide the safe place to which children return to escape the stress of school. Most importantly, parents can help children learn to assume responsibility for learning. The ability to value knowledge is a gift that parents can give their children. One of the best ways to help a child do well in school is to establish a predictable evening routine during which the child is expected to do homework. This means turning off the television and setting aside a quiet part of the home to allow concentration.

During this phase of the family cycle, parents should make strong connections with those institutions that work with their children. Parents who value school have a greater chance of encouraging academic success than those who do not (Garbarino, 1982). Again, close involvement with the schools will help a child develop competence and skills in preparation for later life.

Families with Teenagers

Adolescence is often a time of turbulence for families. It is a period of rapid change for the youth as well as the family. The adolescent is moving toward adulthood and seems to want the whole world to know it. Despite popular lore that suggests the teenage years are stressful, most teenagers endure this period with no more difficulty than they encountered in previous stages of development. Problems, if any, are more likely to be the fruit of family stress rather than an unavoidable consequence of puberty.

Generally, the family's task during this time is to help the young person to grow up and learn skills that will enable him or her to eventually leave the family. The parents assist the young person to develop habits required for work, including assuming greater responsibility and independence. The young person also is learning about sexual relationships, a process facilitated by the parents' role of "sounding board."

Many adolescent "problems" represent the teenager's misguided attempts toward independence and adult autonomy. During this period, adolescents struggle to define themselves and make their own decisions. Parents, however, may not recognize that "problem" behaviors are part of normal development and may focus on inappropriate clothing or make-up, outrageous attitudes, and noncompliance with family rules. An adolescent can display unpredictable behavior, one day playing ear-splitting music, the next day being silent, withdrawn, and brooding. Perhaps most threatening, parents find themselves being challenged and out-reasoned by their formerly manageable child (if they had such a child to begin with). Compliant children may suddenly develop an independent style of logic seemingly contradictory to the facts. Parents may feel uncomfortable or threatened when challenged by children who in the past were obedient, loving, and accepting of parental guidance and direction.

Despite the strife that often accompanies adolescence, teenagers can also be a joy. The process of growing up may be difficult to understand and stranger to watch, but the results can be quite healthy. Teens require support and encouragement during this time. The difficulty for parents is to support the youngster's struggle for independence and maturity while providing necessary structure.

Adolescence is a time of contradiction. The adolescent reviews and repeats all of the previous developmental stages as he or she struggles toward adulthood. Tasks include learning to trust others, acquiring a stable identity, and addressing the questions of purpose in life. Questions of intimacy, relationships, morality, peer associations, and life goals are important as the young person assumes new roles in an attempt to determine his or her future directions.

A significant developmental issue is sexual maturation, which is often accompanied by strong and frequently conflicting feelings. All at once, it seems, the adolescent has grown into a different body, and sometimes the changes can be frightening. The task is to develop a new self-image, but this new view of oneself can seem distressingly fragile. It is no wonder that many young people think of adolescence as a period of embarrassing self-consciousness and self-reflection.

Teenagers demand more privileges and freedom than they have had previously, but they may still have little sense of responsibility for their actions. At this stage much behavior is centered on peer standards because the approval of friends is preferable to parental approval. Parents are regarded as naïve, embarrassingly out of touch, and ancient. The rapid changes suggest that the role of parents during this stage is different from that of previous stages. Their role is more to provide support when needed and back away when they are not needed. Wise parents do not intrude except in cases of need, painful as this often may be to all concerned.

Adolescents loosen family ties by establishing closer relationships with peers, a difficult transition for some parents. As teenagers move toward greater independence, freedom, and responsibility in preparation for leaving home, they are developing skills while remaining within the shelter of the family unit. Unfortunately, some teens leave families prematurely, before they have had the opportunity to develop skills needed for independence.

YOUR ADOLESCENCE

Reflect on your own adolescence, and describe what was going on in your family and how your teen years (or those of your siblings) created changes in the family system.

Families with Young People Leaving Home

When young people leave home, the size of the family shrinks and parental responsibilities change. Young adults may leave the family in a series of slow steps culminating in permanently moving out of the home. This may be a back-and-forth process with the young person leaving and returning a number of times, creating mixed reactions to the transition on the part of the parents. Reactions can range from ecstasy to grief, or a combination of the two.

Parents may face a crisis of their own as they experience their own aging process and changes in their relationship with each other. They can no longer deny that they are getting older since they now have adult children. When parents have focused much of their adult lives on their children, the last child's departure from home provokes a special kind of crisis. Adjusting to the "empty nest" requires that parents replace their traditional focus on their children. Some people pressure their children to produce grandchildren, while others find new hobbies or employment. Some do all three.

During this stage, young people focus on establishing themselves as independent adults, capable of functioning on their own. In some cases, they will be struggling with starting their own families. If they left home early, or had children early, this struggle can be stressful. On the other hand, difficulty finding work or getting into postsecondary education means that many young people delay leaving home, which also can be stressful. The move to independence is compromised by their continued reliance on parents.

When is a child ready to leave the home? This question is difficult to answer. Naturally, some young people leave home before they are ready. Some may run away from home to escape difficult family situations. On the other hand, for middle-class families, some suggest that adolescence is extending beyond the teenage years as children remain at home while they continue school. Many middle-class parents can no longer afford to send their children away from home for an advanced education. However, in families where postsecondary education is not emphasized, youth face difficulty since in Western, industrialized nations, blue-collar jobs are becoming increasingly scarce (Garbarino, 1982).

Issues for Older Parents

Our focus in this book is on social work with families that include children who are living at home. Thus, the other developmental stages of the family will be mentioned only briefly. The next stage describes middle-aged parents who no longer have their children living with them. Their major task is reestablishing themselves as a couple and they may go through a new courtship stage as the partners find new roles and rules in their relationship. This can be a difficult time for couples who find that they no longer have a reason to stay together without the children at home to bind them together.

The final stage, that of the aging family, lasts until the death of one of the partners. The couple must adjust to becoming older and facing death. Couples might become isolated during this stage as friends die or as they are forced by ill health to move to nursing homes or hospitals. This stage is even more difficult if the couple suffers from inadequate financial resources. Another area of potential stress for the couple is the recent trend of older people moving into the residence of one of their adult children. This role reversal, whereby the adult child may take on a caregiving role for his or her parent, can be stressful for everyone.

Middle-aged couples or singles may find themselves caring for their own children as well as their aging parents. These adult caretaker children have been dubbed the "sandwich generation." This role was not unusual in past years when society was less mobile and extended families stayed together. It is more difficult in today's society, in which both partners in a marriage often work full-time.

The above-mentioned developmental stages are generalizations about families based on assumptions that all families have children, remain intact over the lifetime of the parents, and so on. Of course this is not the case. Divorce rates remain high, and there are growing numbers of single-parent families, blended families, and couples marry later in life and therefore have fewer years together as a family. The number of couples who remain childless also has increased. Each of these factors creates specific issues for the family that need to be taken into account when working with families. It is important to remember that each family, regardless of its composition, is unique. In the context of uniqueness, however, the vast majority of families are similar in that families get bigger and then get smaller. Not only do children grow up to form their own families, but family size is affected by divorce and death. At each transition, the family experiences stresses and strains as its members attempt to respond to the changes.

A FAMILY DEVELOPMENTAL ASSESSMENT

Based on your family of origin, complete a developmental assessment by identifying the ages of family members and outlining key developmental issues your family is facing.

VARIATIONS AFFECTING THE FAMILY LIFE CYCLE

Not all families sail through the family life cycle according to the above description. Even the Brady Bunch was a blended family! Economic trends have influenced how families move through the life cycle. More women are actively involved in the workforce now than in past decades; in fact, married women in the workforce exceed the number of full-time homemakers (Eichler, 1997). Poverty is more prevalent among children and women. Female-led, single-parent families often experience severe economic disadvantage, more so than two-parent families or male-led single parent families. Moreover, approximately half of all marriages end in divorce. Live-in relationships occur frequently. Death and desertion may disrupt the family life cycle. Eichler (1997) has identified major demographic patterns in industrialized countries that have an impact on the family life cycle: the decline in fertility, postponement of marriage, a sharp rise in the incidence of divorce during the 1970s and 1980s, and a growing proportion of people living in small households. The diversity of family styles brings with it differences in family development.

Separation and Divorce

Half of all first marriages and 61 percent of remarriages end in divorce (Nichols & Schwartz, 1998). Divorce is a life crisis requiring adjustment by all family members. Divorce has a disruptive impact on the life cycle of the family. It frequently lowers the economic status of family members and demands new coping skills. A couple's decision to separate and divorce is not made overnight. Rather, it is distinguished by distinct stages. The major tasks during divorce are to end the relationship while cooperatively parenting the children. Issues involved in divorce include making the decision to divorce, planning the dissolution of the relationship, separating, and finally, going through with divorce. During each stage, family members must come to terms with personal issues related to divorce. For example, partners must acknowledge their roles in the failed relationship. If the decision to divorce appears imminent, partners must learn to accept the inevitable. At times one partner is more reluctant to divorce than the other. Additional issues include forging new relationships with extended family members and mourning one's losses. Once the divorce is final, the partners must rebuild their lives as single people or adjust to life with a new partner.

Divorce brings with it longstanding issues that affect every member of the family. Of particular concern is the impact of divorce on children. Most children cope emotionally with the separation or divorce of their parents, but for many it still exacts a psychological toll. For a child, divorce and marital separation are comparable to losing a parent through death (Wallerstein, 1983). Wallerstein and Kelly (1980) suggest the major pitfall of divorce for children is the impact on their development. Parents undergoing a divorce often feel psychologically drained and have little emotional energy available to take care of the children's emotional needs. For example, during postdivorce adjustment, custodial parents are less supportive, less nurturing, and more anxious in their relationship with children than they were before the divorce (Bolton & Bolton, 1987; Wallerstein, 1985).

Single parents experience role strain while they balance household tasks, care of the children, employment, and personal lives (Burden, 1986). Mothers who have sole responsibility for their children are more likely to behave punitively toward them (Smith, 1984). Isolation is associated with depression, and depression has been associated with child abuse (Zurvain & Grief, 1989). However, social support may buffer the effect of role strain and poverty for single-parent families (Gladow & Ray, 1986). Mothers in joint custody arrangements fare better than mothers with sole support (Hanson, 1986).

Children between the ages of six and eight often feel responsible for the marital breakup (Thompson & Rudolph, 1992), although guilt is not confined exclusively to this age group. Additionally, children may experience academic difficulties, anger, or other behavioral problems related to the divorce. It is not unusual for children to experience feelings of rejection and anxiety following a divorce, but these emotions are not often acknowledged or dealt with by significant people in the child's life. Divorce is especially hard on young males, for whom it may take up to two years following a divorce for their lives to stabilize (Hetherington, Cox, & Cox, 1978). Thus, children are often victims of divorce, as they suffer long-term ramifications of marital dissolution (Wallerstein, 1985).

Family disruption risks depleting psychological resources available to the child (Garbarino, 1982). For example, many separations and divorces are bitter, and the child's loyalty to both parents becomes strained. The custodial parent (usually the mother) assumes much of the child care and household responsibilities, and her financial resources often become strained. In addition, children who are unsupervised for extended periods of time are twice as likely to belong to single-parent families as to families with two parents (Garbarino, 1982).

Children may experience divided loyalties between the custodial and noncustodial parent, and in bitter breakups a child may be used as a pawn between parents. Custody and access arrangements may be sabotaged, child support payments may be evaded, and allegations of abuse may be made. Some noncustodial parents simply give up the battle and disengage completely from the children.

Thompson and Rudolph (1992) propose several tasks that children of divorce must successfully accomplish in order to move on with their lives:

- *Feelings of anxiety, abandonment, and denial.* Parental support is a critical factor in helping a child overcome negative feelings. A parent must explain to the child what has happened without blaming the other partner.

- *Disengaging from parental conflict and distress, and resuming their regular activities.* Divorce should not be allowed to encroach on the routine activities in which children have been involved.

- *Resolution of loss.* Children must grieve not only the loss of a significant person in their lives, but they may also mourn the loss of other important aspects of their lives such as familiar surroundings and neighborhood friends.

- *Resolving anger and self-blame.* Children may feel responsible for the breakup or blame one parent for the divorce.

- *Accepting the permanence of the divorce.* Children often do not consider divorce final. They may hold onto a reconciliation fantasy long after the divorce. Some children may even scheme to reunite their parents or develop problems aimed at getting parents reunited.

- *Developing realistic hopes regarding relationships.* Children need to recognize that although their parents' relationship failed, positive marital relationships are still possible and that they cannot overgeneralize their parents' failure to all relationships.

Death of a Parent

Some issues related to divorce also apply to families in which one of the parents has died (Wallerstein, 1983). Although the death of a parent in families with young children is rare (Eichler, 1997), it does happen. To children, losing a parent through divorce can seem almost as final as through death. Widowhood is less likely to be associated with the dramatic drop in income that often occurs among custodial parents after divorce. However, widowed parents are less likely than divorced parents to remarry (Furstenberg, 1980). In addition, families that experience the death of one parent are likely to maintain contact with the deceased partner's family and with members of the community (Holman, 1983).

DEVELOPMENTAL CHALLENGES FROM DIVORCE

Discuss the challenges you believe a family experiences immediately after a divorce. Contrast these with what you believe to be the challenges experienced by families who have lost a parent through death. In what ways can a social worker assist the family during and after these critical periods?

Single Parenting

Single parenting can occur for several reasons: death, divorce, desertion, and never having been married. Regardless of the reason for single-parent status, single parents seem to experience common feelings including loneliness, sadness, guilt, and anger (Goldenberg & Goldenberg, 1996). In addition, divorced parents need to decide whether to cooperate with parental contact with the ex-spouse and support contact of the child with the ex-spouse and his or her family (Carter & McGoldrick, 1988).

Forty-five percent of all children in the United States live in a single-parent home at some point during childhood (Garbarino, 1982). Most single-parent homes are mother-led. Children from single-parent households show more problems than children from two-parent homes (Blum, Boyle, & Offord, 1988). They have a greater incidence of behavior problems such as conduct disorders, Attention Deficit Disorder, poor school performance, and emotional problems. This is not to suggest that every child from a single-parent family is destined to experience adjustment problems. Nevertheless, problems of single-parent families are compounded by economic difficulties (Goldenberg & Goldenberg, 1996; Eichler, 1997; Nichols & Schwartz, 1998; Pett, 1982) and fatigue (Okun, 1996). On the positive side of the equation, maternal education ameliorates the negative impact of these stresses (Tuzlak & Hillock, 1991).

Some single-parent families are poorly buffered against conflict and stress that may be acute or chronic. They experience multiple stresses operating simultaneously that overwhelm their capacity to cope. Poverty is a particular concern for single-parent families (Bolton & Bolton, 1987; Holman, 1983) and economic deprivation seems to be a factor when abuse occurs in these families (Gelles, 1989). Poverty also plays a role in many of the social/psychological problems associated with growing up in a single-parent household (Goldenberg & Goldenberg, 1994). Female-headed single-parent families are disproportionately represented among low-income groups. When they have adequate income and support, however, single-parent families can be as viable as two-parent families (Burden, 1986).

Single parents often experience role overload as they are burdened with tasks that are usually divided between two people. Task overload may be reflected in family disorganization, social isolation, and problems in the parent-child relationship (Holman, 1983).

Many interventions with single-parent families will be ecologically based. Issues related to provision of concrete resources and social support should be built into interventions. In addition, single parents may need assistance with stress management, grief counseling and skills related to effective child management. Finally, single parents will benefit from an enhanced informal support network including grandparents and friends.

The special tasks of parents in single-parent families are listed below.

- Develop adequate social support systems.
- Resolve feelings of sadness, anger, and loneliness.

- Cope with stress, fatigue, and role overload without taking it out on the children.
- Develop child management skills that do not result in anger directed at child.
- Develop time management skills that allow for meeting children's needs as well as personal needs.

Remarriage, Stepparenting, and Blended Families

Negative stereotypes about stepfamilies are common to fairy tales, yet, stepparenting is real and not exclusively the domain of storytellers. Despite the bias against stepfamilies, they are neither problematic nor inferior. Some blended families function quite well, while others have difficulty navigating common pitfalls. Because mothers most often are awarded custody, a stepfather family is the most common arrangement (Goldenberg & Goldenberg, 1996).

Embarking on a new relationship requires an "emotional divorce" from the first marriage (Holman, 1983). Divorced adults must deal with their own fears about entering into a new relationship.

In stepfamilies, loneliness is often traded for conflict (Nichols & Schwartz, 1998). In blended families, parents may be engaged in a continuous struggle over child rearing. Conflict may occur over who assumes primary parenting responsibilities for the children and what type of parenting should occur. Rules in stepfamilies may be vague initially, with a lengthy period of time elapsing before roles, rules, and boundaries are reformulated. Children, may feel confused and harbor resentment toward the stepparent whom they consider has usurped the role of the noncustodial parent. Rivalry between stepsiblings may be intense (Thompson & Rudolph, 1992). In addition, children's need to maintain contact with the noncustodial parent can interfere with the custodial parent's desire for a complete emotional break.

Children may have difficulty adjusting to life in a blended family. They may have trouble accepting the fact that their parents will never get together again, and loyalty to both parents may be tested. Divided loyalties are particularly likely when one parent uses the children to direct resentment at the former partner. In addition, children may fantasize about their parents eventually reuniting and try to make this happen. When there are other stepchildren entering the relationship, adjustment becomes even more complicated, since it might involve competing for affection, attention, and material possessions.

There are many tasks for stepfamilies to accomplish in order to achieve successful integration (sources: Thompson & Rudolph, 1992; Visher & Visher, 1982):

- Mourning losses of previous relationships;
- Arriving at a satisfactory stepparenting role;

- Redefining financial and social obligations;
- Agreeing on visitation and custody;
- Establishing consistent leadership and discipline;
- Ensuring that expectations for relationships are realistic;
- Forming new emotional bonds in the family;
- Developing new traditions;
- Dealing with sexuality in the home.

Boundaries in newly blended families need to be negotiated, and this can be a difficult task. Not only must members establish boundaries concerning physical space (sharing, property), but they must also decide how much emotional distance to maintain with new family members and agree upon roles that will work within this new family unit. Adults involved in a marital dissolution often need a clean break from the relationship, yet the presence of children demands that contact with each parent be ongoing and consistent in order for access to be maintained. Additionally, the joining family subsystems (mother-child or father-child) will have learned to operate independently. Changes and adaptations are needed to combine the new family subsystems adequately (Nichols & Schwartz, 1998).

DEVELOPMENTAL TASKS OF STEPFAMILIES

A blended family must accomplish certain tasks as the family subsystems merge. List some concrete interventions the family social worker can carry out to help the family complete each of the tasks listed in this section.

Parenting by Grandparents

In the past decades, parenting by grandparents was most common in African American families, but today it is increasingly common in other ethnic groups (Okun, 1996). Grandparents often assume the role of primary caretaker of children because of substance abuse or other incapacitating conditions preventing their children from being custodial parents. When faced with a choice between seeing their grandchildren placed in foster homes or caring for the grandchildren themselves, grandparents feel obliged to take on parental responsibilities. Grandparents as parents experience a disruption in the family life cycle because they are caring for children at a time when their peers are enjoying the benefits of spare time and relief from some of their financial obligations. Child-rearing practices of grandparents may conflict with modern parenting techniques (Okun, 1996). Also, grandparents may worry about who will care for their grandchildren if they die or become incapacitated.

Regardless of whether grandparents assume primary caretaking responsibilities for their grandchildren, grandparents play a very important role in children's development. Wilcoxon (1991) has identified five important roles of grandparents:

- *Historian* who can link children with the familial and cultural past.
- *Role model* or an example of older adulthood.
- *Mentor* or wise elder who has experienced his or her own life transitions.
- *Wizard* who is a master storyteller.
- *Nurturer* who is the ultimate support person for familial crises and transitions.

Cultural Variations

Cultural traditions influence family life cycle stages. For example, Mexican-American families experience shorter adolescence and longer courtship stages. For other cultures, the involvement of the extended family marks a different relationship and different perspective on such stages as childbirth, launching young adults into the world, and the formation of a new family unit. For example, a daughter in a family from India is expected to live with her parents until she is married, and a grandmother in a Japanese family may take an active role in raising young grandchildren.

DEVELOPMENTAL VARIATIONS

If your family of origin, or that of a friend, was not a typical "middle-class" family, describe how the family's developmental stages differed from the stages described in this chapter.

CHAPTER SUMMARY

One way for social workers to understand families is to become familiar with issues that arise at various developmental stages. Stages of family development include marriage/partnering, birth of the first child, families with preschool children, families with school-aged children, families with teenagers, and families with young people leaving home.

The transition from each stage to the next is associated with a variety of stresses and strains for family members. Understanding these issues enables the family social worker to help families cope with changes that occur as the family matures.

5

Practical Aspects of Family Social Work

There are many practical considerations involved in family social work. In this chapter, we will look at some of these "nuts-and-bolts" topics. We will discuss the importance of adhering to a regular schedule for family meetings while remaining flexible enough to accommodate unforeseen events. Suggestions will be offered for the preparation and care of materials used by FSWs. We will discuss how to decide whether to include children in family meetings, and we will provide tips for handling disruptions and maintaining contact with families who move frequently. Safety issues will be addressed. Within the context of the first family meeting, we will introduce the topics of assessing a family's needs and engaging family members in the helping process. Finally, we will describe ways to orient clients to family social work and to protect clients' confidentiality.

SCHEDULING FAMILY MEETINGS

Prior to the first home visit with a family, the FSW needs to accomplish the following tasks:

- Determine the overall purpose of the meeting;
- Outline specific issues to be addressed during the meeting;
- Contact a family member to set up the meeting;
- Locate the family's home;
- Decide how much time should be allotted for the first meeting.

Adhering to a schedule benefits both the FSW and the family. Changes in the schedule are almost inevitable, but establishing a proposed timetable for visits helps promote steady progress toward the family's goals. Weekly appointments are usually sufficient, but frequency of meetings depends on the goals and needs of individual families. Time for related responsibilities such as meetings with colleagues and supervisors, community liaison and advocacy, documenting, and other related tasks must be worked into the FSW's schedule.

The schedule for family meetings may have to be changed because of unexpected events that are beyond the control of either the family or the social worker. FSWs must develop sufficient psychological flexibility to adapt to changes in plans without excessive distress. A useful tip is to plan carefully but to expect that circumstances may interfere with the execution of these plans. Attention to scheduling is especially important given that FSWs must meet the needs of all the families assigned to them.

Setting Up the First Appointment

In most cases, the social worker's initial contact with the family will be a telephone call to arrange the first meeting. For families who are unreachable by telephone, the FSW will need to write a letter of introduction or drive to the home to make the initial contact.

During the telephone call or visit, both the FSW and the family develop first impressions of one another (Goldenberg & Goldenberg, 1994). The social worker develops an impression of the family's readiness to work and a picture of how family members view the problem. From the family's perspective, first impressions are also important. Clients usually prefer a family social worker who is warm and understanding and who conveys hope and competence. The social worker must be careful not to get caught up in one person's view of the problem (Nichols & Schwartz, 1995).

During the initial contact, the FSW makes an appointment to meet with the family for the first time. For this purpose, many social workers prefer to meet with as many family members as possible. At times, clients may try to exclude family members from this first appointment. They may ask that the social worker see only the child with the problem, or they might try to exclude other family members such as the father or children who do not have a "problem." The general rule is to include as many family members as possible in the first appointment because the number of family members present at the first session affects who will be involved in future sessions (Brock & Barnard, 1992). The social worker can also suggest that the presence of as many family members as possible will help him or her understand the problem more fully and that the presence of the entire family is important because the problem affects everyone.

Allowing for Travel Time

When scheduling home visits, the FSW should be sure to allow enough time to become familiar with the environment as well as to arrive on time at the family home. If time permits, the FSW may choose to make a trial run to a family's home before the first appointment to determine how much time is needed to arrive at the destination, the fastest routes, and issues related to parking safety. A practice run will ensure a timely arrival for the first family meeting. It will also orient the worker to the family's environment.

Traffic patterns, construction delays, bridge openings and closures, one-way streets, and similar situations that affect travel time should be considered when planning the schedule. A current city or county map is a simple but necessary tool for family social workers.

Within an agency, the distance between families' homes is often the main criterion for assigning cases to social workers. To reduce travel time, supervisors of programs that cover large catchment areas may assign family social workers to cases based on geographic location. This practice may not be as desirable as assigning workers based on the best match with family needs, but it acknowledges the impact of travel time on work load planning. Allowing sufficient time between family meetings ensures that a delay in completing one meeting will not result in subsequent delays for meetings with other families. Mileage sheets can be kept on a clipboard in the social worker's car and filled in immediately after every trip.

Many programs require the social worker to document each meeting before beginning the next one. Thus, time and location for accomplishing this task should be considered when setting the daily schedule. Family social workers, searching for suitable places to complete documentation, often become "regulars" at coffee shops, libraries, and other convenient locations near the homes of client families.

Accommodating Family Preferences

Timing of home meetings should reflect the mutual needs of the social worker and family members. For example, fluctuating energy levels should be taken into account to ensure a productive visit. The level of difficulty involved in working with various families should also be considered. For example, FSWs may schedule meetings with their most challenging families early in the day or week. Scheduling that allows for personal preferences and needs can help maximize the social worker's effectiveness and promote personal well-being. Managing a demanding caseload according to an inconvenient schedule can contribute to burnout. In addition, an exhausted family social worker cannot provide the level of service that families deserve.

Families have preferences for meeting times. Ultimately their needs should be the most important consideration when scheduling home appointments. Families have varied lifestyles and routines. Some have stable, predictable schedules and home lives that easily adapt to regularly scheduled home meetings. Others have less organized or chaotic lives that make regularly scheduled meetings unacceptable or even impossible. Parents can have varied work schedules, and the family social worker needs to set up meetings to fit within these schedules. Being sensitive to family preferences, habits, and lifestyles will help the social worker to schedule appointments appropriately.

Because family social work meetings often occur within the home, respect for privacy and accommodation to schedules is crucial. Some families, for example, may not want to meet when young children are napping, while others may prefer to meet while younger children are asleep.

Other people may stop in during a family work session. A family member or the FSW should ask them to come back later.

The dedication of some families to certain television programs is another factor worth considering when scheduling home appointments. Family social workers who arrive during these times may be welcomed into the house but might be expected to wait until the end of a program before beginning activities or discussions. On the other hand, some social workers have found that briefly watching certain television programs with families before engaging in work provides a useful basis for building rapport, particularly with families who find talking difficult.

Scheduling home meetings with parents who work outside the home can be quite complicated. After a day's work, the parents and the FSW may be tired and feel the pressures of impending evening activities. Instead of scheduling every meeting during the evening, the FSW may want to set up an occasional weekend visit. While disruptive to the family social worker's personal routine, meeting at odd hours may be best for some families.

To sum up, the key to scheduling family meetings is flexibility. The FSW needs to aim for a reasonable balance between achieving specific program goals on every meeting and being responsive to the family's immediate needs. Even after the social worker and family have arrived at a mutually agreeable schedule, some meetings may have to be postponed. A family may be unable to benefit from the planned purpose of the meeting on a particular day because of crises such as the threat of eviction, loss of employment, or a child's illness. Under these circumstances, the FSW should attend to the family's immediate concerns and discuss available resources. A crisis may require that the FSW listen to the family's concerns, offer emotional support, encourage active problem solving, or help the family to get help from other agencies. Trying to impose a set agenda upon an unreceptive family can obstruct the helping relationship. As one family social worker phrased it, "Flexibility kept me sane. I had to remind myself that nothing was cast in stone, and that I could really trust my instincts."

PREPARATION AND CARE OF MATERIALS

Another important aspect of planning is preparation and compilation of materials. Materials may be standardized, or they may be created or collected for each meeting. Materials can include activity cards, pamphlets, toys, books, recording instruments, evaluation measures, or referral forms. Preparing for a family meeting may take as much time as the meeting itself, particularly if materials must be gathered or made. The FSW should bring extra copies of materials that have been left with the family in case they have been misplaced.

Materials should be organized and stored so that they can be located and used easily. This is an important ingredient of planning for the FSW who travels regularly between the agency and family homes. Because different sets of materials for several clients will be needed while traveling from home to home and because other forms or materials might also be kept at the office, an appropriate organizational system is needed. Disorganization can result in loss of time, missed opportunities for effective family interventions, and considerable frustration for both the worker and the family. A family social workers may want to keep a file box in the car for case-by-case storage of recent and current paperwork. The FSW can transfer older materials from the file box to the main office files and add new materials for upcoming meetings.

USEFUL MATERIALS

Develop a list of potential materials useful for family social work. Classify the materials used for different age groups, such as toddlers, school-aged children, adolescents, and parents.

The FSW must be careful to protect confidential materials from being misplaced, damaged, stolen, or inadvertently combined with other materials that could be distributed during an appointment. A laptop computer makes it easy for the FSW to record data, provide duplicates for office files, and protect clients' confidentiality. If a laptop PC is unavailable, a separate container or secured portable file box should be used for storage of confidential materials both en route to and during home visits. After each family meeting, confidential materials should be filed immediately in the appropriate secure location. Special care must be taken to keep one family file separate from other family files. This will prevent the FSW from mixing files accidentally.

WHAT TO WEAR

Each community and client population has its own standard of dress, and family social workers should be sensitive to these standards. Clothing should be professional, but the degree of formality can vary. In addition, clothing should be appropriate for the planned activities in a meeting. For example, if the meeting requires the FSW to play on the floor with children or be physically active, clothing should be selected with these activities in mind.

INCLUSION OF CHILDREN IN MEETINGS

The nature of family social work dictates that children will often be the focus of work. Home meetings are often initiated in response to the needs of one child, sometimes called the "target child" or "identified patient." Although only one child may be targeted for intervention, other children in the home may also need help. The FSW should involve the parents in devising a strategy for dealing with children during meetings. The plan might call for the children to play elsewhere, especially when discussion centers on personal adult issues. When the focus is more child-centered, children can and probably should be included in meetings. Obviously the inclusion of children depends on the focus of the session. When no one is available to supervise children excluded from the meeting, special activities may be arranged in another room to occupy their attention. Materials provided by the social worker should include items that can occupy children productively. The FSW should supply materials that will interest the child.

Generally, meetings with parents alone will be easier to manage. As suggested by Satir (1967), "the presence of children might spell anarchy to the therapy process" (p. 136). Nevertheless, the presence of children should be dictated by the purpose of the session, not whether the meeting will be easier. Children could be included in the meeting when they are old enough to contribute to family sessions. Satir (1967) also suggests that social workers take an active role in interviews when there are children. For example, the FSW can model ways of communicating with children. Initially, the FSW may want to assess how parents set limits for the children. In one office-based meeting, for example, a parent sat passively while the child ravaged the worker's office, opening desk drawers and otherwise intruding on the worker's privacy. Rather than imposing limits on the child, the social worker asked the parent to intervene.

This incident opened the door to a discussion of limit setting and discipline. The parent in this example believed that limit setting was a form of abuse. She failed to recognize that her child had developed few social skills and was rejected by his peers. Failure of parents to set limits with children during the family meeting provides valuable information about what goes on in the family and how effective parents are in managing their children's behavior. In addition, the social worker can help parents devise limit-setting techniques with children "on-the-spot," providing feedback as the parent practices the new behaviors.

The presence of children in a meeting can provide the social worker with information about family dynamics, parenting skills, and parent-child relationships. For example, when the presenting family problem involves the children, observing the interaction between parent and child will be necessary for understanding the particular problem. Presence of children is also crucial to observe how parents are implementing the changes made during the work.

Approaches to children during home meetings can include negotiating with them to occupy themselves productively, either with their own activities or those brought by the worker, after which they are rewarded with special attention. In difficult situations, another family social worker may be available to be with the children independent of the meeting with the parent. A coworker can also help coordinate a meeting in which the entire family is present. Observing how parents interact with their children during a home visit helps the FSW to assess the parent-child relationship and to design interventions that will promote positive change.

Sometimes, the FSW may need to ask the parent to arrange for the children to be elsewhere during a home meeting; if this is not practical, the meeting can be conducted at another location such as the agency office. This may be necessary when the parent wants to discuss something that children should not hear, such as marital difficulties or intimate personal problems, or when the needs of one or more children require almost constant adult attention. Parents may talk more freely with the social worker when the children are not present.

When assessing the role of the children within a family, the FSW needs to keep in mind that the family is a system in which each member is affected by factors that affect other members. The birth of a physically challenged child, for example, can influence parental interactions with other children and with one another. In addition, the existence of a serious problem such as delinquency or alcoholism will have a strong impact on family needs and interactions. Siblings of target children also need opportunities to talk about their feelings and have their questions answered honestly and directly. Family social workers often mistakenly assume that because a certain child is not the "problem," that child does not need to be included in the session. Asking a child a question such as "Can you tell me what you are worried about?" may unleash a barrage of concerns. Therefore, family social workers must be sensitive to the dynamics of the whole family and consider all members' needs when conducting meetings.

HANDLING DISRUPTIONS AND MAINTAINING CONTACT

Although most home meetings will run smoothly, the FSW should be prepared for occasions when they do not. Blaring televisions, visits from friends and neighbors, and ringing telephones are all a natural part of the home milieu. The FSW needs to find creative ways of handling such distractions, such as meeting on the front porch or at a restaurant, or having older siblings entertain younger ones. If distractions and chaos continue, the FSW and family need to discuss these obstacles and find a reasonable method for resolving them.

It is important for clients and the FSW to know how to reach each other. Such contact is aided if the client has a telephone; however, if clients do not have a phone another method of reaching the family should be devised. This may involve using a neighbor's telephone or leaving notes at the home. One family worker, after many failed meeting attempts, found that providing the family with addressed, stamped envelopes and stationery to inform her of canceled meetings or unanticipated moves was an effective way to remain in contact. Agency policy may determine whether the FSW provides a home phone number.

Frequent mobility of clients can disrupt schedules. If a family's move is planned and the social worker is aware of it in advance, the appointment schedule can be adjusted. However, some families move without notifying the family social worker, who then has difficulty locating them. At the first meeting, the FSW should request the name and phone number of a person who will always know the whereabouts of the family.

TELEPHONE FOLLOW-UP

Telephone follow-up between sessions is helpful because many parents have additional questions after reflecting on the interview. If the FSW initiates telephone contact, he or she can be more helpful to parents who worry about asking "dumb" questions and are reluctant to bother the family social worker with problems.

When information, instruction-giving, and careful follow-up are insufficient to accomplish the agreed-upon goals, the FSW needs to determine what types of additional intervention may be useful to the parents. The goal is to help parents understand their problems and enable them to change their own behavior in ways that will be acceptable to them. It would be destructive to make recommendations that parents cannot execute. The FSW can judge what can be undertaken immediately, what should be delayed until appropriate preliminary goals have been achieved, and what can be postponed indefinitely. Consequently, the FSW should be willing to adopt alternative methods based upon an assessment of the situation and of parental responses to intervention. Follow-up can help to reinforce new behaviors or help the FSW to decide if further intervention is needed.

SAFETY CONSIDERATIONS

It is impossible for social workers to achieve program goals when their safety is threatened. In some cases, the FSW's safety is threatened by clients who become violent; in others, the risk is created by an unsafe neighborhood. Knowing how to protect one's personal safety is essential in family social work.

Violence against social workers does not appear to be random. Rather, the person committing the violence will often have some complaint against an agency, whether it be real or imagined (Munson, 1993). For example, an aggressive parent who demands that the FSW bypass waiting lists, help acquire special services, or produce unreasonable results may threaten the family social worker. The FSW must be ready to deal with clients' attempts to manipulate, cross boundaries, or attack. A part of the FSW's usefulness to parents depends upon the ability to deflect personal intrusion and impending threat. To protect themselves, social workers must be caring, yet capable of separating involvement on a professional level from involvement on a personal level.

Because families live in all types of environments, from rural areas to inner cities and suburbs, safety issues will vary within and across programs. However, several basic safety guidelines are relevant for all family social workers. To ensure the safest conditions for home meetings, we recommend the following guidelines:

1. Perhaps the most important safety guideline is not to dismiss feelings of danger. When social workers feel vulnerable or unsafe, they should take whatever precautions are necessary for protection. Sometimes FSWs feel awkward about being suspicious of clients' friends or feel uncomfortable and apprehensive in certain neighborhoods. They might underplay the sense of feeling threatened. Ignoring these anxieties can place the social worker at risk. On the other hand, if FSWs are merely unfamiliar with the client's setting or are meeting in an unfamiliar cultural milieu, the source of apprehension needs to be examined before concluding that conditions are unsafe. Becoming acquainted with diverse cultures and neighborhoods allows FSWs to discern real from imaginary danger.

2. A related guideline for safety in home meetings is to become familiar with neighborhoods where home appointments take place. Learning the layout of the immediate area around clients' homes and the usual types of activities that occur there will provide a baseline from which to assess danger.

3. Make certain that the program supervisor and/or other responsible agency personnel are aware of the FSW's schedule of family meetings. The schedule should include the name and location of the family, the date and scheduled times for the meeting, and the expected time of return. When a home meeting is scheduled in an unsafe environment, FSWs can develop a monitoring system such as a call-in procedure when the visit is complete. When telephones are not available, we recommend the purchase of a cellular telephone. As cellular phones become more affordable, family social work programs should consider using them. The following scenario demonstrates how a social worker's failure to let the agency know her whereabouts placed her at risk. She related a situation in which she was eight months pregnant and was taken hostage by an angry father. The incident lasted eight hours, but no one from her agency knew that she was being held hostage or even where she was because there were no call-in tracking arrangements at her agency. She managed to leave the situation after keeping a cool head and talking fast, but after that episode she always let several people in her office know her schedule.

4. Avoid dangerous neighborhoods at night. If this is impossible, arrangements should be made for an escort. For example, one program hired an escort for late-afternoon and early-evening hours. Social workers in the program then scheduled appointments when the escort could accompany them. Another option is to ask a relative or friend to accompany the social worker into the home and to come back again when the family meeting is over.

5. Assess the safest route to and from the client's home in advance. If the most direct route does not have well-lit or well-patrolled streets, a safer route should be chosen. Parking in clients' neighborhoods may also present safety problems. The only available parking may be far from clients' homes or in a high-crime area. If safe parking cannot be found, using a paid driver may be worthwhile. One program serving a high-risk urban community hired a full-time driver who escorted FSWs to all of their meetings. If a social worker feels uncomfortable meeting a family in their home, making arrangements to meet in a public place is acceptable. Further, a social worker who feels unsafe during an interview should leave (Kinney, Haapala, & Booth, 1991).

Clients and communities can participate actively in planning for the safety of the FSW, and this can be an important and useful component of an empowerment strategy. Also, safety planning within the family itself is an important aspect of the family social work process. Besides the above guidelines, several other safety factors should be considered. Since FSWs usually drive to appointments, they need to maintain their cars in good condition. FSWs who must travel long distances through high-risk neighborhoods should ensure that they have enough gasoline. Further, since confidential program materials may be kept in automobiles, it is imperative that they be secured against theft.

The security of personal possessions should be considered when meeting families in the community. The FSW should avoid carrying more money than necessary. Accessories such as purses and jewelry are generally not appropriate for home meetings. Theft of money or other items from family social workers, while rare, can occur. One home-based worker wore expensive clothing and drove an expensive car to family meetings and was advised by the agency to avoid doing so. Preventing incidents from happening is better than having to deal with them once they have occurred. Worrying about confidential items left in a car may also prevent a social worker from devoting complete attention to a family during an appointment.

FSWs should receive training from their agencies on recognizing signs of potential violence among clients (Munson, 1993). All agencies should have clearly established safety protocols for social workers, in addition to offering training sessions on handling violence when it does occur. If a social worker feels frightened during a visit, he or she needs to assess the severity of the immediate risk and should feel free to leave. Erring on the side of caution is best. Circumstances that might require this response include violence in the home, drug use and drug dealing, presence of weapons, or the presence of intoxicated or out-or-control individuals. If a social worker encounters any of these situations during family meetings, he or she must discuss the incident with supervisors and explore alternatives for ensuring safety during future appointments. In some circumstances, home appointments may be ended or situated in safer locations.

Another precaution concerns illness in the home. If a family member has an infectious disease, the social worker should use judgment about being exposed to the illness. When confronted with communicable illnesses, such as hepatitis or influenza, the worker should consult with medical personnel about the advisability of meeting in the home. Sometimes rescheduling a home visit is the best option. The Head Start home visiting program has clearly defined procedures for social workers to follow when confronted with client illness.

Sometimes family members will offer the social worker refreshments such as coffee or cookies. Normally this will not be a problem. Eventually, however, most social workers will come across unsanitary conditions in some homes and will have to think of a graceful way to decline the offerings without offending the family. Within some cultures, offering food to a visitor is a sign of respect. Families would be insulted if the social worker refused their offer. A brief but direct approach is suggested, such as thanking the family for their offer of food or coffee and explaining that the FSW has just eaten or finished a cup of coffee before arriving for the meeting.

THE FIRST MEETING: ASSESSING CLIENTS' NEEDS

Social workers trained in the skills of individual counseling can become overwhelmed when they begin working with families. They may be uncertain about what to expect or how to proceed. It is important to keep in mind that the purpose of the first meeting is to assess the problem and engage the family in problem solving.

The FSW may offset the apprehension of seeing a family for the first time by obtaining as much information as possible before the meeting. Reading family files, if available, is a good starting point, as is reading literature about the family's specific problem. The supervisor can help the FSW understand how to apply specific theories to the family's problems. The FSW should also examine personal values or biases that may affect his or her performance with a particular family and again consult the supervisor. Gaining understanding of any diversity issues is very important before this first meeting.

Keeping the specific family in mind, the FSW may review the principles and techniques of family interviewing. Topics to be explored include: How should this family be engaged? What particular techniques might be useful in engaging this family? How are goals set in a family meeting, and what specific goals might be set in the first meeting with this family? What are the special cultural issues for this family?

After the FSW has formulated answers to these questions, the supervisor can provide useful feedback and direction. The supervisor and other agency colleagues may be willing to role-play the family so the FSW can practice what to say first, where to sit, whether to accept coffee, and so forth. Role-playing provides the FSW with the opportunity to develop new skills and obtain important feedback before actually meeting the family. It is a form of dress rehearsal. The supervisor may encourage role-playing other tasks, such as engagement and goal setting. Even though the reality will differ from the rehearsal, the FSW will have developed a sense of what to expect during the initial meeting with the family.

Basic patterns to look for at the first meeting involve repetitive verbal and nonverbal communications among family members. The FSW should pay attention to indications of conflict, which individuals get involved in disagreements, where family members sit in relationship to one another, who speaks for family members, and so on.

At the start of the first interview, the FSW should introduce himself or herself and explain the agency's purpose. Description of the agency is especially important if the client is not familiar with the agency. Once this has been done, the FSW should engage the family and begin to assess its problems. Assessment involves understanding what the problem is, what is causing the problem, and what can be done to change the situation (Holman, 1983). Ideally assessment is a shared responsibility between the worker and family. The worker collects information by encouraging participation by every family member. This involves getting to know names and developing a sense of how each family member understands the problem. It is important to encourage every member to speak. It is common for parents to speak for the children or for one adult to speak for another. This is an example of a repetitive family pattern that the FSW should note and address. Social workers must understand who is speaking for whom in the meeting and begin to get the spokesperson to allow others to speak for themselves. To do so, the FSW may need to challenge family patterns, especially established patterns of family authority. Understanding cultural norms and ways of communicating can also be important.

INTRODUCING YOURSELF

Describe a situation in which a family requires intervention from a family social worker. Indicate how you would expect to introduce yourself to the family at the first meeting.

The process of identifying problems and learning about the family can be complex and must be planned carefully. The worker can gradually engage the family in activities such as drawing a genogram (family map) or an ecomap (diagram of social contacts). These activities will assist in further engagement of family members, facilitate balanced individual participation in the interview, and help the family to define the problem so that family members can accept the plan for future work. To be comprehensive, an assessment needs to be done from an ecological perspective, looking at the interactions between the family and its environment (Holman, 1983). An ecological assessment should be required for all problems.

Social workers should assess the family's living environment. A tour of the home can reveal much about the family, especially differences between public and private areas. Eating areas are another focal point for the family and give information also suggestive of family style and management. A family that dines together every night around a large table presents a different image from the family who eats dinner on TV trays in separate rooms in the house. Going to the "right part of the house" when assessing a family can be of great value in planning future work with the family, especially if FSWs encourage parents and children to discuss perceptions of different spaces and to describe what the spaces mean to each family member.

Maintaining worker-family communication during a home interview includes sitting where everyone can be seen. Eye contact is critical in engaging family members. It is advisable not to begin an interview until all family members are present. Time-consuming social exchanges can be left to the end of the interview. The tone of the interview will help the FSW decide whether refreshments are a distraction or a gift and can be postponed to the end of the session.

Demarcating the physical space in the home interview is useful so everyone can participate. Someone may stomp out of the room in a rage, retreating to a section of the house where he or she can still listen to what is being discussed. If someone goes into the bathroom and locks the door, however, that is a clear indication that they have left the session and the family will have to problem solve about how to deal with the absence. Such events do not curtail work with the family. Instead, they are examples of natural events that can be used to learn more about the family. Additionally, they can provide opportunities for family members to learn new patterns of behavior.

Increasingly, social workers are becoming technique driven, and various interventions and theories compete with one another. The growing interest in demonstrating intervention techniques can make social workers worry that they will be ineffective if they are not using the latest therapy. However, it seems that therapists are more impressed with techniques than are clients (Miller, Hubble, & Duncan, 1995). For instance, parents report valuing the most fundamental elements of service: support, listening, on-the-spot assistance, and availability of the social worker (Coleman & Collins, 1997).

Basic helping skills of empathy, warmth, and genuineness are crucial to intervention, as is the willingness to ask for clarification when meanings are unclear. Demonstrating these qualities will lay the groundwork for a strong worker-client relationship, often known as the therapeutic alliance (Worden, 1994). Family social workers secure with these basic skills can successfully negotiate both the first and subsequent family meetings with little apprehension. The second interview will be easier and the third interview easier yet. The fourth interview may be more difficult for new FSWs developing critical awareness of their own performance. However, this difficulty and self-consciousness should be welcomed as a positive sign of learning and growth.

DIFFICULT FIRST MEETINGS

Identify potential situations in a first family interview that would be difficult for you to deal with. For each situation, provide two alternative responses to overcome the difficulty.

BUILDING A RELATIONSHIP WITH CLIENTS

The core of family social work is the relationship between the FSW and the family—a relationship that will make it possible for the FSW to provide help to the family. The relationship is the vehicle that carries interventions and makes them palatable to the family. It contributes as much as 30 percent to the effectiveness of intervention (Miller, Hubble, & Duncan, 1995). The first family meeting marks the beginning of a helpful relationship between the FSW and the family. The relationship may be quite brief or long-term.

It is crucial for FSWs to recognize that when there is family conflict, family members may try to get the social worker to side with them in their particular view of the problem. The FSW should anticipate this maneuver and avoid it by empathizing with individual viewpoints without colluding with them. Family work involves maintaining a delicate balance between neutrality and sensitivity to individual experiences. When neutrality does not occur, certain family members can become alienated from the social worker (Coleman & Collins, 1997). Social workers struggle with issues of alliance with individual family members versus advocating for justice for individual family members, especially those disadvantaged or harmed by family dynamics, as in the case of abuse. (These issues are discussed in more detail in Chapters 12 and 13.)

Worden (1994) suggests three crucial elements for developing a strong therapeutic alliance with clients:

- A consensus between the worker and client on the goals of therapy;
- Worker-client agreement and collaboration on implementation of tasks;
- A strong, positive, affective bond between the client and worker.

Keeping these three elements in the forefront will assist the family worker to negotiate the complexities of the first family meeting. The therapeutic alliance will be strengthened further by attending to issues involving ethnicity, gender, and stages in the family life cycle (Worden, 1994).

The first family meeting requires special attention, not only because it is the foundation for establishing a positive relationship between the FSW and family, but also because it will affect the quality and course of later work. Consequently, engaging the family's interest and developing rapport is crucial to the FSW's continued presence in the home. The first family meeting should be time limited, focused, and relaxed.

Another component of the first meeting is instilling a sense of trust to enable family members to express their concerns honestly. Trust is not automatic; it is built gradually as family meetings continue. The FSW can encourage the development of trust by taking a sincere interest in family members' needs and conveying willingness to help and stick by the family during difficult times. Rapport may be achieved quickly with some families, while other families require patience and persistence. The nature of the family and its problems, the purposes of the family work, the personality of the FSW, and life experiences of family members influence how quickly trust and rapport are achieved. How the family feels about dealing with a problem and their perceptions of the problem influence their receptiveness to family work. Building a relationship with a family takes time.

It is important to foster a supportive atmosphere not only between the family and the FSW but also among family members. A high level of rapport and trust facilitates problem identification and effective working relationships, which in turn contribute to positive solutions. Effective working relationships facilitate behavioral changes that stimulate family satisfaction and self-confidence. One role of the FSW is to help clients clarify personal goals and develop a plan for reaching them. The relationship between social workers and clients is so important to family social work that program objectives cannot be met unless positive interaction is established. The therapeutic alliance is strengthened as family priorities are assessed, information is conveyed, support and encouragement are provided, and self-reliance and effective coping are promoted.

TRUST

> Write down one family secret that you have never told anyone in your life. Include reasons why you have not told anyone this secret. Close your eyes, put your pencil down, and spend about five minutes imagining that you must now reveal this secret to a stranger who has just come into your house. What are your feelings about telling this stranger your secret? What must happen (concretely) before you would be prepared to talk to this stranger about your family secret?

Development of a trusting relationship is not always a steady process. Clients who are disillusioned with helping systems will struggle with issues of trust. Thus, progress made in establishing trust during one meeting may be lost at the next appointment, depending on the family's interpretation of intervening events. These events may or may not involve the FSW per se, but may include incidents from the family's life that create suspicion about others' motives. We know of one situation in which trust was undermined when a family received a visit by a children's protective services caseworker for suspected neglect or abuse of the children. Although the FSW's involvement was not related to the investigation, the family projected its distrust and fear onto the FSW.

In the first meeting, and also in later ones, the FSW should be sensitive to the privacy of the family and avoid being intrusive. Workers must convey respect for the family's territory and show appreciation to the family for allowing the worker onto their turf. In other words, family social workers are guests in family homes (Kinney, Haapala, & Booth, 1991). Questions should focus on information needed to carry out program goals, especially during the first meeting. Some families may be eager to share additional information, but usually this will not be the case. If the family chooses to talk about personal matters, the FSW may listen attentively and respond supportively. The FSW may redirect the conversation to program-related topics if conversation becomes tangential or irrelevant. Probing into the personal life of family members during the early phases may undermine the development of a working relationship with a family. A family member who has shared information freely may later regret having shared so much. The FSW should be supportive and nonprobing early in the work.

ORIENTING CLIENTS TO FAMILY SOCIAL WORK

The intensity of the FSW's involvement with family members and their problems can contribute to feelings of personal closeness, yet the relationship must remain at a professional level. FSWs often work with families who are in severe crisis. Many have endured a lengthy history of family problems plus multiple episodes of prior service or treatment from various agencies. Because the family has probably experienced previous failures, it is important that the FSW establish positive expectations for change and convey hope to the family at the beginning. Support should be provided through use of appropriate opportunities for family change.

Reviewing the purposes of family social work and the nature of the activities to be completed promotes work with families. Focusing on family goals can help make each meeting productive. Time may have passed since the family first agreed to participate in family work, and the FSW will need to help the family remember the specific details originally agreed upon. Reminding the family about these details may also stimulate enthusiasm, interest, and participation.

During the first family meeting, the FSW should explain clearly her or his role, including responsibilities and limitations of involvement. When the limits and structure of the relationship are clarified, the FSW and the family can focus on productive work together. Clarification of roles may need to be repeated and reinforced frequently. Some family programs have narrowly defined roles for FSWs, while others permit and even encourage FSWs' flexibility and independence in establishing work-related boundaries. In either case, clarifying FSW responsibilities and limitations helps prevent the possibility of confusion and disagreement concerning the social worker's role.

The family's role in the change process should also be made explicit. Enlisting the entire family as partners in the process, rather than as recipients of service, establishes the idea that family social work is a mutual responsibility of the family and the social worker. The most obvious contribution of the family is availability for the work. Without access and ongoing participation, the FSW cannot perform the roles involved in the helping process.

The family's perceptions and expectations of family work also should be explored during the first meeting. Sometimes expectations are not realistic. The FSW may discover that clients have misunderstood program objectives or were misinformed. Finding out what the family expects and correcting misperceptions during the first meeting eliminates misunderstanding later. Ultimately the whole family should be encouraged to reach consensus on expectations for family work.

The first home meeting might last between one and two hours, depending on the objectives. It should be ended when planned activities have been completed. If the meeting is proceeding smoothly and the family is becoming engaged, the FSW may extend the meeting accordingly. A successful outcome of the first meeting means leaving the family feeling comfortable and looking forward to the next meeting. The second meeting should be scheduled for a time that will be convenient for all family members.

PROTECTING CLIENTS' CONFIDENTIALITY

Family social work offers professional services to families on a potentially more personal level than other service-delivery systems. Because of the nature of the work, maintaining appropriate confidentiality is critical (Collins, Thomlison, & Grinnell, 1992). The following example illustrates the high risk of breaching client confidentiality.

> You receive the Simpson case at a screening and referral. In the first meeting, you inform the Simpsons that you are their new family social worker. They seem a little reluctant to talk, so you encourage them by giving your assurance that anything they say will be held in the strictest confidence. At the time, you believe this implicitly. Later, while you are talking to your secretary, Romalda, you realize that she is typing case notes, including your information obtained about the Simpsons. Still later, in the coffee room of your agency, workers are talking freely about their cases and ask you about your cases. You respond with details of the Simpson case. Later still, you learn that Mr. Simpson has asked for medical assistance and your entry in his file has been shared with various government and medical service agencies. You think with dismay that you might as well have sent the record to the newspaper, only to discover that a sheet of recording has fallen out of your briefcase and been picked up by a neighbor of the Simpsons. You search frantically for the audiotaped interview that you plan to share with your supervisor. Meanwhile, the Simpsons have discovered that what they said to you in strictest confidence is now common knowledge in the social service delivery system. On Friday you meet with your supervisor and give a rundown of your cases. The Simpson case is at the top of your list.
>
> Filled with righteous indignation, the Simpsons complain to your supervisor. Your supervisor gently explains to you the difference between absolute confidentiality, in which nothing your client family says is shared with anyone in any form, and relative confidentiality, in which information is shared with colleagues as required. You realize you will never be able to promise absolute confidentiality as an agency worker and, probably, you will never be able to promise confidentiality at all.
>
> Despite your supervisor's gentleness, you feel that she is convinced of your incompetence. You also feel vaguely resentful; she could have told you about relative confidentiality before.

Guidelines for Protecting Clients' Confidentiality*

1. Do not discuss clients outside the interview (i.e., an open-door of-fice, class, group, meeting) even with changed names and altered identify-ing details. Discussing details about clients with family or friends is not permitted. Social work can be very stressful and social workers sometimes need to "unwind" by talking about their feelings and the stress. The only time it is appropriate to discuss clients is in a private setting with your su-pervisor or colleagues: for example, a case conference. Where discussions involve families, the FSW should be at the office with supervisors and col-leagues, not with family and friends who are not bound by the same rules of confidentiality as the family social worker. Nonprofessionals may lis-ten with interest to a story about families or agencies, but, in the process, may lose respect for the social worker, the agency, or the profession. They could be thinking, "If I have a problem, I will never go to her or any other social worker; it would get all over town," and it might.

2. If a client is not at home when you call, leave only your first name and say nothing about the nature of the business. It may be acceptable to leave your phone number, depending upon how recognizable it is.

3. Social workers must not become involved in discussions with col-leagues over lunch or coffee. At a restaurant or other public places, there is an obvious risk for the conversation to be overheard. Even when names are not mentioned, people might identify the client or think they have. Overhearing personal conversations about work gives others the impres-sion that the social worker is casual about confidentiality.

4. Arrange for phone calls to be taken by someone else when inter-viewing a client at your office. Interruptions lead to a break in rapport and inadvertent breaches of confidentiality. Also, the client may think, "She has more important things to do than listen to me." When in a family home, if using a pager, postpone returning the call so that there is no chance for the family to overhear your phone conversation.

5. Ensure that every interview is private and conducted in a private setting out of the hearing of others.

6. Do not leave case records, phone messages, or rough notes on your desk or in an unlocked car. Case records often have the name of the client prominently displayed on the file, and they may catch someone's atten-tion. Secure records and files before leaving your desk, and make sure that client files are locked up overnight. Clients who observe that the FSW is haphazard in managing files may assume that the FSW will be haphazard in protecting their interests.

7. Clients should not be discussed at parties and social activities. Col-leagues frequently socialize together, and it is tempting to discuss a difficult case or talk about a case to illustrate a common problem.

---

*Items 1–11 reprinted from Collins, Thomlison, & Grinnell, 1992, pp. 186–187.

8. Even if a client seems unconcerned about confidentiality, it must be respected anyway. Some clients may want to begin the interview in a waiting room or initiate or continue a discussion in a public place. In such circumstances, the discussion should be deferred until a private setting can be arranged.

9. Confidentiality about the internal operation and politics of the agency is essential.

10. Before linking a family to other community services, the FSW must obtain permission. When a family gives permission for confidential information to be shared with specific agencies or individuals, information should be limited to that which is essential. Most agencies have developed a release of information form to be used in these situations.

11. In most states, confidentiality must be breached if someone (particularly a child) is at risk of harm. Clients need to be informed of this ahead of time.

CONFIDENTIALITY

Role-play with another student a discussion of confidentiality with a client.

CHAPTER SUMMARY

Considering the practical aspects of case planning helps the family social worker demonstrate the skills of a competent professional. Scheduling enough time for meetings, travel time, and locating clients' homes helps instill client confidence. Planning and preparing ahead for requisite materials and for dealing with children in the home also will alleviate stress for the FSW.

Maintaining client contact may be challenging when working with multiproblem families, who are often seen in family social work. The FSW will need to develop ways of dealing with disruptions and locating clients who move frequently.

Ensuring FSW safety is essential, as most family social work is done in clients' homes. The FSW must be aware of the working environment and take steps to avoid danger, such as refraining from wearing expensive clothes or jewelry into a poor neighborhood with a high crime rate.

The first family meeting sets the stage for all other meetings. A clear introduction of self, the agency, and the purposes of family meetings is crucial. Establishing rapport and trust is the cornerstone of family social work. Finally, client confidentiality is essential for a trusting client-worker relationship.

6 The Beginning Phase

In the preceding chapters, we laid a foundation for discussing the phases of family social work practice. First, we looked at the historical underpinnings of family social work and explored changes in family structure. Next, we applied systems theory and a developmental perspective to family social work. Finally, we explored practical aspects of working with families and offered guidelines for conducting an initial interview. In this chapter, we will continue our discussion of how to establish an alliance with a family and set the stage for positive change. We will begin by describing principles of effective communication, paying special attention to skills needed by the family social worker as he or she begins to work with a family.

Social work takes place in five phases: beginning, assessment, intervention, evaluation, and termination. Each family meeting includes elements of these phases, and the FSW's overall involvement with a family also spans these five phases. In the following chapters we will outline tasks and skills required of the FSW in each phase. The phases of helping are presented one at a time as if they were mutually exclusive, yet in practice they overlap. From the moment of receiving a referral, for example, the FSW begins assessment by reading the referral form or case record. The tasks involved in engaging with a family and assessing its needs continue throughout the FSW's involvement, but they are especially important during the first meetings.

TASKS FOR THE BEGINNING PHASE: ENGAGEMENT AND ASSESSMENT

New social workers often long for a recipe of what to say and do in specific situations. Unfortunately, there are no recipes, just guidelines. It has become cliché to suggest "starting where the client is." A more accurate guideline might be "starting where the social worker is" (Hartman & Laird, 1983), because the FSW influences how assessment and engagement will proceed. The FSW brings to the family an agency mission, as well as skills with which to carry out his or her role.

Several conditions must be met before a family is ready to receive assistance. First, the family has to agree *as a family* that a particular problem requires outside intervention. Second, the family must connect with an agency to deal with the problem. Finally, the agency must decide whether the family's problem fits the agency's mandate. Each of these factors will affect the course of family work.

In some cases, a family's initial contact with the agency is mandated by the court. Even though the family begins as involuntary clients, often the FSW will be able to help them see the merits of family social work so that they will agree to accept help.

The first two tasks of the FSW in the beginning phase are engaging families in the helping process and assessing the problem with which the family is struggling (Worden, 1994).

Engagement involves forming a therapeutic alliance between the social worker and family. Assessment consists of identifying patterns and issues within the family that relate directly to the problem, as well as identifying the connectedness of the family to its social environment. The power of the therapeutic alliance seems to transcend cultural differences (Beutler, Machado, & Allstetter Neufelt, 1994). Rather than looking exclusively at one person's role within the family, the social worker should try to engage all of the family members. This is one reason the entire family should be present at the first meeting with the social worker.

Engagement with the family involves creating a setting where people can safely talk about themselves and about each other (Satir, 1967). The FSW must create an atmosphere that decreases fear and increases confidence of all members. Most important is the development of rapport with the family. Parents may be fearful and lack self-confidence by the time a family social worker enters their home. They may feel that their need for assistance must be a sign of incompetence. Other parents expect to be blamed for the problems that exist. Parents may feel isolated and dejected after having tried to handle the issue for a long time before formal helpers became involved. Conversely, the child with the presenting problem may have been blamed many times for causing the family distress. The child may worry about being blamed further or being removed from the family altogether. All family members may feel hurt, angry, and incompetent.

Thus, during the initial stage of engagement, the social worker must maintain a neutral stance, not confronting individuals prematurely and not making interpretations before all the information is at hand (Gurman & Kniskern, 1981). Minuchin (1974) refers to this early phase of family work as "joining." At this stage, the social worker conveys to the family that "I am like you." Joining helps to bridge the social distance between the social worker and family (Hartman & Laird, 1983).

Engagement and assessment are best accomplished in four steps:

1. Make contact with every family member. The family social worker greets each member of the family, seeking facts that establish his or her distinctiveness. There are no set rules decreeing which person the social worker should turn to first for an introduction, yet gender and cultural issues should be considered. For example, members of some cultures may expect the social worker to speak with the father first. The ordering of introductions should be deliberate. For example, some family social workers avoid turning first to the family member with the identified problem, not wanting to isolate that individual as "the problem." Alternatively, the social worker might validate parental authority by turning to them first. Ideally, the order of introductions should fit the "presenting problem." The FSW makes a personal introduction to the family, including name, agency, how the family came to the agency's attention, and a tentative statement about her or his role.

It is important for the worker to enter into the world of the family, observing family vocabulary and using language that matches the family's style (Goldenberg & Goldenberg, 1994). How members address one another will affect how the social worker addresses them. Regardless of what names are used by the social worker, the names should be selected intentionally. For example, Satir (1967) suggests referring to the parents as "Mom" and "Dad" when discussing parental roles but otherwise using their first names. Additionally, minority families have certain relationship protocols that need to be respected by the worker (Lum, 1992). Special ethnic issues include how to address family members. The social worker's manner of addressing individuals in minority families should adhere to the family's cultural practices. Thus, the social worker needs to learn about the cultural practices of the family's ethnic group and then find out to what degree they adhere to those practices.

2. Define the problem to include perceptions of all members of the family. In clarifying the presenting problem, the social worker speaks with each family member (except infants) to obtain a description of how he or she sees the problem. The FSW should allow each family member to give his or her perspective on the problem without interference from others. Arguments or interruptions should be dealt with politely but firmly (Nichols & Schwartz, 1998). The social worker should attempt to understand each member's perspective based on his or her words and behavior. The FSW can also find out what the family members have attempted to do previously about the problem and what ideas they have for the future. If anger and blaming occur, the FSW must ensure that no one is scapegoated for the problem. The social worker should have strong justification for offering assistance to all family members, as some members may resent the social worker's presence (Geismar & Ayers, 1959).

During the problem definition stage, the FSW should encourage interaction among family members concerning the problem (Tomm & Wright, 1979). This will reveal ongoing family patterns that may have contributed to problem development and clarify why the social worker is seeing the family. By the end of the first interview, the FSW should have established a definition of the problem that does not hold one individual exclusively responsible for either its presence or the solution. This is known as "broadening the focus," whereby the problem and the solution are "owned" by all family members (Nichols & Schwartz, 1998).

In cases of suspected child abuse and neglect, assessing whether any child is at risk becomes a critical first task. Risk assessment of abuse can be difficult, because the best information can be obtained when trust is established and the relationship is strong. The social worker may be suspicious because the family was referred specifically for abuse. In other cases, abuse may be suspected as the work develops. In assessing whether a child is being abused, the social worker should first note any physical signs of abuse such as unexplained bruising and cuts. The social worker should also observe the behavior of the child. Behavioral indicators of abuse may include timidity or aggressiveness, although these signs can indicate other, less serious problems. The behavior of the child in front of a parent should be observed. Does the child seem fearful of the parent? Finally, the parent-child relationship should be observed, especially how the parent interacts with the child. Is the parent irritable and impatient with the child? How much does the parent explain things to the child? Is there an affectionate relationship, or is physical contact avoided?

During this first phase, it is important for the worker to "base all his or her behaviors on understanding and showing respect for the family reality, which includes the value system, cultural context, and experiential nature of all family members" (Alexander, Holtzworth-Munroe, & Jameson, 1994, p. 623). Eventually, problems need to be viewed as problems of the entire family. There are several different ways of teaching the family to view problems within a family framework. Brock and Barnard (1992) propose that one useful visualization is to present the analogy of a mobile to demonstrate how the behavior of one member affects the other members of the family. Ultimately, the problem should be framed within the context of "what needs to be changed" (Brock & Barnard, 1992). Describing the problem as something that needs to be changed sets the stage for the work that lies ahead.

3. Establish goals and clarify an intervention process. The social worker and family members must develop a common goal related to solving the problem. To agree on a goal, the family needs to cooperate with the social worker. The social worker will have assessed the level of motivation in the family and understood what the family hopes will happen (Worden, 1994). Goals should involve the family as a whole, with all members engaged in developing behaviors to eliminate the problem. Concrete ideas and plans can be proposed for problem solving, helping the family to feel a renewed sense of optimism that problems can be resolved.

4. Contract with the family. In this step, the social worker and family reach an agreement on concrete issues such as how often family meetings will be held, who should be present, the length of family meetings, the proposed overall length of intervention, the motivation of each family member, and criteria for judging when goals have been achieved. A definition of the problem should be included in the contract, as well as what everyone can do to address the problem. The social worker and family should reach a consensus on goals and methods (Hartman & Laird, 1983). A written contract lends clarity, formalizes the work that lies ahead, and conveys a sense of seriousness. Contracts should itemize concrete issues such as time and place of meetings that also describe changes in individual and family behaviors that need to be accomplished.

An example of a family social work contract is provided below.

Bob and Anne Smitt, parents of twelve-year-old George, and Cerise Gordon, FSW, mutually agree to work on the following goals.
Focuses of family social work will be (1) parenting skills, (2) husband's unemployment, and (3) child's absence from school.

1. All family members and the FSW agree to meet each Monday in the Smitt home from 6 to 7:30 P.M. for the next six weeks.
2. Ms. Gordon agrees to provide information on parenting classes and job training resources.
3. Mrs. Smitt agrees to attend parenting classes and to work with Ms. Gordon on improving her housekeeping skills.
4. Mr. Smitt agrees to attend parenting classes and to participate in job training seminars.
5. Ms. Gordon agrees to be present when George and his parents meet with George's teacher to develop a plan for him to make up missed work.
6. George agrees to attend school and to participate in the plan to make up his missed work.

BASIC INTERVIEWING SKILLS NEEDED BY FAMILY SOCIAL WORKERS

Many skills and procedures are essential to be an effective helper. Not only will the skills be useful in accomplishing the tasks outlined above, they will also model new behaviors to family members. Basic interviewing skills are necessary for family social work. These skills include

- Listening carefully to expressed family meanings;
- Being sensitive to verbal and nonverbal communication about desires and goals from each family member;
- Recognizing family difficulties related to effective problem solving;
- Promoting skills, knowledge, attitudes, and environmental conditions that contribute to effective family coping.

The role of the FSW involves assisting parents to deal with their children more effectively through the development of problem-solving, decision-making, and parenting skills. Unfortunately, few programs provide training to help family social workers to fulfill these objectives.

Interviewing a group is more complex than interviewing an individual (Shulman, 1992). This is because the maze of problems has expanded to include each individual within the family unit as well as the multiple relationships between individuals. Because of the number of people involved in a family interview, the social worker has less control than in an individual interview (Munson, 1993). Social workers often report feeling overwhelmed by information coming from a number of sources, often at the same time. The complexities present in individual therapy are amplified when seeing a family. An especially difficult task is trying to understand every family member simultaneously and to avoid aligning with individuals in the family (Shulman, 1992). Issues such as male-female roles, ethnicity, and the number of dyadic (two-person) relationships within the family demand that many factors receive attention in a counseling session (Alexander, Holtzworth-Munroe, & Jameson, 1994). Furthermore, the social worker must acknowledge both the advantages and disadvantages of approaching the family from the perspective of an outsider (Hartman & Laird, 1983).

Before family social workers interview families, they must be able to distinguish between a friendship and a professional relationship and between a social conversation and a task-centered family social work interview. If they are unaware of these distinctions, family social workers are likely to lose focus with a family and fail to initiate problem solving.

GUIDELINES FOR EFFECTIVE INTERVIEWS

The following guidelines can help FSW's develop professional relationships with clients (adapted from Kadushin & Kadushin, 1997):

- An interview is deliberate;
- The content of an interview is related to an explicit purpose;
- The family social worker has the primary responsibility for the content and direction of the interview;
- Relationships are structured and time-limited.

A family interview is *deliberate* and has an established purpose and specific goals that are mutually accepted by all participants. Thus, the focus of the interview is on a cluster of family problems, directed toward a solution. To arrive at a solution, the FSW must overcome the temptation to engage in conversations that detract from the task at hand. For example, *extended* "chit chat" can be a waste of time or a way to avoid painful topics. Small talk may be useful initially to allow the family and social worker to get acquainted with each other (Brock & Barnard, 1992). It may also be useful for engaging a resistant family member. Small talk may be appropriate if the FSW uses it to establish rapport and remembers to return to issues after a resistant member has become involved.

When working with members of a different culture, the FSW should initially engage the family in friendly conversation, rather than immediately focusing on the problem. Rules about relationships differ greatly from culture to culture. The dominant Western culture is often considered direct and even rude and disrespectful by members of less aggressive cultures. Family social workers need to be sensitive to cultural variations in how relationships are established in other cultures. When differences do emerge, discussion of these differences can clear up many misunderstandings (Lum, 1992).

As soon as rapport is established, the FSW must identify a specific focus for the work. The longer it takes to develop focus, the harder it will become to focus the work on a specific agenda and accomplish later work. Clients may drop out between the first and second meetings if there is a lack of purpose and direction. Establishing a clear direction, focused on family needs and concerns, gets the FSW's relationship with the family off to a positive start.

The *content* of family meetings should flow from an agreed-upon purpose and move in the direction of addressing the identified problems. Spoken words and planned activities must be related directly to the stated purpose. For example, the FSW who initiates a family meeting with a general question such as "How are things going?" will lead the family in a less productive direction than the FSW who begins by saying, "Tell me how the parenting techniques we discussed last week worked out."

In family work, the FSW assumes *primary responsibility* for the content and direction of the interview. Sometimes this responsibility can be challenging for the FSW who may be reluctant to use professional authority and expertise with the family, particularly if the parents are older than the FSW or if the FSW has no children. Parents may ask the family social worker if he or she has any children. They may want to find out if the social worker can understand what they are going through. They may also be doing their own assessment of the social worker's experience. These questions may create insecurity for workers who are new and do not have children of their own. They do not want to appear incapable. The best response to these questions may be to discuss the parents' concerns. For example, the FSW can say, "No, I don't have any children myself. It sounds like you are worried that because I don't have any children, I will not be able to understand your situation or help you. Let's talk about this."

The relationship between the FSW and the family is also *structured* and *time-limited*. This means that activities are intentional and centered around the task at hand, creating an atmosphere in which family members are expected to work on identified problems. It also means that family social work has a beginning and an end. Thus, the FSW must be able to recognize when a family has achieved its task and no longer requires the social worker's assistance. Similarly, each individual session with the family should be time-limited, depending on the nature of the work that needs to be accomplished.

As much as family social workers try to achieve a partnership with the family, the relationship is seldom reciprocal. The FSW provides leadership, knowledge, and direction to the family. The interests and needs of the clients are primary, demanding that the needs of the FSW be set aside. For example, families may ask the FSW personal questions. The social worker must decide how much information to share, remembering that the needs of the family and the therapeutic focus comes first. Self-disclosure by the social worker to a client must have a definite purpose.

Every action and activity of the FSW must be *intentional*, and words should be selected consciously to have an intended effect. For instance, the FSW may select words based on family interests: if the family is sports-minded, the FSW may refer to the family as a "team." Of course, being deliberate with every word, motive, and action can extract much energy from the social worker.

The FSW-family relationship is guided by clear and firm boundaries ensuring that family needs take precedence over those of the social worker. New family social workers often struggle with the desire to become "friendly" and establish personal relationships with families. This is a natural inclination because family social workers become involved in intimate details of family life and because positive relationships are pivotal to the work. Also, knowing private details about people is associated with intimacy. Family social workers work closely with people in intense and emotionally laden situations. In addition, the FSW may sincerely like clients, and this liking is a crucial ingredient for the work that lies ahead.

Despite temptation, family social workers must retain a professional focus. The helping relationship is different from friendship, because the FSW wields some authority in relation to the family, making a completely equal relationship impossible. Codes of ethics also dictate which behaviors are acceptable and which are breaches of professional conduct. For example, a family social worker arranged to purchase a vehicle from a family, with the family financing the purchase. This was an obvious breach of professional conduct that had to be reported to the agency. Other breaches include sexual involvement with clients (Masson, 1994), taking the family for vacations, or deciding to parent a child from the family in the social worker's home. Social workers should refer to their code of ethics and discuss situations with supervisors when in doubt. A useful guideline is that if the social worker feels the need to keep information from the agency, it needs to be examined for breach of conduct.

Family social workers, thus, must be committed to meeting needs of the family first. The FSW's personal needs are not the focus in this relationship, as attention must be directed to the family's issues. It is natural for social workers to want to do their best and be appreciated, but they should resist comparisons to other social workers, regardless of how families may flatter them by saying "You are the best social worker we have ever had!" or telling them about the atrocities performed on them by other social workers. The social worker should accept a sincere or spontaneous compliment, but the compliment should not draw in negative comparisons with other workers.

Family social work is usually arranged formally concerning time, place, duration, and purpose. Unpleasantness, such as issues requiring confrontation, cannot be avoided and is often necessary to accomplish the tasks contracted for.

PRINCIPLES OF EFFECTIVE COMMUNICATION

The interview is a special type of encounter, and everything said within this encounter conveys a message. All messages should be deliberate. Communication takes place between the social worker and the family, as well as between family members. The process of communication is complex, and experienced FSWs recognize that *"You cannot* not *communicate."* Communication involves more than speaking with words and can include facial expressions, gestures, posture, and tone of voice (Satir, 1967).

Meaning is conveyed at six levels (Tomm, 1987):

1. Content—what is actually said.
2. Speech—how the message is said.
3. Episode—the social context of the message.
4. Interpersonal relationships—the quality of the relationship between the communicators.
5. Life script—self-image and self-expectations.
6. Cultural pattern—internalized values of one's culture.

Effective communication is clear, direct, and honest.

- **Clear** communication is not masked. The communicator says what he or she means.
- **Direct** communication is addressed to the person for whom the message was intended. (Indirect messages avoid conveying personal responsibility and expressing real feelings.)
- **Honest** communication conveys a genuine message.

Simple communication involves sending messages from one person to another, as pictured below:

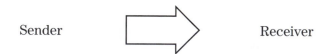

Sender   Receiver

This diagram captures a simple linear communication, such as a parent telling a child, "Pick up your toys." In this message, the linear transmission of the message implies an active sender and passive receiver. However, even in this seemingly straightforward example, additional meaning may be intended or inferred. Imagine that "Pick up your toys" is said by an exasperated parent who believes that the child is thoughtless or careless. The message will then be more than the simple instruction and may contain angry verbal tones and nonverbal behavioral clues revealing the parent's displeasure. The body language of the parent may also seem threatening to the child. Thus, communication involves a circular, interactive process of involvement by participants (Tomm, 1987).

Words contain more than one meaning, and social workers need to realize that the same word can mean different things to different people (Bandler, Grinder, & Satir, 1976). Remember that people seldom select words consciously.

The Communication Process

A thorough explanation of the communication process is given below (Johnson & Johnson, 1994).

- Intentions, ideas, and feelings of the sender are formed before sending a message. The sender *encodes* a message by translating ideas, feelings, and intentions into a message appropriate for sending.

- The sender transmits the message to the receiver through a *channel*. Often the channel is provided by words, tone of voice, facial expressions, posture, and body language (Bandler, Grinder, & Satir, 1967).

- The receiver translates the message by *interpreting* its meaning. Meaning is derived from how the message is conveyed as well as the context within which the message is sent. The receiver's interpretation depends on how well he or she understands the content and context of the message and the intentions of the sender. The receiver receives the message through relevant sensory channels such as sight, hearing, and touch.

- The receiver responds internally to this interpretation of the message. Meanings in a message can include the literal content of the message (denotative level) as well as what is inferred from the nature of the relationship between the sender and the receiver (metacommunication). In other words, metacommunication is a *message about a message* (Satir, 1967, p. 76). Additionally, the receiver of the message will connect the message with past experiences that influence how the message is understood (Bandler, Grinder, & Satir, 1967). The life script or internalized self-image of the receiver also influences translation.

- The receiver then responds to the sender's verbal and nonverbal messages.

"Noise" includes anything that interferes with this communication process. Noise for the sender includes attitudes, frames of reference, emotions, and difficulty in choosing appropriate words. For the receiver, noise can include factors such as attitudes, background, and experiences that influence the decoding process. In the communication channel, noise may result from environmental sounds, speech problems such as stammering, or annoying or distracting mannerisms such as mumbling. Successful communication ultimately depends upon the degree to which noise is overcome or controlled (Johnson & Johnson, 1994).

Influence of Cultural Background

Culture not only affects how people communicate with one another, it also creates unique "noises." For example, ethnicity is often associated with differences in social class. This is because the percentage of nonwhites who are poor is larger than that of whites (Davis & Proctor, 1989). Studies in ethnicity have shown that people differ in their experience of emotional pain, how they show it, how they communicate about what is troubling them, their beliefs about the cause of the difficulties, attitudes toward the social worker, and the intervention they expect (McGoldrick & Giordano, 1996). Social workers who follow practices of the dominant culture may not understand when ethnic families communicate in nonstandard ways.

The FSW must carefully consider factors that affect both the verbal and nonverbal behavior of any person. In family social work, we assume that the behavior of an individual occurs within a family context. Similarly, the behavior of a family must be placed within a cultural context. Personal, familial, cultural, and social background affect behavior, and such factors should be considered when interpreting nonverbal or verbal behavior. For one person, lack of eye contact may suggest avoidance; in another, the same behavior may suggest that the person is listening but is from a culture where eye contact is considered impolite. Similarly, talking face to face may be a sign of interest and concern in some cultures but a sign of disrespect in others.

Many are familiar with different ways individuals greet each other. In some cultures, hugs and kisses are exchanged as a greeting, while in others the same type greeting would be uncomfortable. Initial FSW impressions of a client's nonverbal behavior should be tentative until the FSW learns more about the personal, social, and cultural background of the client. The best way to become familiar with another culture is to ask questions conveying an interest in learning more about the family's background.

The impact of ethnicity is often overlooked, yet ethnic values and identification are usually retained for several generations after immigration. Ethnic family issues may be filtered by gender, roles, expressiveness, birth order, separation, or individuation. Cultural background may also prescribe norms of communication. For example, an emphasis on keeping things "in the family" or the manner of discussing (or not discussing) certain subjects may be handed down from generation to generation, reflecting individual and cultural influences. Space limitations do not permit detailing beliefs and patterns that every cultural group has about the family. Interested readers are referred to McGoldrick, Giordano, and Pearce (1996), Sue and Sue (1990), and Lum (1992).

Methods of Providing Information

The most commonly used intervention at all professional levels is providing information. The FSW must decide what information to provide to parents and how to evaluate the parents' understanding of this information. If parents have not mastered the material, it is the FSW's job to determine what steps must be taken to assure that the parents either develop the understanding necessary to handle the problem or modify their behavior so that necessary clinical goals are achieved.

The FSW must assess the parents' levels of functioning, including the degree to which they can work as a team. Understanding parents' backgrounds helps the FSW decide how to provide necessary information and direct attention to areas of parental concern. Assessment also gives the FSW an understanding about parental strengths and weaknesses that influence child management. Listening to parents discuss their child and related concerns is the best source of obtaining this understanding, although this may require a new orientation for the FSW who may be more accustomed to imposing strict time limits on interviews with parents.

Even simple instructions to parents must be tailored to fit the parents' unique characteristics. A permissive parent, for example, may be unable to stick to a precise behavioral regime for an acting-out child, while an authoritarian parent may find it impossible to negotiate house rules with his or her child. Between these two extremes are the parents who do well with most instructions if the instructions are clear. The FSW must assess parental styles accurately and modify tactics to provide parents with an individualized approach.

The FSW is charged with continually assessing parents to understand their personalized responses to stresses and also their problem-solving abilities. This process applies even in the seemingly simple task of giving instructions. Thus, FSWs must find clear ways of instructing (teaching) and of determining whether the information is understood.

Complex instructions can be provided in written form to parents at the end of an interview. The FSW may suggest a place for the note such as the refrigerator door, so that parents may easily refer to the instructions. Parents should be asked to repeat instructions to verify the accuracy of their understanding. This verbal review is one way to assure that instructions are clearly and concisely presented and understood. It also gives parents an opportunity to ask questions. However, the system is not foolproof and other steps may be necessary as well.

Telephone follow-up is useful, as parents may have additional questions after they have reflected on the interview but be reluctant to ask "dumb" questions or to bother the busy FSW. Another way to assist parents is to encourage them to telephone the FSW freely when needed. Also, reassessment of the situation and discussions with the parents at subsequent visits should be ongoing.

When providing information, giving instructions, and following up are inadequate to accomplish the tasks, the FSW must determine what further assistance is necessary. The goal becomes finding a practical way to help parents understand their problems and change their own behavior if required. The competent FSW can judge what can or must be undertaken, what should be delayed until appropriate intermediate goals have been achieved, and what must be postponed indefinitely. Consequently, the FSW should be willing to adopt alternative procedures based upon an assessment of the total situation.

For various reasons, parents may be unable to comprehend even simple directions. In such cases, other forms of help must be found so that supportive and preparatory intervention can take place. In this, as in all aspects of family support social work, the FSW must solicit feedback from parents so they may participate actively in the evaluation process.

Attending Behaviors

Attending behaviors help the FSW to tune in and focus on people in the interview. They demonstrate that the social worker is paying close attention to what clients are saying and doing. In the process, FSWs must minimize discussion of their personal experiences. Because family meetings are not social situations, the social worker must contain or be in control of self.

Critical to attending is the development of active listening skills. Family social workers must listen carefully to clients and convey an accurate understanding of their messages. Additionally, attending behaviors invite clients into the conversation, because appropriate body language and words to convey interest in what clients are saying. Listening involves hearing, observing, encouraging, remembering, and understanding.

FSWs must use visual attending skills, particularly eye contact and appropriate facial expressions. Maintaining eye contact does not mean staring intensely; instead, it means keeping the client within the range of vision in a continuous, relaxed way. The level of eye contact should respect cultural diversity. In addition to visual attending skills, FSWs use physical attending skills. Ideally throughout a meeting, the FSW faces family members with a posture that is neither tense nor overly relaxed. A tense posture may convey rigidity, and a very relaxed posture may convey too much informality. Different cultures may have different comfort levels concerning distance, and these should be respected. Leaning forward slightly, especially during vital parts of an interview, motivates clients to speak. Body posture and attending should seem natural, not staged or stilted.

Verbal attending skills involve listening closely to what others are stating verbally (content), para-verbally (voice tone and inflection), and nonverbally (body language). With practice, FSWs can isolate the client's "meta-messages" (hidden messages).

These are suggestions, not hard and fast rules. The FSW must be sensitive to cultural differences that require modification of attending behaviors. For instance, members of some cultures consider direct eye contact disrespectful, and others vary as to preferred distances between speakers. Ultimately, the social worker must learn to use attending skills that are culturally appropriate (Lum, 1992).

Self-Awareness

Self-awareness is an important ingredient of family social work. We referred earlier to the influence that values and biases may have on work with families. Every human being has needs, values, feelings, and biases and to be effective, FSWs must assess personal biases that could interfere with effective family social work. In achieving self-awareness, the FSW demonstrates honesty and avoids unethical use of clients to fulfill personal psychological needs. All people have unmet needs or quirks that must be examined to ensure that they do not diminish effectiveness. For example, clients who are experiencing problems similar to those of the FSW can cause feelings of confusion or avoidance in the FSW. There are several benefits of self-awareness:

1. Self-awareness strengthens personal competence whereby the FSW does not need to rely on clients to enhance self-esteem. Work with clients can be honest, without false reassurance from an FSW attempting to elicit positive feedback from clients or fearing that clients may drop out of family social work.

2. Self-awareness encourages appropriate use of professional authority. Family social workers have the potential and opportunity to misuse power, which can occur when a social worker is only comfortable when in control or when coercing a client to comply. Power can also be abused through compulsive advice giving or needing to feel superior to clients.

3. Self-awareness enhances managed use of intimacy. FSWs with unmet intimacy needs or a poorly developed capacity for intimacy will have trouble building worker-family relationships. For example, the social worker who lacks self-awareness may show excessive distancing behaviors or become overly involved with the client.

Self-awareness also helps the FSW acknowledge when personal problems, unmet emotional needs, and critical life events interfere with effective work with clients. Transference and countertransference are important concepts related to self-awareness. Transference occurs when clients relate to FSWs as if they were another significant figure (e.g., parent) in the client's life. Feelings, fears, defenses, and reactions present in another relationship are transferred to the FSW. Countertransference occurs when FSWs transfer their own feelings toward significant others to clients. While such feelings are common within the context of helping, self-awareness allows the FSW to control these experiences rather than vice versa.

Steps can be taken to enhance worker self-awareness. First, workers can undergo personal counseling with the goal of expanding self-awareness. Issues also can be discussed with one's supervisor, and if they interfere with effectiveness or create difficulties in working with particular problems or clients, the caseload can be restricted to clients with whom one can work effectively.

Effective FSWs are in touch with their experiences and feelings and are able to identify and accept a range of feelings and experiences. They are aware of their own values, beliefs, and needs and can develop warm and deep relationships with others. Effective FSWs feel secure enough to reveal who they genuinely are. They accept personal responsibility for their behaviors, receive feedback nondefensively, admit when they are wrong, accept limits placed upon them, and are honest. Effective FSWs set realistic goals with clients, striving for excellence instead of perfection and are aware of the impact they have on others. Becoming an effective FSW is an ongoing process rather than a one-time endeavor. Thus, FSWs are committed to improving their skills throughout their careers.

CHALLENGES FACING THE FSW

Think about types of clients or types of problems that you may find difficult to handle. List these, and write what you would do if faced with each.

CORE QUALITIES NEEDED BY FAMILY SOCIAL WORKERS

Research consistently supports the importance of the social worker's capacity to demonstrate empathy, warmth, and genuineness (Beutler, Machado, & Allstetter Neufelt, 1994). All of these qualities are essential to most helping situations (Lambert & Bergin, 1994), and they are prerequisites for effective social work. Together, they help the social worker to establish a climate of trust and safety in which family members can begin to view their problems in new ways (Lambert & Bergin, 1994).

Family social workers can be reassured by the fact that about 30 percent of change in counseling occurs because of the quality of the worker-client relationship, whereas model and technique contribute only about 15 percent. Strong alliances are formed when families perceive the social worker to be warm, trustworthy, nonjudgmental, and empathetic (Miller, Hubble & Duncan, 1995). This opinion is supported through interviews of parents who took part in a home-based, family-centered program (Coleman & Collins, 1997). Families valued social workers' basic interviewing skills such as listening, support, and teaching. The researchers concluded that "families did not remember the fancy techniques. Instead, they recalled the dignity and respect received in treatment."

Empathy

The FSW uses empathy to communicate understanding of client experiences, behaviors, and feelings from the client's point of view. Empathy is a core ingredient in establishing and developing relationships with clients. Social workers need to maintain empathy with individuals and respect for the family's way of doing things. Family social work "starts where the client is," even when the client's perspective eventually needs to be challenged. Empathy involves seeing the world through another person's eyes, but differs from sympathy or pity. It must be remembered, however, that some ethnic groups do not focus on feelings directly and the worker must find culturally specific ways of seeing the world through another's eyes (Lum, 1992).

When it is difficult to understand what a client feels, empathy should never be faked. Admitting to a lack of understanding is acceptable for FSWs, who can then ask for clarification. Poorly executed empathy includes parroting, verbatim repetition, insincerity, and empathy that is inaccurate. In addition excessive empathy can seem artificial and result in annoying people.

Empathy can be expressed at different levels of depth and effectiveness. A five-level scale has been developed by Truax and Carkhuff (1967) to measure empathy.

Five Levels of Empathetic Responses

Level 1   At Level 1, the responses of the social worker detract significantly from the verbal and behavioral expressions of the client. The response communicates less than the client expressed, and the social worker shows no awareness of even surface feelings. The social worker may be bored, uninterested, or operating from a preconceived frame of reference that does not recognize the client's individualism.

Level 2   The social worker responds but not fully, and subtracts from the noticeable affect of the client. The social worker may show some awareness of obvious surface feelings, but depletes from the client's experience.

Level 3   The social worker mirrors client responses. Responses are interchangeable in that they express the same affect and meaning. The social worker responds with an accurate understanding of the client, but may overlook deeper feelings. The response does not add or detract and shows that the social worker is willing to know and understand more.

Level 4   The responses of the social worker enhance the client's expressions, taking client feelings to a deeper level than the client was able or willing to express. The social worker thus takes understanding of what was communicated to a deeper level.

Level 5   The social worker gives accurate responses to all of the client's deeper and surface feelings. The social worker is "tuned in" to the client, making it possible for the two to explore very deeply aspects of the client's existence.

Empathy at levels lower than Level 3 suggests that the social worker has failed to pick up on key client feelings.

The ability to understand the needs of parents is a prerequisite skill to effective work with families. FSWs often identify strongly with children, and at times this identification may be so strong as to appear anti-adult. Such a position can lead to the view of parents as negative influences on the child, often accompanied by a desire to work with the child alone, isolated from the rest of the family.

A unique perspective is required for effective work with families. FSWs must understand parents' needs and empathize with their feelings. Of vital importance is empathy with the struggle that many parents experience raising children, particularly parents of children with special needs. In addition, the FSW must recognize that parents may feel confused, hurt, and guilty by the time family problems have reached a level where professional help is needed.

To be effective in family social work, FSWs must shift from a child-centered focus to a family-centered one, identifying with both parents and children. In addition, while empathy is an important skill for the FSW to master, family members can also be taught empathy skills to use with one another.

One formula for making empathy statements is:

"You feel _____(emotion) because _____ (restatement of client's experiences and/or behaviors)."

The following procedure has been developed to help in creating empathy statements:

1. "It seems like you feel…"
2. Feeling label
3. Place the feeling in a context.
4. Make the tense of the feeling *here and now*.
5. Check it out for accuracy.

Other stems for empathetic sentences include the following:

"It sounds like…"
"You seem to feel…"
"From your point of view…"
"It sounds like you are saying…"
"Kind of makes you feel…"
"I am sensing up that…"
"If I am hearing you correctly…"
"I am not sure I am with you, but…"
"I wonder if you are saying that…"
"Is it possible that…?"
"Perhaps you're feeling…"

"As I understand what you are saying, you felt that…"
"So, as you see the situation…"
"From where you stand, it seems…"
"It seems to you that…"
"Where you're coming from…"
"Could it be that…?"
"Correct me if I'm wrong…"
"You appear to be feeling…"
"I get the impression that…"

Reflection of Feelings Reflection of feelings is one way of showing empathy. Since client feelings may be masked or unknown, correct reflection of feelings validates feelings and shows that the social worker is listening. This process is a *mirror* that reflects both feelings and content. Reflection may be difficult when several different feelings coexist, but an accurate reflection may help the client sort out conflicting or unclear feelings. Feelings are expressed both verbally and nonverbally, making it necessary to observe incongruence between verbal and nonverbal expression. For example, a client might verbally express comfort in the meeting with the FSW, but at the same time, the FSW may note nonverbal signs of discomfort such as a scowl or a rigid, closed posture.

While reflections help build rapport and trust, some clients may be uncomfortable talking about feelings; for example, some people use intellectualization as a defense. It is important to vary the sentence stems used and to draw from a diverse range of feelings and words.

REFLECTION OF FEELINGS

List at least 25 words that can be used to describe feelings as part of statements to clients.

Examples of Five Levels of Empathy Client (describing her husband's reaction to her decision to find a job) "He laughed at me. My own husband just sat there and laughed at me. I felt like such a fool, so put down."

Level 1: What did you say his name was?

Level 2: Uh huh, I see.

Level 3: You sound upset with your husband.

Level 4: You sound humiliated by his comments.

Level 5: I get a sense that your husband hurt you a lot. It seems to me that you are also feeling angry with him.

Advanced Empathy Using advanced empathy, the FSW shares *hunches* about clients in an attempt to understand client feelings and concerns more clearly. The goal is to facilitate client self-awareness, which, in turn, leads to new client goals and behaviors. Examples of advanced empathy through sharing of FSW hunches include the following:

- Hunches that help clients develop a bigger picture, e.g., "The problem doesn't seem to be just your attitude toward your husband anymore. Your resentment seems to have spread to the children as well. Could that be the case?"

- Hunches that help clients articulate what they are expressing indirectly or merely implying, e.g., "I think I also might be hearing you say that you are more than disappointed—perhaps even hurt and angry."

- Hunches that help clients draw logical conclusions from what they are saying, e.g., "From all that you've said about her, it seems to me you also are saying right now that you resent having to be with her. I realize you haven't said that directly, but I'm wondering if you are feeling that way about her."

- Hunches that help clients discuss topics about which they have hinted, e.g., "You've brought up sexual matters a number of times, but you haven't followed up on them. My guess is that sex is a pretty important area for you—but perhaps pretty touchy, too."

- Hunches that help clients identify themes, e.g., "If I'm not mistaken, you've mentioned in two or three different ways that it is sometimes difficult for you to stick up for your own rights. For instance, you let your husband decide that you would not return to college, though this is against your wishes."

- Hunches that help clients completely own their experiences, behaviors, and feelings, e.g., "You sound as if you have already decided to marry him, but I don't hear you saying that directly."

Nonpossessive Warmth

An important factor in the relationship between FSW and client is the level of warmth and caring shown to the client. Warmth exists when the social worker communicates with clients in ways that convey acceptance, understanding, and interest in their well-being and make them feel safe regardless of such external factors as the client's problematic behavior, demeanor, or appearance (Sheafor, Horejsi, & Horejsi, 1997). According to Goldstein, "without warmth, some interventions may be technically correct but therapeutically impotent" (Hackney & Cormier, p. 65). Establishing a relationship based on feelings of warmth and understanding is the foundation for successful client change.

Warmth is more than saying "I care," although this is nonetheless important. Although it can be conveyed *verbally* by one's choice of words, it is largely displayed *nonverbally*. Examples include (Johnson, 1993, as cited in Hackney & Cormier, p. 66):

Tone of voice:	soft, soothing
Facial expression:	smiling, interested
Posture:	relaxed, leaning toward the other person
Eye contact:	looking directly into the other person's eyes
Touching:	touching the other person softly and discreetly
Gestures:	open, welcoming
Physical proximity:	close

Warmth or the lack of it can have a strong impact on the client and the worker-client relationship. Without it, "a worker's words will sound hollow and insincere and will have no therapeutic impact" (Sheafor, Horejsi, & Horejsi, 1997, p. 149).

Five Levels of Nonpossessive Warmth Five levels of nonpossessive warmth are presented below. Level 3 is the minimal level to be achieved for the effective FSW, while Levels 4 and 5 communicate deep warmth and regard. Levels of warmth that fall below Level 3 fail to convey adequate warmth.

Level 1 The FSW's verbal and behavioral expression communicates lack of respect (negative regard) for the client. The FSW conveys a total lack of respect.

Level 2 The FSW communicates little respect for client's feelings, experiences, and potentials and may respond mechanically or passively.

Level 3 The FSW minimally acknowledges regard for the client's abilities and capacities for improved functioning. The FSW, at the least, communicates that the client matters.

Level 4 The FSW communicates very deep respect and concern for the client. The FSW's responses enable the client to feel free to be himself or herself and to experience feeling valued.

Level 5 The FSW communicates deepest respect for the client's worth as a person and for his or her potential and communicates deep caring and commitment to the client.

Examples of Five Levels of Nonpossessive Warmth Keep in mind that tone of voice and nonverbal behavior are crucial in conveying warmth.

The client says, "My daughter is a bright girl, but she's been getting bad grades in school. I'm not sure what to do."

Level 1: Uh huh. (No eye contact with the client, bored tone of voice.)

Level 2: That's tough. (Some eye contact, flat vocal tone.)

Level 3: You feel angry that your daughter is not living up to her potential. (Eye contact, leaning toward the client.)

Level 4: It is disappointing for you when your child is not doing well in school, and you are worried about her. (FSW looks into client's eyes. Tone of voice expresses concern.)

Level 5: It must be disappointing for you and your daughter that she is not doing well in school. I can see you are worried about her. Let's look at ways we can help your daughter have a more successful experience in school. (Good eye contact, relaxed and open posture, concerned yet optimistic tone of voice.)

Genuineness

The quality of genuineness is perhaps the most difficult to describe. According to Truax and Carkhuff (1967), genuineness refers to a lack of defensiveness or artificiality in the social worker's communications with the client. Barker (1995) defines genuineness as "sincerity and honesty…genuineness includes being unpretentious with clients" (p. 150). Like empathy and warmth, genuineness is conveyed at different levels. Level 3 is the minimum for effective social work.

Five Levels of Genuineness

Level 1 The FSW's verbalizations are slightly unrelated to what he or she is feeling at the moment. Responses may be negative or destructive. The FSW may convey defensiveness in words and actions and does not use these defensive feelings to explore the helping relationship with the client.

Level 2 The FSW's verbalizations are slightly unrelated to what she or he is feeling. The FSW does not know how to manage negative reactions toward the client, nor how to use them constructively in the interview. The interviewing style may sound mechanical or rehearsed.

Level 3 There is no evidence of incongruence between what the FSW says and feels in the interview. The social worker might take a neutral personal stance. The FSW makes appropriate responses that seem sincere but do not reflect intense personal involvement.

Level 4 The FSW presents cues suggesting genuine responses (both positive and negative) that are nondestructive. Responses are congruent, but the FSW might hesitate to express them fully.

Level 5 The FSW freely expresses self but is nonexploitative. The FSW is spontaneous, open to all experiences, nondefensive, and uses interactions constructively to open further discussion and exploration for both the client and the FSW.

Examples of Five Levels of Genuineness The client says, "I'm ready to throw my daughter out of the house. She doesn't listen to a word I say, and she does whatever she pleases."

Level 1: You seem to be overreacting.

Level 2: You need to practice tough love.

Level 3: Teenagers are a handful.

Level 4: I know from a personal experience that it can be very challenging to deal with teenagers.

Level 5: I know it can be challenging and difficult to communicate with teenagers. Let's look at how we can help you and your daughter work toward a more satisfying relationship.

■ **CORE QUALITIES**

> For the client statement given below, provide responses demonstrating one of the following core qualities: empathy, nonpossessive warmth, or genuineness. Create responses that fit into each of the five levels of response.
>
> Client statement: "I don't know what to do. My husband just left me, my son got picked up for shoplifting, and my daughter just told me she is pregnant. If that is not enough, my boss told me that I might lose my job because there is not enough business at this time of year."

DYSFUNCTIONAL BEHAVIORS TO AVOID IN FAMILY SOCIAL WORK

In this chapter we have described a number of skills that are needed in the beginning phase of family social work. In addition to knowing what is helpful in an interview, the social worker should be aware of dysfunctional behaviors that can interfere with effective helping. Accordingly, we provide the following list of behaviors to avoid (Collins, 1989; Gabor & Collins, 1985–86):

1. Taking sides with individual family members;
2. Giving false reassurance or agreement where inappropriate;
3. Ignoring cues about the family's subjective experience of the problem while dealing exclusively with "objective" material;
4. Judgmental responding;
5. Inappropriate use of humor or other responses that inhibit discussion or undermine trust;
6. Premature problem solving;
7. Criticizing or belittling family members and behaving in a condescending manner;
8. Overreliance on "chit-chat";
9. Overprotecting family members by ignoring clear cues to implicit information.

CHAPTER SUMMARY

Family social work takes place in five phases: beginning, assessment, intervention, evaluation, and termination. Specific skills are required for the family social worker in each of these phases. In this chapter, we looked at skills involved in the beginning phase, when the social worker establishes rapport with families. The FSW needs to understand the principles of effective communication and know how to interpret clients' verbal and nonverbal messages. Core qualities required of the FSW include empathy, nonpossessive warmth, and genuineness. The skills and qualities required for effective social work are developed and refined throughout the social worker's career.

7

The
Assessment
Phase

When meeting a new family, the social worker must know what to look for and how to begin assessment. Should the first observations be of the parents, children, or the house? What is the best way to manage time and effort yet obtain a comprehensive understanding of the family? What questions are important to ask? Areas to cover in a comprehensive assessment may be evident, but ways to explore these areas may be less obvious.

The goal of assessment and problem definition is to explore, identify, and define dynamics within and beyond the family that contribute to problem development. During assessment, the FSW must collect enough information about the family to make informed intervention decisions (Brock & Barnard, 1992). Careful assessment will lead to the development of realistic and concrete goals. During assessment, the FSW assists the family (ideally with all members participating) to explore issues of concern. This exploration should lead to a deeper, more accurate understanding of the family's situation.

Each member of the family has a unique perspective on the problem, and every perspective is important. For example, a problem defined by the family as a child spending too much time "hanging out with friends," may be a "conforming" issue for the parents, an "independence" issue for the target child, and an "exclusion" issue for siblings.

During assessment, the FSW must respect the individuality of parents, the coexistence of personal strengths and weaknesses, the influence of cultural and ethnic backgrounds, and the role of the environment (home, occupational, social, and community) in shaping and maintaining attitudes and behaviors. The goal of family social work is to help parents become more effective with their children. The FSW must respect parents from a range of cultural and economic backgrounds. This means accepting diversity rather than expecting all families to look and act alike.

WHAT KINDS OF INFORMATION ARE NEEDED?

Social workers often struggle to decide what information to gather in the first meeting. They will benefit from knowledge of theoretical concepts related to family functioning and the presenting problem. However, different models of family theory emphasize different focuses in assessment. Some theories, for example, emphasize two-person interactions (dyads), while others look at the entire family unit. Perhaps the most important consideration in assessing a family is to remember that each family is unique.

Developing a clear understanding of family problems is necessary for devising interventions. Particularly important is knowing the duration of a problem and how the family has tried to deal with it. In addition, the FSW will be interested in identifying the strengths and resources of the family. Other focuses of attention are family roles, communication patterns, family members' ability to carry out required roles, family closeness, and family rules. A genogram can be used to record this information. Finally, information about a family's relationship with its environment is necessary for successful assessment.

Accurate assessment sets the stage for later interventions and is critical to the success of work with the family. Three techniques are necessary for conducting a comprehensive assessment of families (Holman, 1983): interviews, observation, and the use of checklists or other measurement devices.

During assessment of a family, the social worker attempts to learn about both *content* and *process*. Content is the actual information that is provided to the family social worker. Process refers to how family members interact with one another. Information about the content of family life can be acquired by interviewing family members. Information about process is best obtained through observation. In addition to gathering information and observing interactional patterns within the family, social workers often use concrete tools to assess family functioning.

Family assessment has several purposes:

1. To determine whether a family will profit from family work, and if so, to decide what types of interventions will serve them best and what specific changes are needed;

2. To establish short-term and long-term goals based on realistic objectives;

3. To identify family strengths and resources as well as environmental and community resources that can be employed to move the family toward change;

4. To understand baseline family functioning as a foundation for evaluating the outcomes of the intervention.

ASSESSMENT METHODS

Family social workers need to look at how a family interacts with its environment, rather than attributing problems solely to "sick" individuals. Comprehensive assessment involves understanding how a family interacts with its environment. An ecological assessment identifies the social supports available to the family and the amount of reciprocity between the family and its social surroundings. Some families rely heavily on environmental supports without returning any resources to the environment. Others experience severe gaps in environmental supports that prevent the meeting of individual members' needs. The driving question behind an ecological assessment is "Are the needs of the family being met?" (Hartman & Laird, 1983). Generally, when a family has enough resources for coping with the demands placed upon it, the care of family members will be adequate (Rothery, 1993).

A comprehensive ecological assessment, based on Maslow's (1967) hierarchy of needs, focuses on availability of concrete necessities, such as food, clothing, shelter, medical care, and employment, as well as emotional support and other benefits derived from social relationships (Holman, 1983). Social networks can be informal or formal. Informal supportive persons are an important part of a family's network, and these individuals or groups function as "natural helpers." For some families, environmental resources are not available, while others may be unaware of them, not know how to use them, or refuse to use them. Preparing an ecomap helps the FSW to obtain information about the family's relationship with its environment. An ecomap can display important information about how the family gets its needs met. The ecomap captures the nature of the relationship between the family and the world around them, exploring whether existing resources are adequate to meet the family's needs.

Families have two kinds of needs: basic and developmental (Rothery, 1993). Basic needs, such as food and shelter, must be satisfied for physical survival. Developmental needs are created by stresses requiring change, such as the birth of a new child or a teenager's struggle for independence. Resources to meet needs can be provided either by formal or informal sources. No family is independent of its environment; instead, families rely on a combination of these resources. Some families, however, fail to use a balance of informal and formal resources. Instead, they rely excessively on formal support networks, such as child welfare or social service agencies, and receive an inadequate amount of informal social support.

Valuable information from support networks includes feedback about parent-child relationships, norms, expectations, and child-rearing techniques (Garbarino, 1982). Use of social supports is not only determined by availability; it is also influenced by the family's attitude toward them and its skills to use them.

From a family social work perspective, problems of individual family members should be seen as arising from weaknesses in the family system, including deficient relationships with environmental resources. To understand a problem fully, the FSW should listen to how the problem is described by each family member, as seen from his or her unique viewpoint. Additionally, the FSW will need to observe family members interacting in characteristic ways.

The following example illustrates the use of assessment techniques in family social work.

Joyce Perdue is a family social worker (FSW) assigned to work with the Fryer family. Harry and Lisa Fryer are the young parents of three-year-old twins, Tina and Tommy. Harry and Lisa had married after they learned that Lisa was pregnant with the twins. At the time, they were both sixteen-year-old high school juniors. The marriage and the babies have been stressful for the couple, and they have had difficulty making ends meet. Neither Lisa nor Harry has completed high school. Harry works at a local grocery store, and Lisa cares for the children. The family lives with Harry's parents because they cannot afford to rent an apartment. The couple came to the attention of the family social work agency when neighbors reported that the twins were left outside for long periods of time unattended.

When Mrs. Perdue interviewed the couple in their home, she found Harry and Lisa to be overwhelmed by their responsibilities. Both expressed a desire to finish high school. Lisa reported that the twins were "too hard to handle." She said the twins got into some type of trouble every time she turned her back. For instance, she told Mrs. Perdue that she had found Tommy on top of the refrigerator yesterday. When she tried to get Tommy down, Tina let the hamsters out of the cage. The twins screamed in unison while Lisa tried to recapture the scurrying rodents. Both Lisa and Harry report little satisfaction with their marriage. They have little time for themselves and no extra money.

In performing her assessment, Mrs. Perdue used an ecomap to look at stresses and supports in the couple's current situation. She also asked the couple to complete some simple assessment scales to provide information about their marital and parental satisfaction.

Strengths revealed included love for each other and a commitment to the marriage, love for their children, and support from in-laws. Problems included a lack of parenting skills, need for marital counseling, and insufficient financial resources to allow the couple to complete high school and obtain job training.

Assessment by Interviewing

In an assessment interview, the family social worker meets with as many family members as possible. During these interviews, the FSW uses basic skills discussed in this chapter and in the preceding one. In particular, the social worker relies on the appropriate use of questioning. The content of questions will often derive from some theoretical framework. For example, based on a systems perspective, the social worker could ask, "What effect does your son's behavior have on your behavior toward him, and vice versa?" Most often, the FSW will interview all of the family members who live in the household, because information is less likely to be distorted when all family members are present (Holman, 1983).

"Joining" or engaging with the family and assessing family functioning are overlapping processes. Important information can be gathered by observing how the family engages with the social worker during the beginning phase of the helping process.

Topics to Address in Assessment Interviews During assessment, the family social worker will need to address the following topical areas:

Problem

1. What created the need for intervention? Why does the family need help now? If the family is involved with an agency involuntarily, why were they referred to the agency for help?

2. What problems is the family currently experiencing, both short-term and long-term?

3. How severe and urgent is (are) the problem(s)?

4. What is the family's attitude and motivation concerning the social worker's involvement? If involvement of the entire family seems warranted, how motivated is each member to assist with the resolution of the problem? What does the family expect from the social worker?

5. What other social systems are involved with the family? For what issues? What does each family member perceive the problem to be? Are any family members physically or emotionally at risk?

6. What is the history of the problem? What has the family done to alleviate the problem?

Internal Functioning of the Family

1. What are some areas of family competence, especially psychological and social resources used for daily living as well as dealing with crises as they appear?

2. How would family members describe their family as a whole and their relationships with one another? What is the nature of the relationships within the family? What are the patterns of interaction between family members? What interaction patterns seem to maintain the problem? What are the ongoing patterns and themes in this family?

3. How is the family structured hierarchically? Who has power, and how is that power used?

4. What are the strengths and resources of the family unit and of individual members that can be mobilized to resolve the problem?

5. How does the family communicate? Do family members use repetitive patterns of interaction? Is communication direct, open, and honest?

6. How are family members functioning in their informal and formal roles?

7. How do boundaries operate between individuals, around subsystems such as the parents, and around the family as a whole?

8. Who is aligned with whom in the family, and around which core issues?

Family Life Cycle

1. What is the history of the family? (Compile a genogram with the assistance of family members.)

2. At what stage in the family life cycle is this family? How adequately does the family meet the developmental needs of members?

3. How well are family members fulfilling their developmental roles and tasks?

4. What are the family's usual ways of resolving developmental crises?

Environment

1. What is the nature of the family's relationship with its environment? Do environmental factors nurture or hinder family functioning?

2. What is the quality of the family's interactions with its social environment, including the breadth and quality of outside relationships and the impact of external factors on the family?

3. How does the family get its basic needs met? Which needs are being met and which are not?

4. Who can family members rely on in time of need? What is the nature of contact with support people outside the family in terms of quantity and quality?

5. How dependent or self-sufficient is the family in terms of external resources?

6. How does the family relate to key people, including friends, relatives, teachers, coworkers, church members, and health care workers?

7. What is the family's relationship to other members of their ethno-cultural group?

8. What are the impacts and influences of the family's religious beliefs and values?

9. What aspects of the family's cultural heritage may provide strengths or barriers?

10. What are the formal and informal support systems for the family?

Assessment by Observation

The importance of observation as a clinical skill for family social workers cannot be overemphasized (Holman, 1983). Observation yields information that is essential for understanding families. Unless deliberate use is made of observation, however, much can be missed. Descriptions of family events and dynamics by family members may be contradictory; other times, family members may be unable to describe what is going on because they lack verbal skills or because they do not understand what is happening. Additionally, through independent observation of events in the life of a particular family, the social worker can piece together independent viewpoints into a unified whole. Thus, through observation, the FSW notices physical characteristics and nonverbal behaviors, energy level, emotions, and congruence between verbal and nonverbal expression.

Observation enables the FSW to develop a comprehensive understanding of the ways the family experiences the world. The social worker must note both the content and the process in the family. The FSW observes, for example, subtle signals related to themes of power, authority, and ambivalence about seeking or receiving help. Additionally, difficulties in discussing socially stigmatized topics and inhibitions concerning the direct and full expression of powerful feelings are particularly crucial to look out for (Shulman, 1998). Because FSWs are likely to pick up indirect messages from nonverbal rather than verbal communications, they must observe behavior closely. Observations of family dynamics supplement information obtained through interviews or the use of assessment tools.

Family social work provides special opportunities for observation. During home visits, FSWs have the opportunity to make an ecological assessment encompassing the individual, the family, and the community. The social worker makes mental notes concerning the broader environment in which the family lives, noting such things as proximity to community services (including transportation, medical clinics, and schools), neighborhood safety, and recreational and cultural opportunities. Such information helps place into perspective discussions with the family and also provides a knowledge base to draw upon when connecting the family with existing resources.

Within the home, the FSW takes note of the physical environment of the family. Observing the organization of the home and the availability of resources to meet basic needs allows the social worker to understand client strengths and coping strategies, resources, and limitations imposed by the home environment. Before entering the home, the FSW can create a checklist of what to look for, given the special circumstances of the family. Observations of the physical environment will be affected by special circumstances (Holman, 1983). For example, a family in severe economic crisis may live in a dilapidated house. If the family has an adequate income, however, a poorly maintained house may suggest depression and apathy. Similarly, when working with parents of an active child, the FSW may observe that there are few play materials available and wonder if the

parents lack knowledge of child development or d
money to purchase stimulating toys. Family social wor'
hypotheses about families and later try to validate or re
ample described above, a hypothesis about parents' la
may be validated if the parents mention that they are
ing ends meet.

Besides informing the FSW about environmental and physical resources, home visits offer opportunities for observing how family members interact during their daily routine. In office meetings, professionals
often interview only one member of the family at a time, while in-home
sessions allow FSWs to observe the entire family. Behavior of individual
family members may provide clues as to what kinds of assistance are needed. Careful observation also strengthens documentation and other record-
keeping demanded by many programs.

Data gleaned through observation help the FSW determine how best to
assist the family. Cultural and ethnic differences also need to be factored
into observations of the family. Some cultures have extended family living with them, and others find it disrespectful for certain family members
to be in the same room. Ultimately, observation should be carried out re-
spectfully acknowledging that the FSW is a visitor in the home of the family. Such information should not be used to condemn or make value
judgments on lifestyles.

ASSESSMENT TOOLS

Genograms and ecomaps are preferred assessment tools for most family
social workers. Information in genograms and ecomaps eventually should
be connected with the family's current functioning. Preparing these charts
with the family is a good way to establish rapport. Both types of graphic instruments reveal relationship patterns within and outside the family.

Other assessment devices may be used to supplement genograms and
ecomaps. Family assessment devices serve dual purposes: they provide
the social worker with information about family functioning, and they can
help clients to understand family functioning, discuss family problems,
and set family goals in a focused and structured way.

Family assessment tools include FACES III, which measures adapt-
ability and cohesion (Olson, 1986); the Beavers-Timberlawn Family Evaluation Scale, which assesses family competence, structure, and flexibility
(Beavers, 1981); the McMaster Model, which examines current family functioning involving basic tasks, developmental tasks, and hazardous tasks
(Epstein, Baldwin, & Bishop, 1983); and the McMaster Clinical Rating Scale,
which targets specific areas of family functioning (problem solving, communication, roles, affective responses, affective involvement, and behavior
control) designed to assess the need for counseling (Epstein, Baldwin, &
Bishop, 1983).

Social workers can develop their own checklists for predetermined
purposes. Checklists can be constructed to account for physical resources

in the home, to focus on specific areas of role performance of family members, to assess physical care of children, or to rate the emotional climate of the family. A checklist must fit the needs of a specific family.

Systematic observation, a more formal procedure used both in research and in practice to record actual behavior, may be used when objective information is needed. The family may be helped by seeing the frequency data collected about a particular problem, such as how often tantrums occur. Systematic observation helps parents learn to manage the behavior of hyperactive children or children with other behavior problems, and may be employed to help abusive parents develop positive, effective behavior management techniques. Changing from a punitive, aversive parenting style to a more positive way of responding can be facilitated by self-recording procedures, such as teaching parents to count the number of times they respond positively and negatively to their child. Helping a parent learn to record words that a child with a speech problem says during part of the day may be an important part of an assessment of speech difficulties. Having a parent record the number of times a particular physical therapy routine is carried out can increase compliance with a treatment program.

TECHNIQUES FOR INTERVIEWING FAMILIES

The fundamental goal of family interviewing is to stimulate interaction among family members. In particular, the social worker wants the family to interact naturally, replaying "typical" transaction patterns. In a family interview, communication will seldom be from one person to the FSW. Instead, communication will occur between family members, with the FSW serving as "conductor of the family symphony" (Satir, 1967). A useful technique for stimulating interaction is to ask family members to comment on what various family members have said. Another family interviewing technique involves asking people in the family to describe their relationship with another family member or to describe what they see going on between other members of the family (Hartman & Laird, 1983).

Attentive Listening

Listening requires two activities. First, the FSW must reduce attention to personal experiences, thoughts, feelings, and sensations. Secondly, he or she must concentrate upon the client, striving to *understand*—not to evaluate—what the client is expressing.

Listening involves attentively hearing words and tones of voices, observing nonverbal gestures and positions, and encouraging full expression. Competent listening seldom occurs naturally, yet it is an essential skill for effective family social work. For most clients, being heard and understood by the FSW is a genuinely validating experience that conveys respect while enabling the FSW to gather information essential for assessment and planning. Effective listening also lowers client tension and anxiety. Attentive listening is a powerful tool that can enhance clients' self-understanding, self-esteem, and problem-solving capacity.

The ability to be an effective listener is critical to establishing rapport, building trust, and obtaining information necessary to provide assistance. Listening to words and embedded meanings can uncover concerns, priorities, and resources, as well as strengths and limitations. Families acknowledge the importance of being heard and understood by FSWs. In one home-based, family-centered program, researchers found that

> Parents acknowledge the support they received and reported feeling heard. Listening to both the parents and children was a source of high regard for many parents…"I appreciated having someone that my husband and myself could vent feelings to." "Acknowledging the problems…voicing them out loud is very helpful…knowing that you are not alone." Parents reported a decrease in their isolation and also feeling validated when they felt heard (Coleman & Collins, 1997).

Several guidelines can help FSWs to improve their listening skills. First, the FSW must allow the client time to respond to questions. Second, the FSW should attend to his or her own body language and words to assure that support and interest are conveyed to the client. Third, the FSW needs to remain mentally alert and receptive to the client's spoken and unspoken messages. Inattentiveness can be a cause of misunderstanding. The importance of accurate listening is underscored by clients' positive comments about their FSW: "She really listened to me" or "She heard what I said" (Coleman & Collins, 1997).

Listening may be impeded by many circumstances. For example, a room may be noisy, or a person may speak too softly, or with an unfamiliar dialect. A client might use words the FSW does not understand or that connote meanings different from those of the social worker. Effective listening involves overcoming obstacles and focusing entirely upon the words and gestures of the person who is speaking.

Listening is often regarded as a passive behavior—one person is the active communicator, while the listener absorbs what is being said. In reality, good listening is an active process. The job of the FSW is to ensure that the content of the client's communication, both verbal and nonverbal, is received and acknowledged. The FSW recognizes that what is *not* said is often as important as what is actually verbalized. The social worker must help the family talk in depth about their concerns, not just what is immediately apparent or comfortably discussed. Therapeutic listening helps the clients become more self-aware, slow down, and respect their own wisdom.

Formulating Questions

Interviews contain a mixture of questions and statements (Tomm, 1988). Questions are useful in the early and middle part of an interview, engaging clients more readily than statements (Tomm, 1988). Although the use of questions in interviewing has been discouraged by some (e.g., Egan, 1994), asking questions has both advantages and disadvantages.

Reluctance to ask questions may be related to overuse of questioning by unskilled interviewers. Indeed, the clumsy use of questions can hinder communication between the FSW and the client (Tomm, 1987a). Also, we have been socialized to believe that questions are intrusive and nosy. Yet, well-timed, appropriately worded questions serve many purposes.

Questions are useful for several reasons. First, questions focus and direct interviews and elicit specific information. They help the FSW to gain a better understanding about what the client is saying. Systematic questioning leads clients through problem exploration and opens doors to problem solving. Thus, questions are fundamental to the assessment phase of family social work. Overall, questions can meet the needs of both the social worker and the family—that is, questions may orient the FSW to the family or be used to influence the family to change (Tomm, 1988).

Questions give importance to a particular subject by reinforcing its significance. Questions that focus on a particular topic communicate to the client that the topic is important and should be explored. Questioning can help clients focus on specific problems, keeping the work purposeful and goal-directed. The specific topic is explored with varied questions, depending on family needs and their reasons for seeking assistance from the FSW. For example, if a family's identified goals are to improve communication and to manage conflicts more effectively, questions should target these areas.

Another function of questions is to draw out information regarding family members' feelings, resources, problems, strengths, weaknesses, and so on. Again, the questions communicate that a particular area is very important. Questions can also verify meaning and expression. For example, a client may make a statement about her mother-in-law dropping by unexpectedly. The FSW may follow this statement with a question asking the client how she felt about the visit and discover that the client either was pleased about the visit or angry because the visit was unannounced. Next, questions can systematically lead clients through a problem-solving process, helping them outline actions to take. For example, the FSW might ask a mother, "When your baby was ill, what was his temperature? What did the doctor say?"

For our purposes, there are several categories of questions suitable for family work, namely closed-ended and open-ended questions; indirect questions; primary and secondary questions; clarifying questions; circular, lineal, strategic, and reflexive questions; and focusing questions. Familiarity with these different types of questions will enhance the FSW's ability to assist clients.

The vocal tone with which questions are asked can change their meaning. For example, the same question can be given different meanings through intonation: "Do you spank your children?" Depending on the tone, the meaning could be accusatory, concerned, judgmental, or merely curious.

Closed-Ended Versus Open-Ended Questions Closed-ended questions demand short, abrupt responses such as "yes" or "no." These questions usually start with "can," "do," "did," "are," "have," or "does." Asking a closed-ended question narrows in on specific information and assumes that there are only two possible answers, giving the questioner control of the interview. One disadvantage of closed-ended questions is that they restrict the range of responses and can result in superficial answers or insufficient information. Examples are, "Did you have a good week?" and "Are you employed?" Asking many closed-ended questions in a row is known as the "machine gun" approach to interviewing.

The benefit of closed-ended questions is that they can slow down an over-talkative client. They also control the intensity of an interview and stop clients from disclosing too much at an early stage, before trust and rapport have been established. When there is limited time available for the interview, closed-ended questions allow the FSW to obtain essential data quickly.

By comparison, open-ended questions enable the client to select from a range of responses. These questions usually start with words such as "what," "how," "who," "when," "why," and "where." Open-ended questions invite clients to volunteer information, giving them some control over the interview. These questions also convey trust in the client's ability to answer.

"Why" questions should be used sparingly, as they often ask for reasons that may be out of the client's awareness or may enable the client to intellectualize. They may be interpreted as signifying disapproval, disbelief, or mistrust, making clients defensive by demanding justification, explanation, or a rationale.

Family social workers will obtain more information from children by using open-ended rather than closed-ended questions. Suppose the FSW wants to learn about social relationships. Rather than asking the closed-ended question, "Do you have any friends?" the FSW can elicit more information about the child's social relationships by asking, "What kinds of things do you enjoy doing in your free time?" By using this type of question, the FSW learns not only about friends but also about the child's sport interests, hobbies, and other activities (or lack of activities).

Indirect Questions Indirect questions are statements that have the same effect as a question. Two examples of indirect questions are "I am interested in what you think about…" and "I am curious about whether you could shed some light on…" (Bandler, Grinder, & Satir, 1976). These types of questions do not demand an answer, but they bring an issue to the attention of the listener. If silence is the response, the social worker can intentionally select a family member to respond to the indirect question.

Primary and Secondary Questions Primary questions introduce new topics or new areas and make sense out of the context, whereas secondary questions elicit further information. Secondary questions are useful when the client does not respond or when responses are incomplete, superficial, vague, or irrelevant. If the client's answer is superficial, the FSW may say, "Tell me more about…" or "What do you mean by…?"

The use of secondary questions distinguishes skilled from unskilled interviewers. Unskilled interviewers skip from topic to topic without exploring any topic in depth. By comparison, skilled interviewers first process each response carefully to see if the response is adequate, then follow an area to its logical conclusion. Secondary questions help to keep the interview on topic.

Clarifying Questions Clarifying questions enhance communication by requesting additional information, asking for examples, or attempting to clarify the meaning of what the client has said. These questions are particularly appropriate during early visits in the home or when the client is discussing situations that are open to different interpretations.

A client's use of vague words or words that have more than one meaning is a clue for the FSW to ask a clarifying question. For example, if a social worker is discussing learning activities with a child's mother and the mother says, "Things are all mixed up," the FSW will need to know what the word "things" refers to or what "all mixed up" means. She could begin clarifying by asking, "Could you tell me what things are mixed up?" Once the FSW has an idea of the areas of concern, she will want to clarify what "all mixed up" means to the client. Clarifying questions can prevent the social worker from jumping to conclusions about what was meant. The FSW may discover that the play materials are confusing to the mother or that she is concerned about the child's transportation to a day care center. The statement could also refer to a major event in the mother's life.

ASKING QUESTIONS

Split into groups of three and take turns being observer, interviewer, and client. The observer will time the interview and take notes about what occurred. The task of the role play is to practice effective use of questioning techniques. If a video camera is available for the interviews, the observer should videotape the role-play.

For the first five minutes, the interviewer is to purposefully use questioning incorrectly, asking closed-ended questions, "why" questions, and skipping from topic to topic. Further, the interviewer should not allow much time for the client to reflect or to formulate the best answer to each question. The group will then take five minutes to discuss the impact of these incorrect usages on the client and the interview.

Next, the interviewer is to ask questions appropriately. Both the interviewer and client should take as much time as they need. (*Hints:* Try to ask no more than two questions in a row and then to offer a reflection statement.) After the client has finished responding to the question, the interviewer should wait fifteen seconds before asking the next question.

When discussing the interview, notice the different results of appropriate and inappropriate questioning. What did you learn from this comparison? How difficult was it to use questions in an intentional manner?

Lineal, Circular, Strategic, and Reflexive Questions Tomm (1987a, 1987b, 1988) describes four types of questions that are appropriate for family interviewing: circular, lineal, strategic, and reflexive. According to Tomm, questions can be used for therapeutic and assessment purposes. Selecting an area for examination needs to be done carefully, and "every question and every comment may be evaluated with respect to whether it constitutes an affirmation or challenge to one or more behavior patterns of the client or family" (Tomm, 1987a, p. 4). For example, starting the interview by asking, "What problems would you like to discuss today?" will bring out different responses from asking, "What positive things have happened to you over the past week?" The FSW must carefully note clients' reactions to the questions being posed.

Lineal questions ask for information and assume a basic cause-and-effect sequence. Lineal questions attempt to define problems and seek explanation. Examples of lineal questions include the following:

- What brings you in today?
- How long have you been experiencing these problems?
- What is making you depressed?

Circular questions are based on circular causality and the connections among family members. Circular questions help the FSW to learn about ongoing patterns of family interaction and the effects that family members' behaviors have on one another. Circular questions demonstrate to the family that issues do not belong with individual members—everyone is connected to "the problem" regardless of whether they have a "symptom" themselves.

Circular questions are meant to create change, whereas lineal questions are intended to elicit information (Wright & Leahey, 1994). Circular questions are aimed at developing explanations for problems and identifying relationships between individuals, ideas, beliefs, and events. They can be used to change cognitive, affective, and behavioral domains of family functioning. Circular questions are useful for assessing the role of the presenting problem within the family. Each person is asked questions related to the definition of the problem including who says what to whom.

Examples of circular questioning include the following:

- When Melissa said that she was upset with you, how did you react?
- When you hear your husband yelling at the kids, how does that make you feel?

Strategic questions are directed at change, based upon the social worker's assessment of the situation. The underlying intent of strategic questions is to correct behavior. Such questions challenge or confront patterns within the family. Examples of strategic questioning follow:

- Can you try to see it his way?
- When are you going to tell him what you think?

Reflexive questions ask clients to become self-observers. Reflexive questioning is based on the belief that change depends on the efforts of clients, not the social worker. Examples of reflexive questioning follow:

- What do you plan on doing about finding a new job?
- What do you think you can do to improve your school grades?

Focusing Questions   During an interview, the FSW often needs to help clients focus on a specific topic. Clients may be overwhelmed by multiple problems and unable to sort out what is troubling them. Clients may use vague language to identify concerns, or they may be unable to say what is troubling about a particular situation. Focusing questions help clients to identify problems, set priorities, and establish goals.

One example of identifying problems without prioritizing them: A new mother tells the FSW, "Nothing is going right. The baby cries, she gets up at night, and I'm tired. I miss my job." To help this mother begin to focus, the FSW should ask questions designed to lead the client to prioritize her concerns. For example, the FSW may say, "There are several things that seem to be bothering you right now. Which one would you like to talk about first?" If the FSW sees that the client is unsure where to begin, she may offer a suggestion, such as, "You have mentioned the baby's crying a couple of times before. Would you like to talk about that now?"

In another example, a father of a teenage son tells the FSW, "My son does everything wrong. Nothing is right. He doesn't follow orders. He makes me upset." In this situation, focusing questions will help the father to identify particular times, situations, or behaviors that are troublesome as a way to help isolate the specific concerns. Questions such as, "Could you give me an example of the kind of behavior that upsets you?" might begin to help both the father and the FSW identify specific areas of concern. Once these areas have been identified, the FSW and client can discuss how serious the situations are and decide whether action should be taken.

Decisions to focus with the family on a specific topic can be based on the following guidelines:

- *Severity or urgency.* Is this a topic that needs immediate attention because of the distress it causes and/or because of its frequency?
- *Importance.* Is this issue important enough to the client to discuss and act upon?
- *Timing.* Is this a problem that can be managed at this time with available resources?
- *Complexity.* Is this concern a manageable piece of a larger or more complex problem? Can it be divided into more manageable parts?
- *Hope of success.* If this issue is the focus, can it be managed successfully? If not, is this the right place to start?

- *Generalization effect.* Is this the kind of problem that, if handled, might lead to improvement in other areas of the family's life?
- *Control.* Is the solution to this problem under the family's control? To manage more effectively, will the family have to act or influence others to act?
- *Willingness.* Is the family willing to discuss this topic?

Focusing requires effort on the part of the FSW and the family, particularly if clients seem to be feeling confused or overwhelmed. If the discussion strays from the central topic, the social worker can offer an observation: "I get a sense that you do not want to talk about your own childhood. Can we explore some reasons why this topic may be hard for you to discuss?"

Probing and Prompting

Probing uncovers additional information and is especially important when the FSW has insufficient information to understand family members' concerns or feelings. Probing may help the client to identify resources available in times of stress. For example, parents of a handicapped child may have relied only on each other for support and relief. Probing questions may uncover alternative sources of support such as extended family members, friends, neighbors, and respite care agencies. The FSW can ask, "Is there some member of your family who could help?" or remark, "Earlier, you said your mother could help you occasionally on a weekend." Probing questions help clients look at alternatives that may have been dismissed too quickly or not considered at all.

Prompting encourages behavior to develop and continue and is particularly useful when teaching new behaviors or encouraging clients to attempt actions that they have been reluctant to try. For example, a FSW may place a mother's hands in the right position and guide her through a physical exercise to do with a handicapped child, or she may suggest that the family carry out a group activity they planned but need encouragement to begin. Prompting a client to try something new conveys confidence in the client's ability and helps the FSW assess the client's willingness to try new behaviors.

ASSESSING PARENTING SKILLS

Family social workers will need to assess parenting skills, especially if a child's safety is at risk. The following criteria can be used to assess parenting (Steinhauer, 1991):

1. **Degree of attachment.** Attachment is necessary for the formation of trust, self-esteem, and the ability to develop future intimate relationships. The child's primary attachment should be with the parents. Parents must recognize their child's needs and respond appropriately.

Parents with personal problems such as immaturity or self-absorption are often unable to accurately understand their children's needs. In addition, parent-child relationships should be neither enmeshed nor disengaged.

2. Transmission of values. Parents are responsible for teaching their children to distinguish between right and wrong. Through teaching and modeling, children learn to respect the rights of others and to control their impulses. Morality should be congruent with that of the larger culture while respecting distinct cultural patterns.

3. Absence of rejection, overt or covert. Neglect and abuse are examples of overt rejection, whereas covert rejection is more difficult to identify. It may involve subtle or blatant emotional abuse.

4. Continuity of care. A continuous relationship between parents and child is crucial, and the care should match the developmental needs of the child.

Sometimes the court or a custody lawyer will ask the FSW to assess the ability of parents to care for their children. At other times, the social worker will have to make a decision about whether children can safely remain within their families or whether they should be placed in foster care, at least temporarily. Making these decisions can be extremely difficult.

In assessing parenting ability, the family social worker will need to look at the child's development as well as the history of the parent-child relationship. Sometimes the FSW will need to consult a specialist for expert assessment of child development or diagnosis of psychiatric disabilities in a parent or child. The starting point for assessment, however, should be to determine the quality of the parent-child relationship over time.

Assessment of Child Development

Information on the child's development inclusive of cognitive, emotional, physical, and social abilities should be included in the assessment. Social workers should have knowledge of normative child development to supplement their observations. According to Steinhauer (1991), child assessment should include information about the following topics:

- Behavior in the areas of cognitive, behavioral, emotional, or academic functioning;
- Parental attitudes toward the child;
- Attachment issues pertinent to parent-child relationships, including a history of separations and parental abuse;
- History of psychiatric or social disabilities on the part of the parents, including any evidence of substance abuse or antisocial/criminal behavior;
- History of involvement with social service systems and agencies;

- Risk assessment of child safety in the areas of abuse (emotional, physical, or sexual) and neglect;
- Attainment of developmental milestones;
- Medical/physical history;
- Attitude of parents toward the child and indications of current or past parental rejection and/or hostility;
- Corroboration from external sources regarding the above-mentioned areas;
- School and friendship history.

CHILD ASSESSMENT

Select one child you know, and conduct an assessment of that child.

Assessment of Parent-Child Relationship

The family social worker will need to make a detailed observation of parent-child interactions. Observations should be repetitive and lengthy. The FSW needs to observe how the parent and child relate to one another, noting normative, age-appropriate data. Especially important are the amount and quality of physical and emotional contact that parents and children have with one another. The FSW should also observe the parent's disciplinary style and boundary-setting. Children may express opinions indirectly through play. In addition to relationship issues, the social worker should assess how well the child's physical needs are being met—i.e., whether the child receives adequate nourishment, clothing, shelter, and supervision—and whether the child receives adequate social and intellectual stimulation. Further, the social worker may refer clients to other professionals for in-patient assessment or psychological tests of the parent or child.

Through experience, the social worker may find that there are three levels of parenting capacity (Steinhauer, 1991). At the highest level are families who are functioning well, child development is proceeding normally, and any help provided will be at the request of the parents. In the second category, child development is impaired as the result of a temporary crisis rather than a long-standing, chronic problem. A child-related crisis may have destabilized the family so much that it temporarily lacks the resources to cope. Parents in this category have no chronic emotional or social disabilities and are cooperative with the assistance offered. Parents accept responsibility for their role in the development of the problem and also show willingness to deal with the problem. In the third group, there may be significant impairment in child development. The family's problems appear to be chronic, and lack of parenting abilities is long-standing. Children display significant disturbance in one or several areas of their lives. Parents are significantly disabled either socially and/or emotionally and have a history of unsuccessful social service involvement. Parents are uncooperative and do not accept personal responsibility for their role in problems.

GOAL SETTING

As soon as key problems have been identified, the next step is setting goals. Clear, specific, concrete, and measurable goals, consistent with the family's beliefs and interests, should be itemized in contract form. Goals should be significant to the family and also be achievable and realistic, determined by the family's commitment and resources. A reasonable length of time for achieving goals should be established and an evaluation date set. An explicit understanding of approaches to be used and the responsibilities of various family members and of the FSW also should be a component of the contract. At this time, the social worker should reinforce the importance of regular attendance at the family sessions because some family members may continue to resist intervention (Nichols & Schwartz, 1998).

Intrinsic to family social work is self-determination—the principle that clients have the right and responsibility to determine what they will do. To arrive at a goal statement, the social worker and family must determine the *desired end state*—that is, a description of how the family would like to get along with each other (Bandler, Grinder, & Satir, 1976). To arrive at the desired state, all must understand what the current state is, as well as the resources for arriving at the intended destination. Families should not be manipulated or coerced to accept goals that they do not believe are important. Goals, interventions, and responsibilities may need to be modified in response to changing circumstances.

To assist families with goal setting, FSWs will need to accomplish the following tasks:

1. Recognize that family members are more receptive to change during times of crisis.
2. Move from global, abstract goals to concrete and specific goals.
3. Define clear, concrete, and measurable goals.
4. Help the family identify goals that they would like to achieve first.
5. Assist family members to negotiate with each other regarding behavioral changes.
6. Identify skills and strengths of the family.
7. Obtain a commitment from the family.

If goal setting is done correctly, the work will progress with focus and purpose. Family social work goals stated in clear and specific terms forecast what will be happening once the goals are achieved. In other words, goals identify what the family wishes to accomplish. Although goal setting is ongoing and continuous, the most productive time to set goals is after the problems have been identified and explored. Until the FSW and the family have a shared understanding of the situation, goal setting will be premature.

CONTRACTING

From their first meeting, the FSW and the family will have expectations about what they want to accomplish and how objectives will be met. Contracting can be done on a short-term or long-term basis. For example, short-term verbal or written contracts can help a family get through a crisis (Kinney, Haapala, & Booth, 1991), while long-term contracts focus on results that occur over an extended period of time, such as improved grades in school. The family social work contract is a concrete agreement that specifies goals of the intervention and the means by which to achieve them. The contract should state specific problems, the goals and strategies to alleviate them, and the roles and tasks of the participants.

A contract is an explicit agreement "concerning the target problems, the goals and strategies of...intervention, and the roles and tasks of the participants" (Maluccio & Marlow, 1975). Contracts may begin as recommendations from the social worker to the family about what needs to be done to resolve the problem (Nichols & Schwartz, 1998). They should not be developed hastily; it will take at least a couple of interviews for the FSW to assess the situation and establish a bond with the family.

Contracting should also cover important procedural details such as when and where meetings will take place; how long they will last; what records will be kept; rules governing confidentiality; and who will attend sessions.

Essential to contracting is ongoing accountability between the family and the FSW. Family members are not passive recipients of service; rather, they must be active participants in the entire process. Egan (1994) outlines four basic features of a family contract:

1. The contract will be negotiated, not declared, by the parties involved—that is, helper and family;
2. The contract will be understandable to all involved parties;
3. An oral or written commitment to the contract will be obtained;
4. The contract will be reviewed as the work progresses. If necessary, the contact will be revised.

The FSW is responsible for initiating and structuring discussion about contracting. The first step is to identify common ground between the needs of the family and the services that can be provided. Time constraints limit the social worker's availability for work with a family and must be taken into account. In addition, the mandate of an agency will place further constraints on how social workers enter into contracts with client families. Finally, FSWs should not contract to provide services that are beyond their competence or exceed the agency's capacity and resources.

As mentioned, contracts can change as the work progresses, reflecting the dynamic nature of family social work. Essentially, every time the FSW and family agree on an activity, they have formulated a contract. As the work moves forward, the contract will become increasingly complex, and may eventually address issues in the FSW–family relationship.

A contract makes the family and the FSW accountable to one another. Each assumes an active role and responsibility to fulfill agreed-upon tasks and to work toward negotiated goals. The contract should identify reciprocal obligations and ways to evaluate change.

CHAPTER SUMMARY

The basic interpersonal skills of talking and listening are fundamental to all aspects of human interaction, including family social work practice. To talk and listen effectively, the FSW must use words, vocal tones, and body language skillfully. Active listening conveys respect by demonstrating that the FSW is trying to understand.

The basic helping skills presented in this chapter (observation, listening, questioning, probing, and prompting) should be mastered by all family social workers to make each session constructive. Interactions with families go beyond social exchange, and the FSW must become skilled at using the verbal and nonverbal communication in clinically productive ways.

The family social work relationship is established to achieve certain goals. Goal setting allows the work to develop and retain its purpose. Goals should specify what the client wishes to achieve through family social work, as well as the methods that will be used. Goals should meet the following criteria: they should be measurable, set within a reasonable time limit, consistent with the client's values and abilities, and under the client's control. Strategies for setting goals include identifying general intentions, defining the specifics of the goal, and setting goals that can be reached within a measurable period.

Contracting occurs at the end of the assessment phase. The contract is an agreement between the client and the FSW outlining the goals of the relationship and the means to be used to achieve these goals. The contract can be oral or written and should be negotiated early in the work, but it may change as the work progresses. Without a contract, there is often confusion because the FSW and the family are proceeding without a shared understanding of the work to be accomplished.

Contracts are limited by time constraints and agency mandates. Effective contracts specify what needs to be accomplished and how, the roles of the FSW and the client, and procedural details such as when and where meetings will take place.

8
The Intervention Phase

After the social worker has engaged with a family and assessed its needs, intervention begins. Family social work is a partnership in which the FSW and the family work together to achieve agreed-upon goals. The role of the FSW is to provide support, education, and concrete assistance. Ways of helping may include assisting the family to restructure its daily routines, teaching family members to communicate more directly and effectively, and offering feedback and support as clients practice new behaviors.

GUIDELINES FOR EFFECTIVE INTERVENTION

Change is not always a steady process, and the FSW's interventions with a family can be obstructed in various ways. Intervention will be more effective if the FSW keeps the following considerations in mind:

1. Focus on the family's needs.
2. Respect clients' autonomy.
3. Avoid fostering dependency.
4. Reassess clients' resistance.
5. Maintain professional distance.
6. Set reasonable expectations.

Focus on the Family's Needs

Sometimes it may be difficult for the FSW to focus on the family's needs, particularly when the FSW's schedule conflicts with that of the family. The

FSW may want to schedule a home visit at 4 P.M. so as to finish the work day by 5 P.M., but the client family may prefer to meet with the FSW at 8 P.M. to give the parents a chance to relax after the day's work and spend time with their children. Similarly, the client's behavior or choices may be inconvenient or at odds with the FSW's beliefs. For example, one client insisted on living with her unemployed boyfriend in a high-crime area rather than moving in with her mother in a safer neighborhood. The client got more emotional support from her boyfriend than from her mother. Even though the FSW would have preferred to meet with the client in a safer location, she recognized that her client fared better with her boyfriend than with her mother.

Respect Clients' Autonomy

Clients have a right to make their own choices. The role of the FSW is to encourage and sustain clients to make personal decisions. It can be difficult for the FSW to avoid stepping in and making decisions for the client, particularly if the client's choices are self-destructive, such as refusing to leave a dangerously abusive relationship. Encouraging people to make their own decisions increases their competence and control over their lives because people learn by experience. As one FSW said, "When we support clients by helping them access community resources and by continuing to help them improve their skills, clients become increasingly able to make appropriate decisions and to change destructive life patterns."

In accepting clients' right to make their own decisions, the FSW must always remember that the client is a separate individual with the right to control his or her life. The FSW cannot accept responsibility for client actions. The FSW also must differentiate between his or her personal values and life goals and those of the client, remembering that the goal ultimately is to help the client learn skills. Indeed, effective professionals encourage client self-exploration and self-direction. If the FSW has trouble separating his or her personal needs from those of the client, a supervisor can assist in the self-examination process.

FOCUSING ON THE CLIENT

Think of a specific person with whom you have had difficulty interacting (not necessarily in the context of social work). List some things you could do to establish rapport with this person. Next, list some ways you could show this person that you are focusing on him or her, rather than on yourself.

Avoid Fostering Dependency

A third consideration for FSWs involves client independence. Sometimes the client must depend on the social worker, but excessive dependency can be counterproductive. During periods of stress and crisis, clients may rely on FSWs to help them make and carry out decisions. For example, one FSW helped a depressed client obtain professional counseling. The client needed assistance in finding an appropriate therapist and setting up an appointment. The social worker responded by spending most of a home visit phoning and scheduling the first appointment, though customarily the FSW would just provide information and encourage her client to initiate contact.

While occasional dependency may be acceptable, the FSW should avoid fostering unnecessary dependency. Encouraging clients' independence will strengthen existing competencies and help them develop additional competencies. Family social workers who regularly allow clients to become dependent will harm rather than help clients. One FSW left a family party when a client called her and asked her for a ride. This was not an emergency situation, and the FSW did not place appropriate limits on her professional role. Helping the client find her own transportation would have been more valuable for this client, encouraging her to develop independent coping skills. During the FSW's working relationship with a family, the type and amount of dependency will vary. The goal is for clients to become self-reliant. Keeping this goal in mind helps the social worker judge what level of dependency is appropriate and what is not.

Reassess Clients' Resistance

A fourth consideration for FSWs involves client motivation. Some clients may appear unmotivated to comply with program expectations or to work toward other life goals that are important. Often social workers label this behavior as resistant, but it may occur because of conflict between the FSW and the client over the goals to be accomplished. The FSW who feels frustrated over low motivation should ask, "Are these the client's goals, my goals, or goals of the agency?" Perhaps the goals are not culturally acceptable or personally meaningful to the client. If so, and if the selected goal will benefit the client, the FSW may try to present it in a way that is acceptable to the client. If the goal does not appear to be of benefit to the client, the expectation should be dropped.

Resistance may be a message from the client that the FSW is overstepping the boundaries of the relationship. Resistance can also signal that the issues being discussed are central to the client. If the family is not making progress toward establishing goals, the FSW should attempt to discover what barriers may be preventing them from trying to achieve these goals. Two major barriers to goal attainment are lack of resources and skills. Perhaps helping the client problem solve to overcome or remove the barriers will enable the family to move toward its goals.

If the family is not complying with a required goal in an involuntary program, such as court-ordered treatment for child abusers, program policy and legal procedures will guide the FSW's response. If a client in a voluntary program does not want to attend parent meetings, however, the FSW may change her or his expectations for this family. Alternatively, the FSW may occasionally encourage the client to attend the meetings while focusing attention on other aspects of the program to which the family is attracted.

Maintain Professional Distance

A fifth consideration for FSWs is the nature of their relationships with families. Over time, relationships will change. For example, as positive feelings grow between the FSW and the family, boundaries may become blurred and the relationship may begin to resemble a personal friendship. The FSW may become truly fond of the family and deeply committed to helping. Although positive regard for clients is essential for developing a good working relationship, it should not become confused with friendship. The FSW needs to maintain an appropriate emotional distance. Maintaining this distance is important for several reasons.

The FSW needs to remain objective and goal-focused to help the family become independent and effective. Appropriate distance between family members and the social worker encourages the family to view the FSW as a role model for behavioral change.

On another level, maintaining a professional relationship with a family is a form of self-protection for the FSW. The circumstances of the family's life could become overwhelming for an FSW who becomes too emotionally involved or takes personal responsibility for solving the family's problems. Failure to establish clear boundaries with families can leave the FSW feeling burdened by distressing family situations. Focusing on understanding how the family may feel, without overidentifying, helps the FSW function professionally and effectively.

Set Reasonable Expectations

A sixth guideline for FSWs is to help families feel competent, rather than inadequate. Families may feel that bringing the social worker into their home places them in a vulnerable position, regardless of the purpose of the program. Additionally, families may feel overwhelmed by expectations they fear that they cannot meet. Though the FSW focuses on encouraging and positively reinforcing family strengths, family limitations must also be acknowledged. The FSW must take care to avoid creating feelings of inadequacy.

INTERVENTION TECHNIQUES

Family social workers can use a variety of techniques to assist client families to gain new insights and ultimately to practice new behaviors. These techniques include use of examples, confrontation, refraining, enactment, use of metaphors, and contracting.

Use of Examples

Examples help the FSW explain, describe, or teach a concept to a family. Generally, examples should be compatible with experiences of the family's life. Examples can be used to accomplish several different objectives. They offer reassurance that others have faced the same challenges. A family social worker may tell a worried parent whose child is about to begin kindergarten, "Many parents have these concerns. One mother told me that with each of her five children, she felt some worry as they began kindergarten." Examples can illustrate alternative ways of dealing with a difficult situation. The FSW may tell a parent, "Once when I talked with another mother about a similar situation, she told me that she had tried letting her child take a nap in the afternoon. Your situation sounds similar. Does her decision seem like it would work for you, too?"

Examples can help clients feel at ease with something that has made them uncomfortable. The FSW may say, "I remember a mother who tried three different ways to help her child learn to use the toilet before the child was trained. Like her, you may find that the second or third effort will work, even though the first one did not." Examples in the form of interesting stories are valuable teaching aids because they are likely to be remembered longer than generalized statements.

USE OF EXAMPLES

Develop three examples that would help you to explain a concept or practice to a client. With a partner, practice using examples to explain one of these concepts (such as using time-outs) to a client.

Confrontation

Confrontation is a useful skill for family social workers, but its effectiveness has been questioned because it can be either growth promoting or damaging to a client. Confrontation often is viewed as hostile, unpleasant, demeaning, and anxiety provoking (Brock & Barnard, 1992). FSWs may be reluctant to use confrontation because of potentially harmful consequences, yet confrontation can be helpful under some circumstances. The level of confrontation should be chosen carefully: "Don't use a cannon when a pea shooter would suffice!" Similarly, confrontation is not a verbal hit-and-run; rather, it is used constructively to bring about change.

The goal of confrontation is to raise awareness by presenting information that the client is overlooking or failing to identify. The FSW must find a way to make new information palatable or acceptable to the person being confronted. While confrontation can be a difficult skill to master, particularly for FSWs who are ambivalent about its use, it can also generate change quickly.

A useful guideline in deciding whether to confront clients is to determine what purpose confrontation will serve. Is confrontation planned because the FSW is impatient and unwilling to allow the client to move at his or her own pace? Does the FSW enjoy confrontation or want to impose her or his personal values on the client? Conversely, is confrontation desirable because the FSW is attuned to client feelings and wants to create change? Often confrontation is most useful only after other skills have failed.

Confrontation requires tenacity on the part of the FSW, who must be willing to bring into the open an unexpressed feeling, idea, or issue. Without confrontation by the FSW, family members may persist in behavior that is self-destructive or harmful to others. Confrontation, when used appropriately and in a caring manner, benefits the client. Brock and Barnard (1992) suggest that the difference between a well-done confrontation and a confrontation that is demeaning or hostile can be perceived in the social worker's tone of voice.

Confrontation is appropriate in addressing repetitive client problematic behavior that has not changed through other efforts. For example, the client may be avoiding a basic issue that is troubling or creating dysfunction within the family. Confrontation may assist a family member to recognize self-destructive or self-defeating behaviors or to acknowledge the possible consequences of behaving in a particular way. Further examples of appropriate situations for confrontation include incongruent behavior during an interview that affects the quality of the counseling relationship; failure to assume responsibility for oneself; visible discrepancies between thoughts/feelings and words/behaviors; unrealistic or distorted perceptions of reality.

Confrontation points out discrepant aspects of the client's verbal and nonverbal behavior, bringing them to conscious awareness. The primary function of confrontation is to create disequilibrium in order to permit new behaviors to develop. While confrontation does not solve the actual problem, it does prepare the client to work on the problem.

Confrontation is most effective when a strong client-FSW relationship has been established. A general guideline is the stronger the relationship, the more effective the confrontation. One positive outcome of effective confrontation is a deepening of the client-worker relationship. By using attentive listening and empathy skills to tune in to the client's reaction to confrontation, the FSW may help the client to gain a greater insight and motivation for change. Because of the high emotional intensity of confrontation, it should not be used at the end of a session, when feelings should approach a more even keel.

Confrontation has varied effects, depending on whether the client has the personal and social resources to cope with the information being presented. A client with well-developed defenses may block the impact of confrontation, and the FSW should recognize these defenses and discuss them. Even though some people react poorly to feedback, a social worker who is not honest is colluding with maladaptive behavior.

Successful confrontation occurs in two stages: formulating the confrontation statement and addressing the response of the client. The social worker should prepare for possible reactions such as withdrawal, defensiveness about the FSW's observations, denial, discrediting the feedback, arguing, or finding someone else to collude with.

The following sentence shells can be used for formulating confrontational statements:

"On the one hand, you say _____, and on the other hand you do _____."

"I am puzzled (confused) about what you just said/did ... could you please help me understand?"

"I don't get it..."

Effective confrontation requires that the social worker point out discrepancies, inconsistencies, or contradictions between the client's words and actions. In describing these discrepancies, the FSW must avoid judgmental or evaluative speculations and conclusions. Following a confrontation with an empathic response will increase its effectiveness as a motivator for change.

Levels of Confrontation

Level 1: Giving in to the client. At this level, the FSW either ignores the problematic behavior or makes a weak attempt to confront and then withdraws at the first sign of resistance. The FSW may be overly concerned about being disliked or being attacked, or may not be committed enough to the relationship to become involved.

Level 2: Scolding. The social worker coerces the client into changing by shaming, attempting to induce guilt, or nagging. The FSW risks losing self-control and may lecture the client about proper behavior. At this level, confrontation can be demeaning and manipulative.

Level 3: Describing ineffective behavior. The social worker describes the behavior that is hurting the client or others and identifies possible reasons for the behavior. The FSW may attempt to empathize by conveying a message about how difficult it is to face and take self-responsibility for the behavior, yet the message is straightforward and does not involve lecturing or giving in.

Level 4: Identifying negative consequences of behavior. The social worker identifies ineffective behavior patterns and examines feelings. The FSW also helps the client to identify possible negative consequences of continuing the behavior.

Level 5: Levels 3 and 4, plus soliciting commitment to change. This level incorporates components of Levels 3 and 4 but also challenges the client to accept responsibility for the problem and for making changes. Changes will occur only if the client honestly agrees with the social worker.

▉ USE OF CONFRONTATION

List three situations in which confrontation would be a helpful intervention. With a partner, role-play the use of confrontation with a client.

Reframing

Reframing removes a situation from an old context (set of rules) and places it in a new context (set of rules) that defines it equally well (Becvar & Becvar, 1996). In a reframe, positive interpretations are assigned to problematic behaviors and responses (Satir & Baldwin, 1983). The technique is most successful if the FSW is able to persuade the family that the reframe is plausible and more accurate than the former interpretation (Brock & Barnard, 1992). When problems are understood in a more positive light, new responses are likely.

> What makes reframing such an effective tool of change is that once we do perceive the alternative class membership(s) we cannot so easily go back to the trap and the anguish of the former view of "reality"… it is almost impossible to revert to our previous helplessness and especially our original hopelessness about the possibility of a solution (Watzlawick, Weakland, & Fisch, 1974).

Social workers should use reframing selectively. Not all issues should be reframed. For example, sexual abuse should never be reframed as the perpetrator's attempt to show affection.

Example of Reframing A hyperactive child can be reframed as a challenging, energetic child. Instead of relying on medication, parents may plan more physical activities to help the child "burn off" excessive energy.

Enactment

An enactment is an attempt to bring a family conflict from outside the interview into the here-and-now of the interview. Enactment is useful when a critical family incident has occurred while the FSW was absent. Thus, a problematic scenario is re-created during an interview. In an enactment, family members demonstrate how they deal with the issue while the FSW observes and assesses interaction. Alternative solutions can then be devised.

Externalizing the Problem

Externalizing involves separating the problem from the person, allowing the problem to be viewed apart from the person. In the process, the problem is objectified, not the client, giving the family a better opportunity to gain control over the "problem" (White, 1986). The FSW begins the intervention by asking the family to describe how much influence they have over the problem and how much influence the problem has over them. When families view problems from this vantage (i.e., a double description), their perspective widens, and they are more likely to arrive at a solution (Brock & Barnard, 1992).

Example of Externalizing the Problem Brock and Barnard (1992) suggest that externalizing the problem is an especially effective tool in working with addictions in the family. Thus, the alcohol becomes the "enemy" that the family fights together.

Use of Metaphor

A metaphor is "a figure of speech in which a word or phrase literally denoting one kind of object or idea is used in place of another to suggest a likeness or analogy between them" (Satir & Baldwin, 1983, p. 244). Metaphors are used to help clients understand abstract concepts. They provide information in a non-threatening way and give families some distance from a threatening situation.

Example of Use of Metaphor To help families understand how a crisis can destabilize the family system, the FSW may compare the family to a mobile that gets out of balance when objects are added or moved around.

Contracting

Contracting, which was mentioned in the preceding chapter, can include contracts between family members. Two types of commonly used contracts are *quid pro quo* (QPQ) and good faith (Jackson, 1972). In the QPQ contract, one person agrees to exchange a behavior for one desired by another family member. For example, a mother might agree to drive her daughter and friends to the mall if the daughter washes the dishes without being told. The good faith contract, by contrast, is not dependent on the behavior of another family member. A person is rewarded after contract conditions are met. For instance, if a child completes her homework all week, she can invite a friend over to spend the night on the weekend.

In both types of contracts, the FSW can help family members to make the conditions of the contract as clear and specific as possible.

ECOLOGICAL INTERVENTION

The type of ecological interventions required will arise from an assessment of the family's relationship with its environment, as portrayed in its ecomap. The ecomap is the blueprint for planned change and is the first stage in deciding upon an action (Hartman & Laird, 1983). Not only does an ecomap organize information visually, it also outlines family themes and targets for change. The family should be involved in creating the ecomap. The FSW can ask family members, "What does the ecomap mean to you?" Focusing on the ecosystem will also remove the problem from the level of

individual blame. We should point out at this point that the goal of ecological intervention is to teach clients how to problem solve for themselves, rather than relying on the FSW to do it for them (Kinney, Haapala,
& Booth, 1991).

Typically, the social worker should focus on environmental problems
first (Kaplan, 1986). This will help the family deal first with less-threat-
ening issues, while assisting them in locating community supports. The
type of ecological interventions used depends upon the issues, client
skills, and available resources. For example, one FSW reported that the
following resources were either not available to clients or difficult for
them to locate: mental health treatment, housing, day care, low-skill basic
jobs, transportation, legal services, and religious programs (Goldstein,
1981). Social workers in a different program found that emergency housing, homemaker services, group homes, parent aides, impatient drug and
alcohol treatment, and respite care were difficult to obtain (Kohlert &
Pecora, 1991). The social worker must also help families develop creative
ways to use formal and informal resources. Sometimes families will merely lack information about where resources exist. Other times, family members may have the knowledge, but lack the skills to get connected to
resources. In such cases, the FSW will have to help the family get connected (Helton & Jackson, 1997). The ultimate goal is to help clients learn
how to get needs met on their own. It is tempting and perhaps easier to
take care of clients' needs rather than encouraging self-sufficiency (Kinney, Haapala, & Booth, 1991).

Hepworth and Larsen (1993) list the following ecological interventions
that FSWs can perform for families:

- Supplementing resources in the home environment;
- Developing and enhancing support systems;
- Moving clients to a new environment;
- Increasing the responsiveness of organizations to people's needs;
- Enhancing interactions between organizations and institutions;
- Improving institutional environments;
- Enhancing agency environments;
- Developing new resources.

CRISIS INTERVENTION

A family social worker may encounter many types of crises when working
with a family. Sometimes a crisis can be used to the advantage of the family. At times the FSW may need to create a crisis and at other times to
defuse one (Brock & Barnard, 1992). Two methods exist to defuse a crisis:
the FSW can become triangulated into a relationship, and the FSW can
help the family cope by recalling similar events in the past. One way for the

social worker to become triangulated is to use empathic statements to get the client to direct exclusive attention toward the FSW. The FSW also can help the family to recall times when they have experienced similar crises and have used skills to get themselves out of those crises.

Regardless of the situation, it is crucial that the social worker remain calm throughout the interview. The best approach toward clients in crisis is straightforward. Gilliland and James (1993) present the following model for crisis intervention:

1. Identify the problem.

2. Ensure client safety.

3. Provide support. (Sometimes the support will be in the form of referral to other helping sources.)

4. Examine alternatives. (Alternatives should build on the strength of the clients.)

5. Make plans.

6. Obtain a commitment to try out alternatives.

The goal of family social work is not always to avoid a crisis. Sometimes a social worker may need to induce a crisis to destabilize families, particularly if family members are complacent or lack motivation to change. There are many ways of doing this, such as removing a child from the home. One method of creating a crisis is to amplify an issue in the family (Brock & Barnard, 1992; Minuchin, 1974). The FSW might draw attention to a piece of interaction from an interview and magnify its significance. Alternatively, the social worker strives to change "the affect a family member attaches to a particular experience and assumes that a change in affect will also promote a change in behavior" (Brock & Barnard, 1992, p. 84).

SYSTEMIC INTERVENTION

Systemic interventions focus on the family as a unit rather than on individual members. One type of systemic intervention is teaching family members to solve their own problems through negotiation. Teaching clients to solve problems requires that the social worker function as a facilitator rather than as an expert. As facilitator and consultant, the FSW teaches the family to develop solutions to their own problems rather than relying on outside help.

How to Teach Problem-Solving Skills

Disorganized and unskilled families often lack skills to be able to solve problems adequately. Families must learn how to deal with immediate problems and develop skills to use when the FSW is no longer involved. Problem solving entails seven steps:

Stages of Problem Solving

1. *Define the problem.* A situation is a problem when its resolution is not automatic. Problem definition includes discovering how each person contributes to the problem.

2. *Select goals.* Goal selection should be based on what each person wants to happen.

3. *Generate possible solutions.* Brainstorming can lead to identification of a number of alternative responses that may help resolve the specific problem.

4. *Consider the positive and negative consequences of possible solutions.* Repercussions may be related to time, money, personal, emotional, and social factors.

5. *Decide on a course of action.* Decision making is based on weighing the proposed solutions and consequences and deciding which one is best for the family at that time. The family's priorities and values must be taken into account.

6. *Implement the plan.* Carry out actions called for by the proposed solution.

7. *Evaluate.* Review the results and decide whether goals were met. If the strategy did not work, return to stage 3.

Teaching problem-solving skills not only helps families resolve their immediate problem but also gives them the tools for dealing with future concerns. Families with problem-solving skills are on their way to becoming independent and self-reliant.

Teaching clients to solve problems demands that the family social worker serve as a facilitator rather than an expert. Instead of defining a family's problems and then providing solutions, the FSW encourages family members to identify their own needs and goals. When a family has difficulty applying problem-solving skills, the FSW simplifies the process. In some situations, if a family can only vaguely define a difficult situation, the FSW may initially take a more active role in identifying a problem, gradually involving the family. The eventual goal is to empower the family to assume this responsibility as they develop the skills to do so.

In considering solutions to problems, family social workers will often have more knowledge about topics than does the family, thus placing the FSW in a position to offer help. The shift in philosophy to facilitator does not mean such information will not be shared. Rather, it means that clients will be encouraged to generate unique solutions on their own and to consider consequences. In decision making, the FSW will sometimes need to state an opinion or even to ask that something be done; usually, however, the FSW encourages the family to decide. Clients develop more independence as they improve their coping and decision-making skills.

In the early stages of problem solving, more direction from the FSW may be necessary. Later, however, the family social worker becomes less directive as the client assumes more responsibility. One agency described how its services to families changed over time: at first, "doing for," then "doing with," and, finally, "cheering on."

How to Teach Communication Skills

Teaching communication skills is an important aspect of family work because dysfunctional communication can interfere with effective problem solving (Kaplan, 1986). Effective problem solving requires that communication among family members be congruent, direct, honest, and clear (Satir, 1967). By examining communication patterns, the FSW will be able to see how family members experience their relationships with one another, how they express intimacy, and how they convey information (Satir & Baldwin, 1983). Improving communication in families entails teaching new skills. These skills may be taught by instruction or demonstration (Bodin, 1981).

Changing dysfunctional communication patterns is a three-step process. Family members should discuss communication, then analyze their behaviors and emotional responses, and look at the impact of their interactions on relationships (Watzlawick, Beavin, & Jackson, 1967).

Metacommunication is "communication about communication" or a "message about a message" (Satir, 1967). Metacommunication is particularly useful in working with families because it allows people to check out the meaning of what another person has said. While families communicate a lot, they seldom spend time looking at underlying messages to one another (Hepworth & Larsen, 1993). Discussions of communication are most effective if done in the here-and-now when the interaction is fresh in the minds of family members. Metacommunication requires the FSW to pay close attention to the ongoing family interaction, stop the communication process, and then engage the family in a discussion of the events that have occurred. The goal is to get the family to replace dysfunctional patterns of communication with healthier patterns.

Systemic intervention also focuses on the family interactions, particularly communication strengths and deficits. Training to improve families' communication skills emphasizes active listening, empathizing, and use of "I" statements.

Listening and Empathizing Family members can be taught to actively listen, or paraphrase, what the speaker has said in order to signal that the message was received. For instance, a wife may tell her spouse, "I feel angry right now because you were late and did not call." Her husband, using active listening, could say, "You are mad because I did not telephone to say I would be late." Rather than arguing with the speaker, the listener has restated the angry message and communicated to his wife that he heard what she said, thus supporting her communication. Also, if the paraphrase is incorrect, the speaker has an opportunity to give feedback and clarify her message. This type of listening communicates empathy to the speaker.

Use of "I" Statements Using "I" statements to communicate a message, especially a message likely to put the listener on the defensive, can reduce family conflicts. The angry spouse in the previous paragraph may say, "You are a thoughtless bum; you come home late all the time and never call!" Alternatively, she can use an "I" statement to express the effect of her husband's behavior on her feelings: "I feel angry and frightened when you don't call to tell me that you'll be late, because I worry about your safety." The general format for making "I" statements is "I feel (*speaker's feelings*), when you (*family member's behavior*), because (explanation)."

Developers of one family-centered, home-based intervention model provide the following guidelines for using "I" messages (Kinney, Haapala, & Booth, 1991):

- Describe behavior, not persons.
- Use observations, not inferences.
- Use behavioral descriptors, not judgments.
- Avoid the use of generalizations such as *never* or *always*.
- Speak for the moment.
- Share ideas, and do not give advice.

If the listener uses active listening to be empathic, the speaker may respond by offering a solution, such as, "Could we make a deal that I won't worry if you are less than an hour late, and that you will call if you will be more than an hour late? The listener might modify the solution or offer alternatives until a mutually agreeable solution is found. Active listening and use of "I" statements can be modeled and practiced, with the FSW giving feedback.

The FSW should be alert to communication deficits in the interaction. For instance, a family member may talk too loudly or softly, too quickly or slowly, or use a tone of voice that is monotonous or hostile. The FSW also may watch for ways to help members improve their nonverbal communication. For example, the FSW can help family members practice communicating with relaxed posture, a warm and smiling facial expression, and appropriate eye contact (Hepworth & Larsen, 1993).

How to Explain Circular Causality

To help family members understand circular causality, the FSW must be able to identify recurring interaction patterns. The FSW can use a flip chart to draw a diagram illustrating the family's circular patterns, especially those related to specific issues. Each person's feelings and behavior should be noted on the diagram. The simplest patterns consist of feelings-behavior-feelings-behavior and so on. The FSW should explain these patterns, pointing out the relationship between feelings and behavior. For example, a father scolds a child, the child feels hurt, the child pouts, the father feels frustrated, the father scolds, and the pattern continues. It is helpful for a family to see how they go around in these maladaptive circles. After explaining the circular pattern, the social worker will need to find out if there are any family rules or myths that perpetuate these patterns. For example, a parent may believe that the only way a child will listen is if the parent yells.

When clarifying a circular pattern with a family, the FSW should explore underlying feelings, such as fear or anger. The FSW then points out evidence of emotional distress and get members to label specific feelings. When feelings are out in the open, particularly fears and hurts, they can be addressed. The worker can then encourage the family to offer each member reassurance and support.

After the dysfunctional patterns have been identified, the FSW should then get the family to think of helpful *adaptive* patterns to deal with problem situations. The FSW should reinforce family members' constructive suggestions, coach families to try new behaviors, and assign tasks as homework (Tomm & Wright, 1979).

▪ COMMUNICATION SKILL TRAINING

Caitlyn Jones is a fifteen-year-old girl who is having trouble in school. Her older brother and sister left home before they had finished high school. Her brother Ryan got into trouble with the law, and her sister Jamie became pregnant at age seventeen and moved in with her boyfriend's family. Caitlyn's parents, Bob and Kerrie, are worried that Caitlyn will also leave home early and drop out of school. Caitlyn feels she has been pressured by her parents to do well in school. She has been struggling with her classes and is fearful of failure. Write some "I" statements Caitlyn could use to communicate her feelings to her parents, as well as some active listening responses her parents could offer. With three other students, role-play a session with the Jones family (one student should play the FSW and the other three should be Caitlyn, Bob, and Kerrie). Negotiate some solutions to Caitlyn's problems.

WORKING WITH ENMESHED OR DISENGAGED FAMILIES

Satir and Baldwin (1983) describe an exercise called "Ropes" that provides clients with a concrete, visual depiction of family relationships. Each family member ties a short rope around his or her waist. Longer ropes form links between family members. This exercise helps families to recognize the complexity of family relationships. It can be used with any family as a starting point for discussing relationships and boundaries.

Establishing Boundaries

In working with enmeshed families, FSWs strive to strengthen boundaries between family members and increase the autonomy of individuals (Nichols & Schwartz, 1998). The social worker encourages family members to speak for themselves. While one person is speaking, the FSW must not allow interruptions from other members of the family.

In much the same way, FSWs can help families to establish boundaries around sibling or parental subsystems. For example, topics such as sex or money may be declared off-limits to children. Similarly, children should be allowed time and space for play, without parental interference.

Disengaged families avoid interaction; therefore, the FSW must challenge their efforts to circumvent conflict. Family members must begin to make more contact with each other, even if such contact is conflictual at first.

Dealing with Dysfunctional Family Alliances

Dysfunctional family alliances include, but are not limited to, disengaged marital relationships, enmeshed relationships, triangulated relationships (often a child triangulated into a marital relationship) or inappropriate relationships with people outside the family (Hepworth & Larsen, 1993). Intervention can remedy a problematic relationship, strengthen an underdeveloped relationship, reinforce a functioning relationship, or loosen an enmeshed relationship. Before any of these goals can be accomplished, the family must first be able to describe these relationships, understand their impact on the family, and decide to change them. A well-constructed genogram should highlight the nature of these relationships, and family members can then be encouraged to discuss ways to address problems. Family sculpting (discussed in Chapter 2) is another way of pointing out the structure of family relationships. After family members recognize how their relationships are structured, they will be prepared to discuss what they want to change, how to make the changes, and the consequences of making the changes.

A strong parental alliance is necessary for family well-being, and social workers should try to enhance the parental alliance by negotiating an agreement on parenting standards (Brock & Barnard, 1992). The FSW can ask parents how each of them plans to handle a specific child-related issue that has emerged. This discussion should take place without the presence of the children. Once the parents have arrived on a decision, they should act upon their decision together. If similar issues arise between interviews, (the FSW can give the parents a homework assignment of working out a solution privately and then jointly acting upon the issue.

Working with Family Rules

Every family has rules that govern behavior. Some family rules are explicit, while others are unspoken. Openly discussing these rules makes it possible to revise them. Satir poses several questions to ask when looking at family rules: Are the present rules impossible to follow? Are the rules up to date and relevant to a changing situation? What are the rules governing roles of males and females? What rules surround the sharing of information? What are the family rules about what members can say about what they feel, see, and hear? (Satir & Baldwin, 1983).

In discussing rules with a family, the social worker must help the family to examine their rules. When the rules are unclear, they need to be brought out into the open. When rules are outdated or unfair, the social worker must help the family make a decision about whether to keep such rules. The FSW can start by emphasizing that all families operate according to a set of rules, many of which are unspoken. An example of a family rule is that everyone is supposed to eat dinner together. After making certain that family members know what the term *family rule* means, the FSW can then begin to discuss rules. The social worker should have an idea of what areas the discussion of family rules should cover. For example, in a family in which the activities of children are not monitored or supervised, the FSW may direct discussion to rules concerning parental involvement with the children.

GENDER-SENSITIVE INTERVENTION

Gender-sensitive intervention involves support and education, as well as instruction in problem solving. Key elements of this approach are helping families to

- Recognize and change the destructive consequences of stereotyped roles and expectations;
- Avoid promoting dependency and submissiveness for women and children;
- Encourage women to build positive self-esteem, and encourage men to become actively involved in child care and household duties.

Intervention from a gender-sensitive perspective does not advocate neutrality for the family social worker, as does traditional family therapy. Gender-sensitive family work places the FSW and the family on an equal footing. Family members are empowered to recognize their own skills and abilities, changing the whole family in a positive way by building on the strengths of individuals. This is congruent with the emphasis in family social work on supporting family members. Support and education, as well as problem solving and contracting, are key elements of gender-sensitive practices.

Applying this supportive approach, while utilizing a gender-sensitive perspective, helps families become aware of gender issues of the 1990s. Young girls still grow up in a world that gives them very different messages from the ones that boys receive about their value, roles, and life opportunities. Yet traditional therapy often fails to take this social context into account when dealing with the problems of women and girls. For example, a traditional therapist may treat a woman's depression and anger in response to an abusive relationship as psychiatric symptoms, encouraging her to adapt rather than to change her situation. Family social workers need to understand families, and women in particular, within a modern social context rather than a traditional psychiatric model. The FSW can teach a woman to differentiate between her problem and someone else's problem, helping her to realize that every failed relationship in her life is not her fault.

Family social work helps families recognize and change the destructive consequences of stereotyped roles and expectations in the family. Traditional therapists have assessed mental health of women and men differently. Healthy women are expected to be more submissive, less independent, more easily influenced, less competitive, more excitable and emotional, more preoccupied with their appearance, less objective, and less interested in math and science than healthy men. For women, a significant hurdle in counseling has been the male standard of behavior that traditionally guides what is "healthy" and "normal." It is imperative that FSWs present an egalitarian view of relationships. In the intervention phase, this translates to having adults share in child rearing and household tasks.

Gender-sensitive family social work avoids promoting dependency and submissiveness for women and children. Women often feel their role is to nurture and support others, rather than to recognize their own needs. Women who are employed outside the home often find themselves trying to keep up with all the demands of work as well as home, resulting in exhaustion or "burnout."

For women who have been abused, healing starts with recognizing their will to survive. Putting their problems in a social context also boosts women's self-esteem. Effective family social work helps women build self-esteem, stand up for themselves, and assume greater control over their lives. It helps men to value their roles of equal partner and parent, encouraging them to become actively involved in parenting and household chores. Client strengths and competence are emphasized. Indeed, the key to helping women and families is to focus on strengths rather than weaknesses. In family or couple work, this means giving equal consideration to the skills, aspirations, and careers of women and men.

A gender-sensitive FSW working with couples who are experiencing a troubled marital relationship should explain that there are two key ingredients for a successful marriage:

1. A good marriage requires a supportive, nurturing relationship involving genuine commitment and caring for each other. This is an indirect way of saying that partners need to develop intimacy in order to achieve marital satisfaction.

2. A satisfying marriage also requires equal sharing of instrumental tasks within the household. When children are involved, there should be equal sharing of parenting tasks, such as assisting children with homework, taking children to dental appointments, and spending creative playtime with children. Both parents need to understand that the time and energy they invest in child care pays big dividends in terms of family functioning. Furthermore, the male's role in raising children has to be enhanced to that of an equal partnership with the female. This means that women need to avoid making men feel incompetent when caring for children, and men need to become active partners in doing tasks such as cooking and laundry.

Problem Solving Within a Gender-Sensitive Intervention

A problem-solving approach complements a gender-sensitive perspective. Gender sensitivity assumes equality of family members, and problem solving encourages participation of all members in solving common family problems. What affects one member affects everyone. Mutual problem solving helps family members negotiate solutions to problems that are acceptable to everyone.

In teaching families about problem solving, family social workers help families identify concerns and goals, set priorities, and develop a plan for resolving difficulties. Problem solving promotes clients' self-esteem and well-being, and the use of this model can enhance a family's ability to independently address its own needs.

In the course of personal and work life, family members have goals, as well as problems or stresses. Problem-solving strategies can be used to reach goals, meet challenges, or deal with stresses and problems. Parents should be taught problem-solving skills so that they will have a better understanding of the processes and strategies involved in thinking through a problem and carrying out proposed solutions.

The social work profession has a long history of using a problem-solving approach. The problem-solving model is based, in part, upon an assumption that parents' day-by-day situations are often as complex and demanding as those of many professionals. Therefore, the preparation and training given to many professionals in problem solving is appropriate for parents. Problem-solving skills are essential for anyone who needs to identify, assess, and resolve problems. By teaching parents problem-solving skills, the FSW helps assure that parents can develop positive parent-child relationships.

PROBLEM-SOLVING APPROACH

Keeping in mind the Jones family described in the previous exercise, outline the steps of a problem-solving intervention for this family.

CHAPTER SUMMARY

During the intervention phase of family social work, the FSW provides support, education, and concrete assistance. Effective intervention requires that the social worker focus on the family's needs, respect client autonomy, avoid fostering dependency, reassess client resistance, maintain professional distance, and set reasonable expectations.

Specific intervention techniques available to the FSW include use of examples, confrontation, reframing, enactment, use of metaphors, and contracting. Intervention techniques should be chosen to meet the needs of the family.

The FSW needs to recall the assessment phase and use the ecomap when presenting ecological interventions.

Family social workers frequently encounter families who are experiencing crisis. It is important that the FSW remain calm and help the family sort out its challenges.

Systemic interventions help FSWs and families to think about the family as a whole. Systemic interventions are particularly helpful in teaching problem-solving and communication skills to families.

Family members need to find a balance between disengaged and enmeshed relationships. The FSW can help families set rules that will bring them closer to achieving this balance.

A family social worker needs to be gender-sensitive, working with the family in a supportive and educational role. Gender-sensitive and problem-solving approaches can be implemented simultaneously for effective interventions with families.

9 Promoting Behavioral Change

Assessment of each family's needs should guide the FSW in outlining goals and selecting interventions. For many families, the most useful intervention is teaching parents how to modify their children's problematic behavior. Often changing behavior is more important than searching for the underlying causes of the behavior, because whatever created a problem in the first place may no longer be relevant (Kaplan, 1986). Further, families may need the FSW's help in learning ways to cope with stressful daily events and crises.

ADVANTAGES OF A BEHAVIORAL FOCUS

Behavioral interventions are compatible with developmental assessment of families. The demands of different developmental phases require family members to change and adjust. Behavioral interventions involve continuous reeducation and are most effective when children are young (Thompson & Rudolph, 1992), but the basic premises are also useful for later stages of the family life cycle. Reeducation helps parents to develop a positive relationship with their children that will strengthen the family to get through challenging developmental phases, such as adolescence.

Behaviorally focused family social work has several advantages over traditional family therapy. It provides structure and practical strategies for parents to use with their children (Kilpatrick & Holland, 1995). By contrast, the techniques taught in office-based therapy sessions may seem far removed from a family's day-to-day experiences (Gordon & Davidson, 1981).

Behavioral interventions are based on the idea that behaviors are shaped and maintained by interactions between people. Behavior can be changed by altering responses that maintain the behavior. Because parents can control many aspects of their children's environment, particularly when children

163

are young, they are in an excellent position to produce behavioral change in children. Behavioral change occurs first with the parent and later with the child. Essentially, parents are trained to become their child's "therapists."

In behavioral interventions, the FSW teaches parents to intervene with the child's behavior directly and immediately. Parents live with the child and are a stable, continuous treatment resource. If parents learn to deal with their child consistently, even when the FSW is not present, behavioral change can be reinforced. Parents with varying degrees of parenting skills can be taught to use the fundamental principles of behavior modification and social learning theory.

APPLICATION OF BEHAVIORAL TECHNIQUES

Children often act differently in various settings, suggesting that the actions of adults send varying messages to children regarding what type of behavior is permissible. An exception is aggressiveness that remains constant in different settings; a child who is aggressive at home is also apt be aggressive with peers. Children with behavior problems expend a great deal of energy trying to control their environment. They are at risk of developing habitual patterns of problem behavior.

Behavioral techniques have been used successfully for such diverse problems as temper tantrums, hyperactivity, homework avoidance, bed-wetting, disobedience, delinquency, and aggressiveness (Alexander & Parsons, 1973; Baum & Forehand, 1981; Foster, Prinz, & O'Leary, 1983; Webster-Stratton & Hammond, 1990). Social workers have taught parenting and child management skills to parents who physically abuse their children. Behavioral treatment is effective for teaching child management techniques (Sandler, VanDercar, & Milhoan, 1978; Wolfe, Sandler, & Kaufman, 1981) and self-control techniques (Denicola & Sandler, 1980; Isaacs, 1982).

Parents of children with behavior problems often possess poorly developed parenting skills compared with parents of children who are functioning adequately (Patterson, DeBaryshe, & Ramsay, 1989). A more positive approach is to view parents as having skill deficits that can be overcome with the assistance of the FSW.

Intervention with children's behavior problems requires careful assessment and clearly defined techniques. The FSW teaches parents how to understand and consistently apply behavioral skills with their children.

Before teaching new skills, family social workers must understand the environment in which families live. The environment can affect how well parents learn new skills and how likely they are to continue using them. Some families particularly those who are poor, experience more stress than others. Low-income families often lack access to community, financial, and personal resources. Accordingly, they may feel alienated from mainstream society and lack trust in formal helpers (Kaplan, 1986). When they do connect with community supports, the experience is likely to be negative. Lack of support networks and material resources allows problems to grow because resources are lacking to handle crises on the spot.

Information, concrete resources, and emotional support may be absent. Many high-risk families tend to have limited contact with people outside the family. Aversive events, such as being laid off from a job, dominate life in these families, making it difficult for them to deal effectively with daily family events. Until the family's environmental deficits are addressed, parent training may not be effective.

Behavioral interventions with families are based on the idea that behavior is either maintained or extinguished by its consequences. Rewards strengthen the connection between a stimulus and a response. Simply put, this means that positive behavior, not negative behavior should be reinforced. Material reinforcers (toys, coins) or social reinforcers (praise, attention) can be used.

In poorly functioning families, positive and negative reinforcement mechanisms are present but often reinforce the wrong behavior. Parents of aggressive children may condone fighting (Patterson & Fleischman, 1979). Abusive parents tend to rely excessively on aversive methods of behavior control, such as spanking, and fail to use consistent and positive child management techniques (Denicola & Sandler, 1980). Microanalytic (minute-to-minute) observation of interactions between parents and children may help the FSW find ways to modify behavior and thereby reduce the risk of child abuse.

The Oregon Social Learning Center has provided research-based data concerning behavioral family treatment. Based on microanalytic observation of interactions within families, researchers have noted the ways in which responses shape interactions. Social learning theory resembles circular causality yet distinguishes more clearly between an antecedent event and its consequences. The social learning model focuses on the here-and-now and makes minimal use of history.

Families with antisocial children tend to have fewer house rules; parental permissiveness often leads to aggressive behavior. Aversive parental behavior responses such as spanking or yelling negate prosocial child behavior and promote ongoing coercive behavior such as whining and tantrums. Parents of antisocial children are more likely to give aversive consequences for coercive child behaviors; thus, abused children have higher rates of coercive behavior than other children. Negative reinforcement increases the likelihood of high-intensity negative responses. For example, the child throws a tantrum in the grocery store and does not stop screaming until the parent agrees to buy her candy.

BASIC PREMISES OF BEHAVIORAL INTERVENTION

In behavioral interventions, the focus is on family relationships and interaction patterns rather than the intrapsychic life of individual family members. Nevertheless, the FSW's relationship with the family is very important. The FSW models appropriate social behavior, coaches members in positive communication skills, and helps them learn a set of behavioral contingencies to be used consistently in family interactions (Kilpatrick & Holland, 1995).

Given the premise that parents are the best therapists for children, planned changes in parental behavior should lead to changes in children's behavior.

Behavior problems are learned responses that become set and intensified with ongoing reinforcement. Much of the reinforcement in families is unintentional, as members are seldom aware of how behavior is reinforced and maintained. Being self-aware and tracking child behavior is often difficult for parents. Without awareness, however, imposed consequences can produce unintended effects. For example, in some situations, scolding may reinforce a child's behavior because the child is receiving attention from the parent. At other times, parents might ignore or reinforce unacceptable behavior, making it difficult to eliminate the behavior. Further, positive child behavior might also be ignored or not reinforced.

Many parents do not know how to implement behavioral consequences effectively. They may fail to follow through on threats or natural consequences. Punishment may be delayed, thereby defusing effectiveness and creating confusion for the child. On the other occasions, the level of punishment may not match the level of the problematic behavior, being either too mild or too severe.

When parents respond negatively toward their children, their children are likely to behave negatively in return. In some families, negative behavior receives more attention than prosocial behavior. Positive behaviors do not receive adequate attention. Behavioral intervention teaches parents how to reward prosocial behaviors and ultimately alleviate problem behaviors. Ideally, positive behavioral changes by either the parent or the child will create a spiral of positive family interactions. Interventions should be tailored to fit the specific circumstances of individual families. The goal is to develop rewarding parent-child interactions through positive changes in behavior, decrease reliance on coercion and aversive control, and teach effective communication and problem-solving skills.

PRINCIPLES OF BEHAVIORAL CHANGE

Techniques for producing behavioral change are essential skills for FSWs. These techniques are based upon the principles of behavior modification and social learning theory that explain how behavior can be increased, decreased, or maintained and how new behaviors can be taught. The social learning approach gives families a structured method for dealing with a range of family problems. Family social workers who are skilled in behavioral approaches have much to offer parents.

The basic principles of behavior modification address the effects on behavior of its antecedents and consequences. Though most attention has been focused on consequences of behavior, especially on positive consequences or reinforcement, attention should also be directed to the effects of a family's immediate environment. This environmental focus can be used to make homes safe yet stimulating for young children. A FSW who brings toys or other activities to keep one child entertained while she talks to the parent and sibling changes the child's environment positively. What we say to each other also can increase the likelihood that a behavior will occur. Parents who know how to give clear and unambiguous directions and follow through on them, for example, will be more likely to obtain cooperation from their children than parents who give confusing, contradictory directions.

Behavior is reinforced or extinguished by its consequences. Positive, reinforcing consequences increase the likelihood that a specific behavior will be repeated. When a child is rewarded with praise or material reinforcers for completing homework, he or she is likely to continue doing homework. Punishing a behavior decreases the likelihood of recurrence of that behavior. For example, a child who is criticized by parents for leaving toys around might pick them up. However, parents and social workers need to remember that positive consequences work better than punishment. The rule should be "whenever possible, use positive reinforcement." Negative reinforcement occurs when a behavior represents a means of avoiding or escaping an aversive event that one would have expected to occur (Wilson, 1995). For example, a child may run away from home to avoid hearing parents fight.

Parents naturally use positive consequences in some situations; for example, they praise and encourage a child who is learning to walk or talk. But as child behavior becomes more complex or problematic, parents often need help in knowing which behaviors require favorable attention and which should be ignored or punished. Parents may unintentionally become negative in their interactions with children because of lack of skill or frustration and need help in shifting from unpleasant interactions to more positive and enjoyable ones.

Behavioral interventions are compatible with developmental and systems perspectives on family life. Teaching parents to use reinforcement effectively involves helping them learn to judge the appropriateness of the child's behavior, based on knowledge of child development. The FSW should be sensitive to the needs of the parents as well as those of the children. For example, the FSW may discover that parents' needs and problems interfere with their ability to parent. The FSW must consider the effects of intervention on other family members and be alert to the possibility that children's behavior may be influenced by family subsystems, such as a widowed grandmother who lives with the family and attempts to take over the parental role. A broader ecological focus goes beyond asking what consequences could change a child's behavior to asking questions about environmental conditions. For example, does the physical environment (including the interfering grandmother) make it possible for the child to comply with parental requests?

To implement behavioral interventions effectively, FSWs need to understand the principles of behavior management. In addition to mastering the material in this chapter, the FSW must keep abreast of new developments and available resources. For example, several excellent, comprehensive parent-training programs exist to help parents deal with many child-management problems. The procedures are especially important for parents of children with handicapping conditions and parents who have a history of abusing or neglecting their children.

TEACHING AS AN INTERVENTION TECHNIQUE

One of the most helpful interventions is teaching families specific skills. In one study, a parent reported appreciating the opportunity to learn "the different ideas on how to handle behaviors going on, for example breaking power struggles by offering choices." In the same study, another parent said, "I learned how to intervene, trying different techniques of discipline" (Coleman & Collins, 1997).

Teaching should be based on an assessment of each family's situation. Steps involved in teaching include:

- Giving clients a rationale for learning the skill;
- Demonstrating the skill;
- Having clients practice the skill;
- Providing feedback (Brock & Barnard, 1992).

The opportunity to learn new skills can be offered as a way of overcoming problems. For many clients, this approach will seem new because their previous experiences with counselors have focused on analyzing the past (Kinney, Haapala, & Booth, 1991).

There are several ways to teach parenting skills. The FSW can *share information* with clients, *model* a specific behavior, or use *contingency management*, which involves showing parents how to reward positive behaviors and to ignore or punish behaviors that they want to discourage (Kinney, Haapala, & Booth, 1991).

After learning a new skill, parents need to apply it. They will be more likely to practice a skill when they see that it produces positive results. Often they may also want to understand the rationale for using the skill, particularly how it will benefit them. When the family is motivated to learn the skill, the FSW should model it and ask family members to describe what they observed. Because a skill involves a series of complex behaviors, the FSW should break down the skill into manageable parts and have the clients learn components of the skill one at a time. Opportunities for teaching and demonstrating skills can be identified "on-the-spot" in the home. The FSW can capitalize on "teachable moments" and use a crisis or other timely event to inject a teaching moment. The final stage of teaching is having the family or individual practice the skill and receive feedback. At this stage, the FSW should offer positive comments as well as corrective suggestions.

Sharing Information

One way to teach parents is to share information. For example, a FSW working with new parents could provide them with the following information to help smooth the transition to parenthood.

1. Parents must learn to anticipate and adapt to the needs and rhythm of their child. For example, stimulating a child immediately before bedtime will make it hard for the child to fall asleep. Similarly, scheduling baby pictures at a time when the infant would normally be napping is not recommended.

2. Parenting requires a new level of self-sacrifice. Parents must recognize that their previous lifestyle is changed forever once children arrive. Each stage of child development also requires additional change in parental lifestyles.

3. Raising children often creates new stresses in a relationship. While the parents' relationship may become closer, there will be times when each partner feels unloved, unwanted, isolated, or rejected. The couple must learn to discuss with each other the effects of parenting on their relationship including changes in their energy levels and sex life. They need to openly discuss concerns about being an effective parent. Financial worries also have to be addressed rather than ignored.

4. Some of the problems of new parents cannot be resolved immediately. Waking up four times a night to feed the baby decreases the likelihood of an active sex life for the parents. Sleep disruption will continue until the baby begins to sleep through the night. However, despite the inability of parents to change the situation, being able to talk about their frustrations can help ease their tension.

5. Stress, financial worries, and lack of sleep can lead to conflicts and feelings of frustration. Thoughts of hitting the child or leaving one's partner are common. If they remain just thoughts, they are normal. However, they become problematic if acted upon.

6. Parents need to learn to love their children. The bond between the parents and the child is not automatic; it takes time and work to make it happen. An important aspect of the parent-child relationship is the match of temperaments. For example, an active baby is a challenge for calm, slow-moving parents. Love can grow despite differences in temperament, but it is likely to require more patience from the parents.

7. Parents need to set aside time to enjoy their children. Caught up in the daily stress of parenting, they may miss some of the pleasures that a child can give. Thus, parents must learn to balance the work of child care with opportunities to relax and play with their children.

8. Unresolved personal issues will create additional stress for parents. Distinguishing between ongoing personal or couple issues is important. Naturally, different issues will require different interventions. For example, a woman who was sexually abused during childhood may suddenly have flashbacks and bouts of anxiety when a daughter is born or when the daughter reaches a certain age. These types of stresses require assistance from a psychotherapist.

9. Parents need to provide a variety of stimulating experiences for their children. The experiences must be age-appropriate and involve shared parent-child activities such as reading aloud, playing board games, and skating.

10. Parents should reinforce a child's attempts to be independent, thereby supporting the child's development of a positive identity. The overarching developmental task of childhood is to separate from the parents and move toward maturity. Parents may find their children's struggles for independence difficult to handle, as they fear for the children's safety. Other parents may believe that attempts at independence are signs of rejection. Also, studies suggest that some parents allow boys more freedom than girls.

11. The demands on parents increase, rather than decrease, during early family developmental stages. For instance, having a second child does not just double the work involved in raising one child, but seems to increase the parents' responsibilities exponentially.

12. Children need to be both independent and dependent at the same time. This can be confusing for parents and children alike. To reduce the confusion, FSWs should share information about child development, including dependency needs at different stages.

13. If both parents work outside the home, they may feel torn between the demands of their jobs and those of their family. For example, a mother who works outside the home may be pressured by her husband, extended family, and neighbors to sacrifice her career for the sake of her family. Men are less likely to experience this type of pressure.

Modeling

Modeling is used to demonstrate a specific behavior for family members. This technique is particularly useful when family members cannot imagine carrying out a particular action or when they cannot begin an activity. Modeling is also useful when family members lack necessary skills to take action or when they are hesitant to try out a new behavior. Examples of situations appropriate for modeling include demonstrating how to ask a spouse to help with child care, or how to comfort a sad child.

Family social workers can model effective behaviors for parents. Other models may be provided through videotapes or meetings with peers who have experienced similar problems and have developed the skills to deal with those problems. In Chapter 5, we discussed communication skills that social workers can use with families. The FSW can model these skills to the family. Through modeling, the family can imitate the social worker's communication style and practice using the skills within the family.

After modeling the behavior, the FSW should encourage the client to practice the behavior to assure that the client understands what was modeled and that the client can imitate the behavior of the family social worker. The FSW can provide corrective feedback if necessary. Such practice helps ensure that the client will remember the behavior and provides the FSW with the opportunity to correct any errors in the client's performance, as well as to reinforce and encourage the client's behavior.

MODELING

List three situations in which modeling would be a helpful technique. Pick one of these and practice it with a partner.

Contingency Management

According to the premises of behavioral family work, behavior should change when contingencies or reinforcements are altered. Before this can happen, the FSW must carry out a careful, detailed assessment of the problem and find out how often the problem behavior occurs before change. Information to be gathered includes antecedents and consequences of the problem behavior. Problems must be defined in concrete, observable, and measurable ways. Based on this information, strategies are planned to alter the antecedents or consequences of the behavior. To track change, the FSW must measure the frequency of the problem behavior before and after the intervention. A step-by-step procedure for producing behavioral change is outlined below.

Step 1: Define the Problem Clearly Three aspects of the problem must be identified. First, the FSW and parents must identify the antecedents—the events that immediately precede the behavior. Second, the behavior must be described in concrete, observable, and measurable terms. Third, the FSW and parents must identify *consequences* of the behavior, such as parental responses that reinforce the behavior.

The entire family should participate in problem identification to help members understand the role they play in provoking or reinforcing the behavior. However, input by parents should be the focus of the first interview. Initially, the presence of the child may interfere with finding out critical pieces of information (Gordon & Davidson, 1981). Parents may want to discuss the situation in private. Also, until the child's behavior is reframed and understood by the parents as a learned behavior to which they contribute, parents may label the child as "bad" or as the "problem." Clearly this is detrimental to the child.

One way to understand the behavior is to ask parents to describe a typical day, requesting detailed and concrete information. Parents can use checklists or charts to record the family's behaviors. The FSW may want the child to attend the second meeting so that parent-child interaction may be observed. When assessment is done in the agency, some agencies provide observation rooms with two-way mirrors so that social workers can observe and record family interaction patterns.

Parents can identify problem behavior easily, but they often have more difficulty identifying antecedents to the behavior. In other words, the parents may label the child as "bad" but be unable to provide specific examples of conditions in which problem behaviors occur. In such cases, the FSW must help parents describe the specific problematic behavior; for example, if the child throws tantrums, what specifically does that child do when throwing a tantrum (e.g., cry, yell, hit, throw things) and how often does the tantrum occur? The behavior must be understood in terms of frequency, intensity, duration, consequences, and social context. Parents should clearly describe the antecedents to the behavior, the behavior itself, and the consequences. Videotaping parent-child interactions is helpful in teaching parents.

Step 2: Observe and Measure Behavior After the specific behavior targeted for change has been identified clearly and concretely, the FSW must establish ways to observe and record the frequency and duration of the behavior. Everyone involved should know the frequency of the behavior before intervention to determine whether there has been improvement. At this stage, the family social worker must teach parents to use checklists, charts, and questionnaires to record the actual behavior, as well as its antecedents and consequences. A sample chart is shown in Figure 9.1.

Parents require training to recognize when the behavior is occurring and when it is *not* occurring. They must also be taught to notice their own behaviors before and after the behavior of the child—that is, whether they are providing positive or negative attention to the child or are ignoring the child. Ultimately, the FSW wants to make certain that the behavior of the child is an appropriate response to the behavior of the parent and vice versa. Once parents are taught to observe and count child behaviors and to notice their subsequent responses to these behaviors, they will become more "self-aware" and understand their contributions to the child's misbehavior.

The FSW should help parents become aware of ways in which they reinforce problem behavior. For example, parents may spank the child for aggressive behavior, thereby modeling aggressive behavior and confusing the child. Events that occur outside the family home may also reinforce the child's problem behavior; for example, peers may encourage the child to skip school. Problems outside the home will require meetings and planning with all involved parties to make certain that the response to the behavior is consistent. The focus of family intervention is on changing parent-child interactions. It is more helpful to recognize the efforts that families are making than to criticize what they are doing wrong.

In sum, parents are instructed to conduct a "three-term contingency" measurement (Gordon & Davidson, 1981), which involves the following tasks:

1. Observing and describing the antecedents of the behavior (that is, events that set the stage for the behavior). Parents should record observations over a one-week period. Insights gained by the family during this information-gathering phase will be an impetus for change.

2. Describing the behavior in concrete and measurable terms.

3. Determining the consequences of the behavior—the specific events that follow the behavior.

Step 3: Design an Intervention Measurement should extend past assessment and continue throughout the designed intervention to see whether

FIGURE 9.1   Behavior Chart: Frequency of Temper Tantrums

Date	A.M. or P.M.	Duration	Comments

the intervention is producing the desired results. The family must be capable of implementing the intervention, and the intervention must meet the needs of the family. The FSW should use the following guidelines in helping clients to choose an intervention:

1. Ensure that the intervention does not strain the family's resources. For example, material reinforcers should not be used if the family's finances are limited.

2. Assess the quality of the marital relationship. Will the parents be able to work as a team?

3. Identify personal issues for the parents, such as depression or substance abuse, that could interfere with their ability to follow through with an intervention.

4. Assess the child's ability to cooperate with the intervention plan. The child should be motivated and have sufficient personal resources to follow through on the plan. Even young children can benefit from behaviorally focused interventions if reinforcers are appropriate and the desired behavior is within the child's developmental capabilities. The FSW must also be aware of "environmental noise" (stress and other learning distractions) that may interfere with the intervention (Gordon & Davidson, 1981).

Together with the parents, the FSW must identify which behaviors should be increased and which should be decreased. Positive reinforcement accelerates behaviors that would otherwise occur infrequently. The child must value reinforcers selected. (Social workers will find that children are remarkably willing to let parents know what reinforcers should be used in their program.) During intervention, parents must learn to respond *immediately* (with positive reinforcement, punishment, ignoring, and so on, depending on whether the behavior is to be increased or decreased) to the child's display of the problem behavior. When reinforcing behaviors to be increased, the parents may gradually withdraw the reinforcers with the expectation that the desired behavior will become more durable once it is well established. Changes in their child's behavior will be the parents' reward, but the FSW may ask parents to think of ways to reward themselves also (a night out without the children, for example). Parents of children with behavior problems often experience little joy because they are over-focused on the children, and their own relationship may thus suffer from lack of attention. Applying contingent punishment can diminish behavior. One example is time-out—isolating the child when a problem behavior is shown. Other ways of diminishing problem behavior include issuing verbal reprimands or ignoring the behavior. Time-out can be replaced by positive reinforcement; for instance, children can earn tokens or points for good behavior.

Step 4: Teach the Family How to Support the New Behaviors Evaluations of most interventions have usually looked at initial changes but have seldom considered whether improvements persist. Many therapists rely upon a "train-and-hope" approach, assuming that changes made during intervention will remain intact long after treatment has stopped (Stokes & Baer, 1977). If parents are to continue using their new techniques over time, they must learn to apply skills in different settings and in new contexts or situations (Foster, Prinz, & O'Leary, 1983). Parents must also learn to maintain the changes despite facing environmental stressors that could erode gains made in treatment (Steffen & Karoly, 1980). Thus, the FSW must prepare the family to continue working after the FSW is no longer present. The FSW can ask parents to describe what they have learned and how they expect to reinforce the changes.

ASSISTING PARENTS IN SETTING RULES

Parents need to know how to set rules for children, how to determine when rules are needed, and how to enforce rules when children are not compliant. Parents must learn a set of procedures for enforcing rules consistently, and they must establish consequences for noncompliance. Rule setting and enforcement can be described in terms of several manageable steps.

- First, parents must convey to the child the specific rules and the rationale for each rule. The explanation must match the cognitive ability of the child.

- Then parents should offer the child choices of appropriate behaviors, and the child should be informed of the consequences of choosing inappropriate behavior.

- If the behavior persists, the parent must firmly tell the child that if the behavior occurs again, there will be a specific consequence.

- If the behavior continues, the parent must stop the child and impose the consequence *immediately*. This procedure must be followed every time the child breaks a particular rule. Consistency is imperative. Inconsistent enforcement of rules does not produce behavior change in children.

The following principles of natural and logical consequences have been identified by Grunwald and McAbee (1985):

1. The consequence should be directly related to the behavior.
2. The consequence should be meaningful to the child.
3. The consequences of the behavior should be known ahead of time.
4. The child should be aware that there is a choice between appropriate behavior and behavior that will lead to negative consequences.
5. The consequence should take place as soon as possible after the behavior has occurred.
6. The consequence should usually be of short duration.
7. The consequence should not be a lecture; rather, it should involve some action.
8. As many family members as possible should agree to the action.

BEHAVIORAL INTERVENTION WITH A FAMILY

Imagine your supervisor asks you to work with the Smith family, who are experiencing problems with thirteen-year-old Christina. The problems center on Christina's desire for more independence. She would like to go to the mall with her friends on Saturday, but her parents are worried that she is not old enough for this privilege. Christina feels that her father is too bossy and domineering, while her mother is a "doormat." Christina reports that her father spanked her when she sneaked out of school early to go to the mall with her friends. Christina also reports that her brother Thomas, age fourteen, is allowed to attend a football game with friends without adult supervision every Friday night. She feels she is being treated unfairly.

Working with a partner, develop a plan for carrying out the following steps to address the problems of the Smith family: (1) define the problem; (2) observe behavior; (3) design an intervention.

ADDITIONAL BEHAVIORAL TECHNIQUES

A wide variety of behavioral interventions can be used by family social workers. The specific interventions chosen should address the needs of each family. Several types of behavioral interventions are described below.

Extinction

Extinction is a behavioral technique designed to eliminate undesirable behavior. Clients are instructed to withhold attention from the individual who is behaving inappropriately and not reinforce the problematic behavior through inadvertent types of reinforcement. Extinction is useful for behaviors such as whining, crying, tantrums, and sleep disorders (Thompson & Rudolph, 1992). Extinction is a slow method. The annoying behavior must be *consistently* ignored. All family members must cooperate with the extinction plan, and they must persist even when it does not produce immediate results (Davis, 1996).

Time-Out

Time-out is an indispensable parenting technique used to weaken problematic behaviors of children. When used correctly, parents substitute time-out for physical discipline. Parents often observe that their children's behavior tends to spin out of control as parents lose patience. Time-out entails removing the child from a stimulating environment and placing the child into a setting that provides little stimulation. During time-out, parents have a chance to regain composure while the child calms down. Children can spend time-outs in a chair or a quiet room. The child's bedroom should not be used for time-out, because the child may associate the bedroom with upsetting incidents and resist going to bed.

Time-out can be used when children break rules set by parents. Immediately after the rule has been broken the parent should place the child in the time-out spot. The length of time in the spot will depend upon the child's age, but should range from between five and fifteen minutes.

Davis (1996) recommends the following tips for applying time-outs:

- Decide which behaviors qualify for time-outs. Then parental expectations should be specified as clearly as possible to the child. Typically, time-outs are used for temper tantrums or other noncompliant behavior.

- Determine in advance which quiet settings would be the most appropriate for time-out.

- Decide the point when time-out will be used.

- Let the child know in advance what behaviors are acceptable and which ones are unacceptable. Calmly explain the purpose of the time-out.

- Do not argue with the child when imposing a time-out.

- At times, the child may have to be physically taken to the time-out spot. The parents must be prepared to take the child back if he or she leaves prematurely. Parents should realize that if the child resists the time-out procedure, ensuring that the child remains in the quiet spot can be both frustrating and exhausting. Parents may need to remain physically close to the child but distant enough not to stimulate the child's behavior further. Parents need to be assured that once the child becomes accustomed to the consistent use of time-outs, the child will become more compliant.

Role-Playing

Role-playing allows the client to act out a real-life scenario and develop skill and confidence in dealing with it. It is appropriate for situations in which the client has difficulty being assertive. For instance, a parent offended by the abrupt manner of her child's schoolteacher may be reluctant to ask the teacher questions about the child's school performance. During the role-play, the FSW may take on the role of schoolteacher while the mother asks the teacher questions. The mother may then try out both roles. For instance, she can be the mother asking the teacher pertinent questions; she can then take the role of teacher while the FSW models some additional questions the mother could ask.

As an intervention technique, role-playing has several benefits. Through a role-play, clients can learn how their behavior appears to others (Thompson & Rudolph, 1992). Role-playing helps clients practice skills and anticipate the probable consequences of a particular behavior. Role-playing can also be used to help the FSW understand clients' problems with their social environment, such as conflicts in the workplace or with a neighbor.

Role-playing can be used in several ways in working with a family. One way of staging a role-play is for the FSW to play a role, with clients playing themselves. Another method is to have two people reverse roles and act out a problem scenario. The latter method helps each person to practice using empathy to understand the other person. Role-playing can also be used to rehearse skills relevant to a situation, much the same as rehearsing a play before performing it.

Role-play is a safe form of behavioral rehearsal, involving practicing a new behavior without the fear of consequences. During behavioral rehearsal, the FSW and significant others provide feedback to the client. After the behavior is practiced in a safe environment, the client will be prepared to try out the actual behavior in the real world (Davis, 1996).

ROLE-PLAY

List three situations in which role-playing would be helpful to clients. Pick one of these and practice it with a partner.

Self-Control Training

Self-control training can be used with individuals who are able to as-sume some responsibility for their own behavior (Thompson & Rudolph, 1992). Self-control training is helpful for anxiety reduction, truancy, stut-tering, and to some extent, hyperactivity. Steps involved include (1) se-lecting the behavior to be changed; (2) recording for a week when the behavior occurs, the setting, and the antecedents and the consequences; (3) setting a realistic goal; (4) changing the antecedents and the setting related to the behavior; (5) altering the consequences that reinforce the behavior; (6) recording changes; and (7) devising a plan to ensure that the changes continue.

Assertiveness Training

Conflicts within families often occur because members do not know how to disagree appropriately or how to be assertive with each other. Instead, they rely on passive or aggressive behavior. When individuals are passive, others can easily intrude on their rights. Aggressive individuals intrude on the rights of passive members and attempt to get their needs met through anger. Learning assertiveness skills can help family members deal with one another and with people outside the family.

Parent Training

Parent training, unlike other models of family work, accepts parents' def-inition of the child as the problem (Becvar & Becvar, 1993). Parent training assumes that the problem identified by the parents should be targeted for change. However, while the model explicitly states that the child is the focus of change, parents must learn to respond differently to their chil-dren. Parent training helps parents to become aware of antecedents and consequences to their child's behavior and to exert control over them. Par-ent training can occur in a group session outside the home or with indi-vidual families either in the home or the office.

Parent training relies on checklists, observation in the home, and in-terviews. The family social worker can work with parents to devise a checklist specific to the child's problem behavior. Observed behavior could include temper tantrums, working on homework, completing household chores or staying dry at night, just to name a few. Many of the observed be-haviors will occur at home, and often in the parents' presence.

Parents should be taught how to observe and record the following as-pects of their child's behavior:

- Count how many times a behavior occurred within a particular time period. The time period selected can be short or long, depending upon the problem. For example, if a child is to do homework between 7:00 and 8:00 every evening but avoids homework by leaving the room, going to the bathroom, or playing with pets, the parent can observe and record the avoidant behavior during the one-hour period. Alternatively, if the parent has been instructed to record the occurrence of a child's temper tantrums, the length of time needed to observe the child's behavior could be as long as a day or more. The family social worker and the parent can develop a chart for recording frequency of behavior.

- Note how long a behavior lasted. Some behaviors can be measured by how long they last. For example, a parent may record how long it takes a child to comply with the parent's request to do the dishes.

- Record the severity of the behavior. In this type of observation, the family social worker must help the parent devise a scale to measure a particular behavior. Examples could include how well a child washes the dishes or how loud a child's whining is in reaction to a parent's denial of a privilege.

Parents also need to become aware of events that precede the target behavior, as well as how they respond to the behavior.

The following example addresses parent training used with Harry and Lisa Fryer, a young couple with three-year-old twins (discussed in Chapter 7).

Harry and Lisa were sixteen-year-old high school juniors when their twins were born. Their inexperience at parenting was addressed by the family social worker (FSW), Joyce Perdue. Mrs. Perdue's assessment revealed that Lisa was the primary caregiver while Harry worked in a local grocery store. Lisa reported that the twins were unmanageable much of the time. She reported that the children refused to take naps or go to bed at night without a tantrum. When they were awake, the twins either fought with each other or teamed up against their mother to get into mischief, according to Lisa. For instance, while Lisa talked on the phone one day last week, Tina drew pictures on the living room wall with crayons while Tommy climbed the bookcase, sending books and knickknacks crashing to the floor.

Harry tried to provide Lisa with some relief after he got home from work, but he was frustrated by the twins' lack of compliance with their parents. Harry said that the twins were "basically healthy and happy but totally out of control."

Mrs. Perdue helped the couple apply rewards for compliant behavior. For example, the twins could earn a Popsicle for dessert after lunch, or a trip to the park. The couple learned that rewarding the twins' good behavior was likely to increase it. The FSW also helped Lisa and Harry learn to use extinction whenever possible, discouraging negative behavior by ignoring it. In situations when extinction was not possible, the Fryers learned to use time-out. For instance, when Tina and Tommy fought with each other, the parents were to redirect their behavior by putting each child in a time-out chair.

The Fryers learned these new parenting behaviors by observing Mrs. Perdue as she modeled them. Lisa and Harry then practiced the behaviors while Mrs. Perdue observed and offered feedback. As the couples' parenting skills improved, Mrs. Perdue warned the couple that they might see an increase in the twins' undesirable behaviors before positive changes occurred. This was exactly what happened. But the Fryers continued using their new skills and gradually observed an improvement in the twins' behavior. Mrs. Perdue then helped the parents to establish a few simple rules to provide a routine for the twins and to guide their behavior. These rules included no hitting others or destroying others' property, bedtime at 8:30, and so on. The Fryers reported a much calmer and happier family life as their parenting skills improved.

Contingency Contracting

Contingency contracting is useful in working with children because it relies heavily upon input by all concerned parties. A contract is developed, through mutual negotiation, identifying what behaviors individuals will perform and when. Usually the contract specifies who is to do what for whom, under what circumstances, when, and where. Rewards are established such that if all parties successfully carry out the contract, mutually positive rewards will follow. All participants must understand what they will give and what they will get if the contract is followed.

Contingency contracting involves six steps (Thompson & Rudolph, 1992):

1. Identify the problem to be solved.
2. Collect data to find out baseline frequency of behavior to be changed.
3. Set goals that all parties agree upon.
4. Select methods for achieveing the goals.
5. Assess results for observable, measurable change.

Families with teenagers may find contingency contracting useful. The contract is used to specify appropriate behaviors and corresponding rewards and consequences. Both the teen and parent have input into what behaviors they want to include, and disputes may be negotiated. When a family has just begun to use contracting, simple issues should be selected. A sample contract is shown in Figure 9.2.

Relaxation Techniques

Progressive relaxation is a useful technique to deal with generalized anxiety or anxiety that is triggered by specific situations. For generalized anxiety, the person is taught the skills of relaxation. For situation-specific anxiety, the person learns to relax while visualizing anxiety-provoking situations. In deep muscle relaxation, the individual relaxes the muscles, one group after another, until a state of deep relaxation is achieved. Typically, people are instructed to start by tensing with their toes, and then gradually move to major and minor muscle groups up the body. Muscle tension should occur for about five to ten seconds, followed by a complete release of tension. There are tapes or scripts that can teach progressive relaxation. Alternatively, the FSW can script a relaxation session for clients, recording it on audiotape so the user can pay full attention to the directions.

FIGURE 9.2 **Contract for a Child to Complete Homework**

Homework Program

	Mon.	Tues.	Wed.	Thurs.	Fri.	Sat.	Sun.
Brings books home from school. (1 point)						/	/
Starts homework at 7:00 P.M. without arguing. (3 points)							
Keeps television off during homework. (2 points)							
Stays in one room to do homework until 8:00 P.M. (1 point)							
Total points							

I, _____, agree to do my homework regularly based on the conditions set above. I understand that I will earn points based on the agreement above. When I earn _____ points, I will be able to cash them in for _____.

_____   _____
Mother's signature   Father's signature

_____
Child's signature

Relaxation techniques can be useful for many situations. For example, a parent may be anxious about a pending job interview or court case. The anxiety may be interfering with sleep or contribute to a parent's irritability with a child. Similarly, a child may be acting out in response to school stress or worry about conflict at home. Relaxation techniques can help clients to cope with stressful situations.

Giving Homework

Change begun in family meetings should continue when the FSW is no longer present. One way to encourage continuous progress is to assign "homework" for clients to do between sessions. Assignments can take many forms but have a threefold purpose:

- To get family members to behave differently;
- To collect information about family behavior outside between meetings;
- To emphasize self-responsibility to create change.

Assignments should be based on the work done in an interview and are useful in bridging gaps between sessions. Tasks should be geared toward the ability and motivation of the family, and they must be outlined clearly. Assigning homework to families helps them take responsibility for behavior change and will prepare the family to continue working when the FSW is no longer available to nudge them along. Examples of homework include developing a list of household tasks, charting behavior, or continuing to use an agreed-upon parenting technique. Charting behavior can help family members become aware of how often the behavior occurs and helps the family to monitor progress made (Kinney, Haapala, & Booth, 1991).

Homework that is assigned should be related to the assessment of the family and work that is being done. For example, if the family is socially isolated, a homework assignment for family members could be to use a community resource or nurture an outside relationship.

For homework to be effective, the FSW must start the next interview by reviewing how the homework went. If the social worker discovers that the family did not do the homework assignment, he or she will need to find out the reasons for nonperformance. Reasons may range from open resistance to not understanding the instructions. When homework is assigned regularly, families eventually learn to expect the social worker to assign a task at the end of each interview (Hartman & Laird, 1983).

AVOIDING PITFALLS IN BEHAVIORAL INTERVENTIONS

In applying behavioral interventions, family social workers must be careful to avoid some common pitfalls. For example, Johnson (1986) suggests that defining problems as interactional may cause some clients to feel that the entire family is an object of blame. Also, certain interventions may seem to favor one family member over another, rather than treating family members equally.

In one study, parents discussed their perceptions of alliances and power imbalances that may develop during family social work. First, parents expressed concern about the possibility of having their parental power undermined by the FSW. Second, alliances between the social worker and family members were sometimes viewed as problematic; for example, if the FSW formed alliances with children, parents perceived these alliances as a collusion against parental authority. Conversely, other parents were pleased when the FSW developed a working relationship with a child, because they felt that the child was receiving special attention (Coleman & Collins, 1997). Family social workers must be prepared to discuss alliances and power issues openly with clients so that potential problems can be avoided.

The following FSW behaviors can interfere with the success of behavioral interventions and should be avoided:

- Blaming individual family members or the entire family for difficulties.
- Taking sides or aligning with individual family members.
- Telling clients what to do instead of helping them arrive at their own solutions.
- Relying on negative consequences rather than positive reinforcement.
- Using technical language that the family cannot understand.

By becoming familiar with how people learn and by developing skill in balancing family and individual needs, FSWs can help create an atmosphere in which all family members feel heard and understood, expectations are expressed in straightforward language, and family members participate actively in the process of change.

Tips for Producing Behavioral Change

- Understand learning theory, including reinforcement principles.
- Decide on a parent/family education model that fits the family (for example, behavioral model, parent effectiveness training model).
- Ask for and anticipate concerns of the parents and children.
- Provide a clear rationale for changes.
- Teach basic life skills, such as money management, child management, consumer skills, communication skills.
- Discuss skills in concrete and specific nontechnical language.
- Model appropriate behaviors and skills to parents.
- Reinforce family motivation and acknowledge positive change.
- Get the family to generate their own solutions.
- Recognize and reinforce development of skills.

CHAPTER SUMMARY

In this chapter we discussed how to assist families by focusing on behavior change. A behavioral focus offers a practical approach for working with families, especially families who are experiencing behavioral difficulties with children.

Behavioral interventions are based on the idea that behavior is either maintained or extinguished by its consequences. In behavioral interventions, the focus is on family interaction patterns rather than the problems of individual family members.

Familiarity with behavioral change techniques is essential for all family social workers. These techniques are based on principles of behavior modification and social learning theory that explain how behavior can be increased, decreased, or maintained and how new behaviors can be taught. Indeed, teaching clients specific skills is one of the most helpful behavioral interventions. Methods of teaching include sharing information, modeling, and contingency management.

Assisting parents in setting rules is another useful behavioral technique. Parents need to know how to determine when rules are needed, how to set rules, and how to enforce them. Additional behavioral techniques discussed in this chapter were extinction, time-outs, role-playing, self-control training, assertiveness training, parent training, contingency contracting, relaxation techniques, and assigning homework.

10 The Termination Phase

Termination is the final phase of the helping process. Ending family work constructively sets the stage for continued positive change, yet termination is often overlooked as an essential part of the helping process (Kaplan, 1986). The central focus of termination is evaluating whether work with the family has resolved the presenting problem (Lum, 1992). A related purpose is ensuring that progress is sustained—a process that can occur only if families develop the skills they will need to solve problems independently after the FSW's involvement has ended.

Family social work is often short-term because many families seek assistance during periods of crisis and are motivated only to solve their immediate problems. Plans for termination or transfer to another helper should be negotiated with the family early in the helping process. Some agencies automatically impose time limits on family social work, making the termination date clear and explicit. The FSW should initiate the countdown to the final appointment well in advance of the last scheduled contact by periodically reviewing with the family the progress made to date. Families may need the social worker's help to work through a number of important issues during the termination stage: denial, anger, sadness, and "letting go."

Termination can occur in several ways:

1. Termination by mutual agreement following successful resolution of presenting problem(s).

2. Termination on clients' initiative at the end of a contractual period of specified length. Contracting for a specified period provides a time framework that may make intervention efficient.

3. Sessions seem to reflect no progress. Termination should be by common consent.

185

4. Clients show active resistance, questioning process and outcomes. One or more clients are openly uncooperative and may be hostile.

5. Repeated cancellation of appointments or failure to keep them without formal withdrawal by clients.

6. Direct withdrawal, usually via a telephone call stating clients' decision to terminate with or without stating reasons.

Ideally, when work is unsatisfactory, the FSW should end the relationship after holding a final session to review what happened.

The best time to terminate family work is when the presenting problem has been resolved and both the family and the social worker are satisfied with the outcome. In practice, however, termination often occurs in unanticipated ways. Many families drop out of a program or terminate prematurely, before the desired outcome has been achieved.

Clients may experience a range of emotions as they approach termination. Most authors emphasize feelings of separation and loss, implying that termination creates a grief reaction. We believe that this case may be overstated, yet social workers may find that some clients are reluctant to terminate. They may bring up new problems or claim that the old problems have worsened. Other clients, especially involuntary clients, may welcome the end of the working relationship.

Social workers also react to termination in a variety of ways. Some may be reluctant to stop services. Termination for these social workers will be easier when they acknowledge limits to their responsibility for people's lives (Gambrill, 1983). That is, FSWs should accept that after the end of family work, responsibility for decision making rests with the family.

In this chapter we will examine issues related to who takes the initiative to terminate: the family, the FSW, or both. Because the decision to end family work does not necessarily mean that the family will stop contact with all agencies, it is important to look upon referral as an important aspect of the termination process. Specific suggestions for phasing out and concluding family social work follow.

REASONS FOR TERMINATION

List some reasons for advising a family to terminate family social work.

PLANNING FOR TERMINATION

Successful termination requires skill on the part of the FSW. The first step is for the FSW to discuss impending termination with the family at the outset of work, usually during contracting. Although some worker-client relationships may end abruptly or unexpectedly, termination ideally should be anticipated and planned from the beginning of involvement in the program. The manner in which termination is handled can influence how well the family sustains changes made during the helping relationship. Satisfactory termination to one helping experience also may predispose a family to seek help again if they need it.

Generally, the process of termination should parallel the end of each family meeting. For example, about ten minutes before ending an interview the FSW can tell the family that ten minutes remain, address unfinished business, and use the remaining time to summarize the session. Arrangements for the next session will be made. Every week the social worker and family will repeat the process of reviewing what family members have achieved and how the family can continue making progress (Kinney, Haapala, & Booth, 1991). Termination of the overall working relationship follows similar steps, except that there will be no further sessions.

POSSIBLE REACTIONS TO TERMINATION

Much has been written about ending helping relationships, most of it focusing on negative aspects. For the majority of clients and their social workers, however, termination is essentially positive because it can be used to focus upon accomplishments. Positive reflection will increase clients' self-confidence and reinforce feelings of personal competence. Families may be eager to try out new skills learned in the helping relationship. Similarly, when social workers feel they have achieved their designated goals with clients, their self-esteem increases, renewing them for future work.

Problems with termination can arise if the FSW has not maintained clear boundaries with the family. For a family social worker who has become over-involved, termination may provoke anxiety. The FSW may grieve the loss of the relationship or worry about the family's future welfare. While most terminations produce a mixture of feelings, family social workers who have maintained professional objectivity will be able to deal with their emotions more effectively than those who have not. Of course, it is inappropriate for a social worker to end a professional relationship only to strike up a personal relationship with a former client.

Family social workers often establish intense and meaningful relationships with families and may feel hesitant about initiating termination. Termination means letting go and moving on. The FSW's feelings can range from grief to joy or include a mixture of both. Terminating with some families may bring relief, while discontinuing with others may elicit feelings of sadness and loss. Through experience, the FSW will anticipate feelings to address at the time of termination. Family members' feelings can range from pride and satisfaction to anger, sadness, or regret. The FSW can recognize signs suggestive of difficulty at terminating: for example, a client may predictably cancel appointments as the date of each appointment draws closer. It may be difficult to schedule a final meeting when family members have canceled several times previously. Sometimes the FSW will need to remind the family that time is running out before conducting one final appointment.

Clients may try to halt termination in the following ways:

- They may become overly dependent on the social worker.
- They may report that former problems are starting to reappear.
- They may introduce new problems.
- They may find substitutes for the social worker (Hepworth & Larsen, 1993).

Most of these concerns can be handled by contracting at the beginning and by exploring the family's feelings about termination near the end. Referrals to other agencies and nurturing informal support networks are two important ways of easing termination. Families may be especially reluctant to terminate when goals have not been met. Short-term programs seem especially vulnerable to family dissatisfaction with the services. A parent in one short-term program stated, "I disliked the shortness of it. We're quite dysfunctional. In order to get a habit established, we needed long-term help" (Coleman & Collins, 1997).

Alternatively, termination can be a time of celebration, especially when concrete, positive change has occurred. The FSW should be aware of the limits of family social work and encourage the family to transfer to another helper if and when appropriate. Rituals associated with closure and evaluation should promote a sense of satisfaction with progress made.

STEPS IN TERMINATING

Five steps are required for constructive termination: (1) recital; (2) inducing awareness of change; (3) consolidating gains; (4) providing feedback to the FSW; and (5) preparing the family to handle future problems.

1. *Recital*—As the helping process draws to a close, the social worker and each family member should be given an opportunity to comment on their experience in family work with an emphasis on discussing what has changed (Bandler, Grinder, & Satir, 1976; Worden, 1994). Doing so will help family members understand what changes have been made and what has happened to produce these changes. Lum (1992) calls this *recital*, a technique that involves reviewing important incidents of family work.

If negotiated goals have not been achieved or additional problems have emerged, the recital may point to the need for referral to a different agency or to another social worker within the same agency. In either case, the family should summarize their perceived progress to date so that they will be able to help the new social worker understand the situation. In a planned referral, the FSW will speak personally with the new social worker after receiving the family's permission.

As mentioned earlier, routine and ongoing review of the family's progress throughout intervention will make the final summarization easier (Barker, 1981; Tomm & Wright, 1979). Negotiating for a predetermined number of sessions alerts families to the eventual end of intervention and sets a contract to track change. While an open-ended contract may be more typical, we suggest a time-limited, well-developed focus for work, allowing for flexibility with regard to the frequency and duration of sessions. Periodic reviews give family members an opportunity to express satisfaction or dissatisfaction with the progress being made, and it also allows the family and the social worker to make changes as the work proceeds.

2. *Inducing awareness of change*—After family members have discussed with the FSW their reactions to the social work process, they can receive feedback from the worker's perspective. As the FSW and family compare their perceptions of the process, family members will develop both a conceptual understanding and the tools with which to produce further change. These reflections can be a powerful source of self-esteem for family members.

Professional helpers want to be effective, and many have entered social work to fulfill a sincere desire to promote healthy social and family functioning. Because of this, they may develop a sense that credit for the change belongs to the social worker. It is unfortunate that failures are usually attributed to clients, while successes are claimed by social workers. Pinpointing the source of the change can be difficult because change often involves being in the right place at the right time, doing the right things with the right people. In fact, for years researchers have been trying to isolate factors that create change. Regardless of where the FSW believes the change originated, it is essential for the family to receive credit for making the change (Brock & Barnard, 1992; Wright & Leahey, 1994). To accomplish this, the FSW can ask family members what *they* did to create the change (Brock & Barnard, 1992). Social workers need to be humble in discussing their contributions. When family members are reminded of their own part in creating change, they will feel competent to meet future challenges.

It is natural for social workers to accept praise—success is a major source of professional gratification. Nevertheless, the family social worker's professional responsibility is not complete until termination has been conducted satisfactorily. Families struggle with the pain, conflict, and pressure of their problems and deserve credit for making changes. When change occurs with a child, parents should recognize that they are primary caretakers for the child in the present and future. Giving recognition for progress increases the chance that the positive effects of family social work will persist. To do otherwise conveys the message the family cannot manage without the social worker.

If a family is distressed by lack of progress at termination, social workers must find a balance when discussing negative and positive aspects of the work. Negatives should be presented as goals to work toward in the future. Social workers may also want to explore with their supervisors possible reasons why the sessions were not successful. Perhaps the goals were too high or unrealistic. Resistance to change may have been increased by the FSW's inability to understand the family members' hesitancy. In many cases, social workers have explained lack of movement by claiming that families were unmotivated, rather than trying to understand how they may have contributed to the problem.

Social workers need to acknowledge difficulties in working with families. Overburdened families sometimes will not benefit from complex or fancy interventions. It is important that the FSW believe the family has worked hard despite making little change. It is also important for the social worker to reinforce family strengths. Even though we are encouraging family social workers to credit families for change, the FSW can also relish successes. Family social work is rewarding when the family social worker is a partner in the change process.

In Figure 10.1 we present a checklist for termination. Social workers and client families can complete the checklist together to determine whether termination issues have been addressed. The checklist consists of sixteen factors that are useful in evaluating clients' readiness for ending family social work. If a family, together with the family social worker, can answer "Yes" to most of these statements, then termination is appropriate and timely.

3. *Consolidating gains*—The third step of termination is talking about the future, emphasizing how to maintain and build upon the goals achieved. Helping the family develop strategies for attaining future goals is an excellent method for consolidating gains. When appropriate, the FSW can help the family make a transition to other community supports.

Reviewing family accomplishments is also an important component of the FSW's self-evaluation. Client behavior is one factor in determining a successful outcome, but other factors are also important. The FSW can note the professional learning accomplished while working with the family. The FSW's professional development is advanced through learning new skills or improving existing skills, regardless of whether the case outcome is positive or negative. The FSW may articulate the learning in various ways: "I persevered," "I learned how to work with a suicidal individual," or "I have developed more skills in teaching parents how to manage difficult child behavior."

Termination should be viewed as a transition, not an end. Describing termination in this way to clients produces the sense of a new beginning and a recognition of all that has been accomplished. Participating in a helping relationship requires faith—in oneself, in families, and in the helping process. Family social workers may not witness clear evidence that they have helped families change or achieve desired goals, but their efforts may make some important differences in their clients' lives. Additionally, some interventions may have no immediate impact, but may exert an influence in the future. Some of the greatest benefits to families may come in the form of increased confidence, new skills, or supportive social networks that enable clients to see themselves differently and help them respond to challenges later. Believing that their efforts have not been in vain diminishes the regrets FSWs feel about ending their work with a family.

4. *Providing feedback to the FSW*—It is important to provide formal closure to the intervention by holding a face-to-face discussion. During the final session, evaluation of case outcomes may be conducted. Gurman and

FIGURE 10.1   Checklist for Terminating Family Social Work

	Yes	No
The presenting problem has been eliminated.	☐	☐
It has been made manageable or tolerable for the family.	☐	☐
The changes made can be measured effectively.	☐	☐
Positive changes have been made in psychosocial functioning.	☐	☐
Family members are communicating more effectively.	☐	☐
Family members are safe from abuse.	☐	☐
Formal support networks are available, and the family knows how to use them.	☐	☐
The family has an adequate informal network upon which to call when in need.	☐	☐
Family or individual members have been referred for specialized services in the community.	☐	☐
The family has agreed to be referred to specialized services.	☐	☐
The family has learned skills to function in their daily routine.	☐	☐
Basic physical needs of all family members are being met.	☐	☐
The social worker and family have evaluated the family's progress to date.	☐	☐
The family is satisfied with the service rendered..	☐	☐
All family members are better off as a result of the work.	☐	☐
The family has gone through recital of the changes they have made.	☐	☐
Family members have acknowledged the role they have played in creating change.	☐	☐

Kniskern (1981) recommend evaluating the progress of the entire family unit, as well as the subsystems that may have been experiencing problems (e.g., the marital subsystem and individual family members' functioning). The first step involves evaluating with the family their perceptions of success. The FSW can ask family members, "What did you find most helpful during our work together?" and "What did you want to happen that did not occur?" It gives the family an opportunity to highlight the highs and lows of the process and also shows them that the social worker is receptive to feedback. The social worker should not react defensively to feedback but express appreciation and inform family members that their contributions will help the FSW in future work with families. Additionally, measurement instruments or other assessment tools may be used one last time to provide comparative data to add to the evaluation.

5. *Preparing the family to handle future problems*—A final step in termination is to ask the family to anticipate upcoming changes or challenges that could cause setbacks (Nichols & Schwartz, 1998). The social worker should ask the family to describe how they plan to handle such situations. The FSW can also use this theme to reinforce family strengths and newly developed skills. Another method of preparing families for the future is to gradually extend the time between family meetings and thereby encourage the family to lessen their reliance on the program.

Some agencies expect social workers to make a follow-up visit to clients after termination. Such a follow-up can provide a "booster shot" during a time when the family is vulnerable to relapse. Follow-up services can help families through transitional periods (Lum, 1992). During vulnerable periods, the FSW may become re-involved with a family for a brief period of time to prevent the family from slipping into old patterns. Vulnerable periods depend upon family characteristics and the type of problem experienced.

The following example illustrates a successful termination of family social work.

> Lindy Stein and her parents Mary and Todd participated in family social work with their family social worker (FSW), Betty Chess. The family initially became involved with the FSW agency when fifteen-year-old Lindy ran away from home and was gone for a week. Prior to running away, Lindy was truant from school on numerous occasions and rebellious toward her parents and her teachers. Her grades had dropped from an A average to Cs and Ds, and she had been charged as a minor in possession of alcohol.
>
> Mrs. Chess determined during the assessment that Lindy was reacting to her parents' separation and subsequent divorce. The divorce was difficult for the couple, who were angry with each other and had put Lindy in the middle of their fighting. Lindy's behavior was a response to her frustration and her inability to communicate her needs and feelings to her parents.
>
> Mrs. Chess intervened by helping Lindy to learn to communicate her feelings to her parents. As Mary and Todd began to realize how their conflicts were affecting their daughter and contributing to her problems at school and at home, they recognized the need to arrive at a truce. Mary and Todd consequently agreed to allow Mrs. Chess to refer them for family counseling so that they could effectively coparent Lindy.
>
> As Mrs. Chess prepared the family for termination, she set aside time for the Steins to provide a recital of their experience in family work, followed by her own summary of the family's gains. Holding a termination session allowed Mrs. Chess to provide closure and to receive feedback from the family. She asked them to evaluate what had been most and least helpful during family social work. At the end of the termination session, Mrs. Chess asked the family to anticipate future problems and to describe how they planned to address them. This review of the skills learned allowed Mrs. Chess the opportunity to congratulate the family on their improved communication skills. Mrs. Chess referred the family for counseling to enable the Steins to consolidate their gains and to continue to improve their interactions. She also reminded the Steins that they could schedule "booster sessions" with her whenever they felt the need for follow-up services.

■ SUGGESTIONS FOR THE FUTURE

Using a family from your field placement or work setting as an example, list some suggestions you could make to help the family maintain positive gains after termination.

When becoming involved at a later date with families, the FSW can refer to follow-up contacts as "consultations" or "booster shots." Family members are likely to work through their problems more quickly if they feel that they are in charge of the changes, with the family social worker serving as information provider and encourager on a short-term basis. The social worker must take care to identify the consultation as a sign of health rather than an indication of failure.

TIMING OF TERMINATION

The best time to decrease the frequency of sessions is when progress has been made, goals have been reached, and the family shows signs of stability. Most families agree to termination when they can identify improvement in their problem-solving capacity. If families find termination difficult to accept, the FSW may ask a paradoxical question such as, "What would each of you have to do to bring the problem back?" to give family members a better awareness of the changes made (Tomm & Wright, 1979).

The frequency of sessions may need to be decreased when a family seems overly dependent on the social worker. At times paraprofessionals have acted in a supportive capacity with family members only to become their major support system because other supports have not been nurtured. To avoid fostering dependency, the FSW can mobilize formal and informal supports for the family while concurrently decreasing the frequency of sessions. If the family resists decreasing the frequency of sessions, the FSW should discuss concerns and solicit support from all family members (Tomm & Wright, 1979). Family members may worry that if appointments are discontinued altogether, they will be unable to cope. By asking, "What do you think will happen if we stop meeting?" and by openly discussing family members' anxieties, the FSW can often prevent the worst-case scenario from occurring.

Premature Terminators and Dropouts

Sometimes families terminate indirectly. Some may simply not be at home for a scheduled meeting, and others may call and cancel at the last minute. Other times individual family members do not show up for a scheduled meeting with the FSW (Barker, 1981). Another hint that families are considering dropping out is when they express dissatisfaction with family social work and talk about practical problems of participating in family sessions, such as missing work, having to reschedule other appointments, and so on.

When the social worker begins to notice a pattern forming (several missed appointments in a row) we suggest raising the topic for discussion.

The difference between families who stop work prematurely and those who merely drop out is that premature terminators try to give the social worker notice and a reason for leaving. It should be remembered that as many as 40 percent of families terminate work after six to ten sessions (Worden, 1994) but perhaps fewer for home-based services. When a family announces its decision to terminate, the FSW should acknowledge the decision and elicit information about reasons for termination. In such cases the work may be stopped because of client absences, resistance, the social worker's inability to take the family further, or personality conflicts between family members and the social worker. Information garnered from clients will help the FSW differentiate between timely, appropriate termination and inappropriate or premature termination.

One type of premature termination occurs when clients display sudden improvement; this is referred to as a "flight into health" (Tomm & Wright, 1979) or "faking good." Families may "fake good" when they view change as threatening. They may tell the FSW that their problems have been resolved, and there may even be a temporary cessation of problems lasting for a short period of time. If the family specifically states that they would like to end work, but the FSW believes that termination would be premature, the FSW should move into the *recital* step of termination to review problems and even renegotiate a new contract. In doing so, the FSW and family can encapsulate the changes, identify problems that still exist, and sort out what goals need to be achieved. Eliciting specifics of the family decision may be helpful. The FSW can try to find out when the family decided to quit and what factors prompted the decision.

While termination can sometimes be averted, sometimes premature termination may be unavoidable. In such cases, the FSW must accept the decision to terminate without applying inappropriate pressure, even though the FSW disagrees with the family's decision (Tomm & Wright, 1979).

Avoiding premature termination can be more difficult with court-mandated clients, who often wish to avoid any work beyond what has been required by the court. They may suddenly become resistant the day a court order ceases to exert authority over them. One way to prevent this outcome is to encourage family members to discuss their reaction to being ordered into treatment. Court-mandated families who drop out of family work must also face the consequences of their decisions. Premature termination may mean that child welfare authorities or the courts will have to be notified.

Ideally, termination may take place after the presenting problems have been resolved. The family's ability to cope with problems, not avoid them, is an important indicator of readiness to terminate (Freeman, 1981). Movement toward termination occurs smoothly if the beginning and middle stages of treatment have concluded successfully. Effective family social workers often set mini-goals and suggest that progress toward a goal be evaluated within a specified number of interviews. However, the most important decision for family social workers concerns when to end. Ideally, termination should occur after goals have been met.

In some agencies, the FSW must assess whether the family needs further help or whether they can resolve problems on their own. Regardless of how termination occurs, the social worker should initiate an honest discussion of everyone's perceptions of what was achieved during family social work.

Tasks for Family Social Workers During Termination

- Recognize limitations and functions of family social work.
- Understand differences between family social work and family therapy.
- Help the family identify goals to be achieved after family social work ends, and explain the different roles of other helpers compared with family social workers.
- Identify community resources that can support the family after termination, and help the family link to these resources.
- Encourage the sharing of feelings concerning termination.
- Identify the strengths of the family and its members.

Dysfunctional Behaviors to Avoid

- Unwillingness to discuss termination with the family.
- Postponing termination even when postponement is not warranted.
- Avoiding discussion of family members' feelings about stopping work.
- Minimizing the role that family social work played in creating change.
- Reluctance to credit family for its efforts in resolving problems.

HOW AND WHEN TO REFER CLIENTS TO OTHER PROFESSIONALS

Referral to other professionals may be necessary for a variety of reasons. Specific skills are needed by the FSW to assist families in making a smooth transition from one professional to another. Major reasons for referring families to other professionals include the following:

- A family may need assistance from a specialist. It is unrealistic to expect family social workers to be experts in all areas. Assistance from other professionals may be needed when problems are complex. Referral can be either for consultation or for in-depth treatment. The role of the FSW after referral will vary from that of a treatment collaborator to that of a former helper. For example, if an adult within a family is sexually abusing a child, it is important that specialists in offender treatment be consulted. The FSW may refer the family for consultation with a psychiatrist but may continue to meet with the family until the consultation is complete.

- A family member may have a problem that should be assessed at an institution with the resources available to assess and treat the particular problem.

- A family moves out of the social worker's catchment area but needs continued assistance. Referral to a social worker in the new area may be indicated.

- Family social workers should not think of themselves as inadequate if they must refer a family. Referral requires extensive knowledge of resources within the community as well as good counseling skills with families.

Clients need to be prepared prior to referrals. The FSW must explain the reasons for referral and how the family may benefit from it. For example, if the FSW has determined that the family's problems include a family member's alcoholism, the family social worker can refer the individual alcoholic and the family for addiction treatment. To facilitate the referral, the FSW can provide a summary for the new helper and possibly give a copy to the family. Selecting an appropriate referral source is essential, and colleagues and supervisors can offer suggestions about which agencies can best meet the family's needs.

For families who have established rapport with their social workers, referral to other helpers may be difficult. The comments of a mother about what she did not like about a family social work agency illustrate this difficulty:

> We did not like being turned over to someone else. We are not machines; we are people. [FSW] had established an excellent rapport, she was trusted, she was effective, and when *they* thought she was done, she was pulled out without out consultation. Not any consideration to the workability of the dynamic. These are intimate, profoundly personal issues...if I don't like them, I don't want them in my family...I want to accept help, but I'm simply not a case, I'm a human being...It's really detrimental to take out someone who is working well with a family...if [FSW] had stayed six months, [child] would never have been in placement for a year and it would have saved [the Agency] thousands of dollars (Coleman & Collins, 1997).

As this mother's comments show, switching to a different FSW can be difficult for some families. They may be emotionally attached to the first social worker and not want to go through the stages of trust building and engagement another time. Referral may be more effective if the FSW participates in the family's first meeting with the new social worker. This personalizes the referral and helps alleviate family members' anxieties about starting with someone they do not know and must learn how to trust. Before the actual referral, family social workers should encourage family members to express concerns or ask questions about the upcoming referral. Likewise, the new helper should clarify with the family why the referral was made and attempt to clear up any misconceptions the family may have. Thus, referral is smoothest if both the family and the new helper are given adequate explanations.

EVALUATING RESULTS OF FAMILY SOCIAL WORK

Although positive and even dramatic results may be obtained during family social work, success is measured by the positive changes that are maintained or continue to evolve weeks and months after termination. We encourage social workers to obtain follow-up information from the family. A focus on outcome directs the FSW to orient work toward change, to focus on problems that can be realistically changed, and to think of how the family will cope on their own (Haley, 1976). In a follow-up contact, the FSW should explain that this is a normal pattern of practice (e.g., "We always contact families with whom we have worked to get information on how they are doing"). It is also important to follow up with a clear and specific purpose in mind, such as reinforcing changes made in family work. To reinforce an emphasis on outcome, we suggest conducting follow-up sessions face-to-face.

■ EVALUATION AND FOLLOW-UP PROCEDURES

List some procedures that would help you evaluate the effectiveness of your work with a family.

The degree of change achieved in family social work should be assessed at all levels: individual, parent-child, marital, and family system. Gurman and Kniskern (1981) suggest that a "higher level of positive change has occurred when improvement is evidenced in systemic (total family) or relationship (dyadic) interactions than when it is evidenced in individuals alone" (p. 765). That is, change in individual family members does not logically require change in the family system, but stable change in the system does require both individual change and relationship change; also, relationship change requires individual change.

Another measure of outcome is evaluation of practitioner performance. The competence of the FSW is central to the success of family social work. Just as setting goals for family behavioral change assists in the change process, so too does setting goals for one's professional performance assist

FIGURE 10.2   Family Social Worker's Self-Evaluation Form

I developed the following new skills in working with this family:

Skills in working with specific problems areas:

New techniques of intervention:

Self-awareness of strengths and problem areas:

With this family, my best work involved:

With this family, I could have done the following better:

with skill development. An example of a self-evaluation form is provided in Figure 10.2.

CHAPTER SUMMARY

In this chapter we described the process of terminating the family social worker's relationship with a client family. Termination involves summarizing the family's accomplishments, reviewing problems that remain, and making decisions about further work, follow-up, or referral. Termination may occur for three reasons: termination is predetermined and time-limited; the family's goals have been accomplished; or the family or the FSW decides not to continue.

Steps for successful termination include (1) recital of the family social work process with the client family, (2) inducing an awareness of change, (3) consolidating gains for the social worker and the family, (4) providing feedback from the family to the FSW, and (5) preparing the family to handle future problems. If termination is described as a transition, rather than an ending, it may seem more palatable both to the family and to the FSW.

Contracting for a specific number of sessions at the beginning of family work sets time limits to encourage completion of goals. When adequate progress has been made, the FSW can begin to decrease the frequency of sessions as a way to help the family prepare for termination. Referral to another professional may be necessary in some cases.

Giving families credit for the positive changes they have made is an excellent way to increase clients' self-esteem, feelings of competence, and motivation for independence. When families have made little progress during family work, the FSW can acknowledge family members' positive efforts toward solving their problems. The FSW may seek supervision or consultation for help in determining the causes of a lack of progress. Implementing systematic evaluation and follow-up procedures helps the FSW to analyze his or her performance and set goals for improvement.

11
Gender-Sensitive Practice

Historically, men have held more power than women. Men wrote laws, controlled property and money, and were recognized as heads of households, while women did most of the work within the home and received little recognition or respect for their contributions. These patterns have been changing within the last few decades as growing numbers of women have entered the work force and the political arena, but imbalances of power remain. Because of long-standing patterns of gender inequity, family social workers are likely to encounter situations in which women are oppressed and abused.

Expecting women to adapt to oppressive situations is inappropriate; instead, family social workers should empower them to assume greater control over their lives. Empowering women can mean helping them find ways to change or leave oppressive relationships and to gain a broader awareness of the options available to them. Accordingly, gender-sensitive interventions are well suited to family social work, particularly work with families in which women have been oppressed or abused by their partners.

Gender-sensitive family social workers question some of the views held by traditional family therapists, particularly their emphasis on circular causality. They disagree with the idea that women contribute to their own abuse. Instead, they attribute the abuse to imbalances of power between men and women.

To implement a gender-sensitive approach with clients, FSWs must be willing to question their own assumptions about men and women. They need to become familiar with the ways in which society reinforces unequal treatment based on gender. Gender-sensitive social workers take an ecological perspective on family dynamics, recognizing the influence of a family's social environment on its internal functioning. Finally, gender-sensitive social workers recognize that changes in families can lead to changes in society and that social change can improve life for families.

GENDER-SENSITIVE PRACTICE VERSUS TRADITIONAL FAMILY THERAPY

Gender-sensitive family social work is based on a feminist view of how families operate. The feminist perspective on families has been described as "an attitude, a lens, a body of ideas about gender hierarchy and its impact rather than a specific model or a grab-bag of clinical techniques" (Carter, 1992, p. 66). In many ways, feminist theory is a philosophical foundation upon which family social workers can base gender-sensitive interventions. Feminist theory, as it applies to family social work, advocates sensitivity to the problems created when rigid, traditional gender roles are assigned to family members. Feminist social workers recognize the detrimental effects of power imbalances and gender-based inequality in family relationships.

Feminists have challenged some of the basic assumptions of traditional family therapists, noting the influence of cultural and historical biases on the development of family theory (Nichols & Schwartz, 1998). Feminist theorists have criticized the inherent sexist biases of the pioneers of family therapy, who emphasized the value of characteristics in which males are socialized (rationality, independence), while depreciating characteristics (such as nurturing and interconnectedness) typically associated with female socialization. Early family theorists also endorsed a "normal family structure," often premised on gender inequality. Advocates of feminist social work practice believe this male-constructed view of the world interprets behavior associated with females as suggestive of weakness, passivity, masochism, and inferiority.

During the 1980s, feminists began to criticize family systems theory for some of its sexist tenets, particularly the assumption that if all participants in the system contribute to a problem, they do so from positions of *equal* power. Feminists find family systems concepts of circular causality, neutrality, complementarity, and homeostasis problematic. Circular causality, which implies that members engage in a never-ending, repetitive pattern of mutually reinforcing behaviors, is regarded by feminists as a sophisticated version of blaming the victim and rationalizing the status quo (Goldner, 1985a).

When applied to situations of family violence, circular causality suggests that the perpetrator and victim are equally involved in producing and maintaining "the problem." Feminist therapists challenge mainstream family theory by insisting that women are *not* equally responsible for their own abuse. They assert that attributing abuse to circular causality subtly removes responsibility from the abuser while implying that the victim contributes to the problem by playing into the interaction pattern that results in abuse.

Similarly, systemic notions of neutrality, which emphasize that all parts of the system contribute equally to the production and maintenance of problems, overlook differences in family members' power. Feminists disagree with the idea that social workers should avoid holding one family member responsible for a problem. By remaining neutral, they argue, traditional helpers contribute to the maintenance of the status quo.

Feminists also challenge *complementarity*—the view that gender disparities are acceptable because men and women play separate but equal roles in family life. According to traditional views, men are responsible for the economic well-being of the family, while women are responsible for care and services provided to family members. In order words, under the traditional model, wives are responsible for almost everything that keeps the family operating smoothly, such as housework and child care (Eichler, 1997). Feminists point out that while the homemaker role is esteemed in the abstract, actual work is denigrated (Pogrebin, 1980). Moreover, women are socialized to assume responsibility for the emotional well-being of the family. Goldner (1985a) alerts us to this bias: "We think of mothers as gatekeepers, regulating the interaction between the family and the outside world, and also as switchboards, regulating communication patterns within the family" (p. 39).

A major concern about gender bias in family work is the long-standing tendency of the helping professions to blame mothers for problems of other members or the family as a whole. Mothers have been looked upon as the crucial (and often only) socialization agent of children (Mackie, 1991). The practice of mother-blaming is both pervasive and disturbing (Caplan & Hall-McCorquodale, 1985). Issues such as attachment disorders (Bowlby, 1969), schizophrenia (Weakland & Fry, 1974), and more recently sexual abuse (Trepper & Barrett, 1986) have all been laid at the doorstep of poor "mothering." Mothers have been blamed for participating in their own abuse. In the literature, mothers are described as either overinvolved or remote. They are either incompetent or overcompetent. They are either overemotional or cold. In the etiology of child problems, mothers are emphasized as contributors to the disorders, but fathers are ignored, even when the problem originates from the father, as in the case of sexual abuse. Mothers have been blamed for the difficulties of adult men (Caplan & Hill-McCorquodale, 1991).

A central tenet of family systems theory asserts that the family, as a living organism, attempts to maintain a balance or homeostasis. This view of family functioning eliminates individual responsibility, because all behavior is understood as an attempt to maintain homeostasis. Family homeostasis and mother-blaming work together to preserve the antiwoman bias evident in family systems theory.

Family social workers should take special note of how homeostasis has been used to explain family problems, particularly when the problem involves victimization. For example, family systems theorists who discuss the causes of intrafamilial sexual abuse have interpreted the father's behavior in positive terms (i.e., a misguided attempt to show affection), while suggesting mothers should be assessed for inhibited sexual desire. Not only are fathers given positive intent for the abuse, mothers become responsible for maintaining homeostasis. Again, in the words of Goldner (1985a), "Insofar as all roads lead to Mom, her excesses and deficiencies will indeed make an enormous difference in how life flows around her and how the children develop" (p. 40).

DIFFERENT PERSPECTIVES ON FAMILY PROBLEMS

Think of a family with whom you are familiar. How would you assess this family's problems? Redefine the problems to include dimensions of power and gender.

The Ecological Orientation of Gender-Sensitive Practice

In assessing family problems, gender-sensitive family social workers recognize the influence of the economic, political, and social environments in which people live, as well as the prevailing social attitudes and expectations that frame gender roles. By recognizing the social context of gender roles and associated traits, FSWs can better understand why men abuse their partners emotionally and physically. Additionally, they realize that women may remain in abusive relationships because of feelings of powerlessness, helplessness, and lack of control over their lives.

Traditional family systems theorists have failed to recognize how family problems are connected to socially prescribed gender roles and power imbalances, and thus have not acknowledged how the interactions between family members are affected by the larger social system (Goodrich, Rampage, Ellman, & Halstead, 1988, p. 12). Feminists point out that trying to assess a family's problems without regard to ecological embeddedness "is like watching a parade through a key hole" (Goldner, 1985a, p. 34).

The larger social context needs to be considered when looking at family dysfunction. Feminists suggest that cultural values and beliefs about gender influence how families function, with the larger cultural context playing a role in wife battering and child abuse.

SOCIAL VALUES THAT PERPETUATE FAMILY PROBLEMS

Family violence is not new, nor does it represent a backlash against feminism. In an investigation of family violence from colonial times to the present, Pleck (1987) suggested that three central societal values have hindered attempts to eliminate family violence. These values include beliefs about family privacy, family stability, and conjugal and parental rights.

Family Privacy

Over time, there has been lack of agreement about how much families should be left to their own devices without outside intervention from the state. Some of the value placed on family privacy is based on the belief that intimate family relationships should be free from state intrusion and interference. As stated by Pleck (1987), "Modern defenders are likely to argue that the family has a constitutional right to privacy or insist that the home is the only setting where intimacy can flourish, providing meaning, coherence and stability in personal life" (p. 8).

In the same fashion, behavior within families is often viewed differently from behavior outside the family. "When we think of the family, and then think of the world that surrounds it, we tend to think in terms of contrasts" (Goldner, 1988, p. 24). For example, abuse of family members is sometimes attributed to family dynamics, but similar behavior directed toward a neighbor is viewed as assault.

Social isolation has become the downside of family privacy. Many families seen by family social workers are socially isolated, making access to social resources difficult. Privacy removes problems from scrutiny and keeps family members from sources of social support and information.

Family social workers must identify their personal beliefs about family privacy and decide what impact their beliefs and agency mandates may have in working with families. When families are involuntary clients, the family social worker must cross the line concerning privacy. If a family social worker is uncertain about how to deal with issues of privacy, he or she may be governed by politeness instead of dealing with family problems. Drawing artificial boundaries around the family inhibits family work.

Efforts to safeguard family privacy affect social work practice, especially when abuse is suspected. Notions about privacy may protect abusers from legal consequences and prevent victims of family violence from using resources to escape the abuse.

Family Stability

Keeping families together is a central goal of family social workers. When working with people involved in abuse, however, FSWs may be forced to choose between two basic values: the autonomy of the family and the protection of children (Giovanonni, 1982). Making this choice is difficult because the measure of success for family social workers is often keeping the family together.

Traditionally, one way of ensuring family stability has been to reinforce established gender roles by keeping the male at the "head." Encouraging the independence of women has been viewed as a threat to the family unit (Cherlin, 1983). Gordon contends that "the concept of the autonomous family, in fact, as it is manipulated in contemporary political discourse, is generally used in opposition to women's rights as autonomous citizens" (Gordon, 1985, p. 218). Family social workers need to examine personal biases about gender roles, to consider what it means to empower *every* member of the family unit.

Traditionally, social workers' struggle to preserve family stability in situations of gender-based abuse has sometimes meant keeping the male in his traditional role as family patriarch. Family social workers must decide whether the goal of preserving family stability meets the needs of every family member, particularly those who are vulnerable. Does failure to preserve the family make the intervention a failure?

The desire to maintain family stability has frequently led family social workers to make mothers the focal point of intervention, because traditionally women have assumed responsibility for family well-being. A mother may feel pressured to keep the family together even at great personal emotional cost. Moreover, the family's economic welfare may be at risk. As recounted by Goldner (1985a), "She knows that she has much more at stake and much more to lose if things don't work out than the man she married...the breakdown of the traditional family has too often meant a new kind of freedom for men and a new kind of trap for women" (p. 41).

Conjugal and Parental Rights

From a feminist perspective, marriage is a relationship based upon an unequal distribution of power, usually with the male as the dominant partner. "Truly, position is power" (Munson, 1993, p. 362). The husband is often the primary wage-earner, and his position is validated politically, socially, and economically. He is usually physically more powerful, a fact that makes potential abuse of his power threatening to other family members. In patriarchal societies such as ours, both women and children have traditionally been considered possessions of the father, making them vulnerable to boundary violations and violence (Armstrong, 1987; Nelson, 1987). Feminists therefore consider the traditional husband as the benefactor of the marital relationship at the expense of the wife.

Power hierarchies within families are influenced by both gender and generation. These factors play an important role in how families are structured (Goldner, 1988), providing fundamental organizing principles of family life. Power comes from socially endorsed *conjugal and parental rights*. Just as there are special privileges and power imbalances outside the family, there are "private" power imbalances and special privileges inside the family. Women have power over children, and men have power over women (Mackie, 1991).

EFFECTS OF SOCIETAL VALUES ON FSWS AND CLIENTS

Three central societal values influence the FSW's role: family privacy, family stability, and conjugal/parental rights. List three of your beliefs concerning each value. Describe some of the effects these beliefs may have on your work with clients.

POWER IMBALANCES IN FAMILY RELATIONSHIPS

One of the strongest critiques of family therapy by feminists is the assertion that by failing to challenge the imbalance of power in families, family therapy has sanctioned this imbalance (Dye Holten, 1990). Because feminist practice is primarily concerned with power and its distribution, feminist theory looks at inequality in family relationships. A fundamental aim of feminism is to ensure that power used in family relations is appropriate and healthy.

Under the law, husbands, wives, mothers, fathers, and children have certain rights and obligations. A second source of power concerns gender norms established by society. Gender power is changing as traditional role definitions change. Changes in gender roles may create confusion in families, and members may face conflicts as roles change. A third source of power involves access to knowledge and resources. People can increase their personal power base by improving their formal education and obtaining more resources, such as money, information, or social support. Women usually have less economic power than men, and economic dependency becomes especially potent with the arrival of children (Mackie, 1991). However, when wives have greater status or money than their husbands, divorce is more likely to occur.

Personality differences influence the distribution of power in family life. Members with high self-esteem, for example, are likely to have more power than those with low self-esteem. People who are outgoing, talkative, and assertive are also considered to have greater power and control than those who are not.

Another important source of power involves factors such as age and the present stage of life. Changes in life situations that affect personal power are sometimes difficult to understand and constitute potentially stressful life events. For instance, an unemployed husband may not have the same status and power he enjoyed while working. The loss of power from a change in life situations may be accompanied by sadness, anger, or both.

A final source of power influencing family members can be described as "emotional factors." Family members vary in their ability and willingness to give or withhold love and affection. Motives also vary on this dimension, with some family members exerting control with manifestations of love, affection, dominance, force, denial, or rejection.

Not all power discrepancies in families are destructive. For example, parents should have more power than their children (Brock & Barnard, 1992). Every family has unique power dynamics based on age, sex, education, personality, and life situations. Couples need to be acutely aware of these factors in exercising power with each other.

Power is not diminished or lost when it is shared with others. In fact, shared power provides balance in families, and satisfaction is highest when all family members feel they share in the family's power. A family council or regular marital review is one way families can equalize power distribution. Emotionally healthy families use power to support one another, while troubled families use power to distort, control, or dominate. Appropriate use of power helps members reach their potential and provides maximum benefit to family members.

Regardless of how power relates to gender in the family, social workers need to be sensitive to issues of power. For example, some parents, in discussing their experiences in a family-centered program, reported feeling resentful when social workers allied themselves with some family members at the expense of others. Forming an alliance with a child was often perceived as a sabotage of parental authority (Coleman & Collins, 1997).

Gender-sensitive FSWs strive to model egalitarian relationships with families. Rather than taking an authoritarian role, they try to empower family members. Thus, they demonstrate the benefits of sharing power rather than appropriating it for oneself.

SOCIALIZATION AND GENDER ROLES

Families provide a socializing environment for children. Mothers and fathers interact with their children differently. For example, mothers are more likely to feed, clean, and protect children whereas fathers tend to play with them more (Mackie, 1991). Similarly, mothers often are more involved in the daily routine of child care and discipline.

Children are often treated differently based on gender. Parents cuddle female infants and talk to them, and they handle male infants less gently and play with them more. Boys are more likely to be spanked as a form of discipline, whereas girls are more likely to be verbally reprimanded. Achievement is expected more from male children than female children. Parents are also more likely to punish behavior that deviates from social expectations of the child's gender and reward behavior that fits the mold of the specific gender. For example, parents are more likely to discourage independent activities of girl children and to discourage dependence in male children. If parents observe a male child struggling with a problem, they are inclined to let him find his own solution. With a female child, they are more likely to take over and solve the problem instead of letting her do it alone. Boys are often pressured to cover up or deny feelings of sadness and vulnerability (Pollack, 1998).

GENDER ROLES

Think about your family of origin. How did your family encourage traditional gender roles for its members? How was flexibility of roles encouraged?

Overall, fathers are most responsible for the sex typing of the children. Researchers have noted that fathers are more likely than mothers to reinforce stereotypical gender behavior in children.

How parents relate to one another will also affect children's perceptions of their own gender. For example, Pogrebin (1980) suggests that how the family allocates roles regarding household tasks and paid employment affects children's competence, their ability to overcome stereotypical notions, and their occupational choices.

Feminists note that despite the fact that many families are headed by dual-career couples, role arrangements within the family often have remained static. Most people acknowledge that men *should* contribute equally to domestic duties, but the reality is different. In the words of Eichler (1997), "There is an amazing inelasticity in men's contributions to household tasks; no matter how much there is to do, men do the same amount" (p. 60). Thus, women often continue to shoulder the burden of family and household responsibilities even when they also hold jobs outside the home.

Influences on children's gender role socialization are pervasive. Some of the influences are subtle, while others are blatant. Family social workers need to be attuned to biases involved in child-rearing and to recognize how sexist biases handicap both male and female development.

To be gender-sensitive is to be aware of the different behaviors, attitudes, and socialization experiences associated with growing up male or female, especially differences in power, status, position, and privilege within the family and in society in general. Gender-sensitive family social workers strive to empower clients and enable them to move beyond prescribed sex roles to roles in which they have expanded options.

NONSEXIST CHILD-REARING

Describe behaviors that you consider inappropriate for girls but appropriate for boys, and vice versa. For example, some people would find it inappropriate for male children to play with dolls. Indicate why each behavior is inappropriate.

DIVISION OF LABOR IN FAMILIES

Relationships between men and women often change after the birth of the first child. A woman who remains at home with an infant, even for a short period, often falls behind her spouse with regard to career advancement. The man becomes the "breadwinner," while the woman assumes the traditional role of housekeeper and mother. Child-rearing removes women from public roles while men gain power.

Marriage and parenthood have a different impact on men and women. Regardless of the labor status of the partners, females continue to do most of the work within the home. Domestic involvement encompasses housework, child care, emotional support of family members, and maintenance of the family's social status (Mackie, 1991). Traditional norms dictate that the first priority of women will be the family.

Domestic responsibilities are not distributed evenly in the family. This appears to be related to conjugal power. Housework and child care limits the amount of time in which a parent can pursue personal interests and career development. Men "help" out with the housework, while women have the primary responsibility for ensuring that jobs get done. In addition, men are said to "baby-sit" their own children. There are indications, however, that women's movement into the workforce has increased their conjugal power (Mackie, 1991).

Men's lives can be broadened and enriched when they nurture children and assume responsibility in family relationships. Unfortunately, some men resist changes in their roles. One explanation for the increase in divorce rates over the past two decades is that more women have been refusing to take sole responsibility for familial nurturing and communication, household tasks, and child care. Instead, they expect their husbands to share these duties. Only when a male assumes equal responsibility for these tasks can the marital and parental relationship evolve into an equal partnership. Dissatisfaction develops when a woman anticipates an equal partnership, and although her partner may verbally agree, little change actually occurs.

The challenge of getting men to take housework and parenting seriously has been described as "troublesome, problematic, and complex" (Braverman, 1991, p. 25). In the 1990s, most wives worked approximately 1.5 hours more each day than their husbands, including part-time jobs, housework, and child care. This amounts to an extra month of twenty-four-hour days per year. Only about 20 percent of husbands share equally in housework and child care (Carter, 1992). In order to preserve marriages, husbands and wives have constructed myths that support the egalitarian ideal of marriage, while in reality playing stereotypical, traditional roles (Carter, 1992). For example, the wife is responsible for laundry, while the husband tends the car—hardly an equitable arrangement. Laundry consumes approximately four hours per week, while responsibility for the car demands only four hours a month. Women have changed their roles drastically, but male roles seem to have remained static.

Gender-sensitive social work seeks to empower women to assume greater control over their lives, rather than to adapt to oppressive circumstances. The following example illustrates a gender-sensitive approach to assisting a family.

Jorge and Liz Martinez have four children, ages nine, seven, five, and three. The family came to the attention of the family social work agency when neighbors reported that the oldest child, nine-year-old Anabella, was left home as primary caretaker while both parents worked. The FSW, John Preston, learned that Mr. Martinez worked as a city employee and Mrs. Martinez was employed full-time as a legal secretary. Both were required to work long hours, putting in overtime several nights a week. Mrs. Martinez reported feeling overwhelmed by her schedule. In addition to her job, she was responsible for the care of home and family. She turned to her daughter Anabella for help.

Mr. Martinez felt that his wife should take care of the household, as his mother had done when he was growing up. He believed that his contribution to the family was to keep a stable job and bring home a weekly paycheck, as well as maintain the yard and make car repairs. After all, Mr. Martinez explained, his own mother had raised nine children, kept a spotless home, and never complained.

The FSW asked Mr. and Mrs. Martinez to make a list of the tasks they performed and the amount of time involved in each. Mr. Martinez was surprised to discover that doing the laundry took his wife four hours per week, while maintaining the cars took him only four hours per month. The FSW also helped

Mr. Martinez reassess his traditional expectations of family life in the context of a nontraditional household with a full-time working mother. Although Mr. Martinez still did not feel comfortable doing "women's work," he began to understand the bind his wife was in. The family did not have much extra money, but they decided to pay Mr. Martinez's sixteen-year-old niece to baby-sit and do light housekeeping after school.

DIVISION OF LABOR BASED ON GENDER

Based on your own family of origin, complete the following list of household chores, allocating percentages to each parent. Put a check mark next to each task that you feel should be assigned on the basis of gender.

Task	Percent Done by Mother	Percent Done by Father
Buy groceries.		
Prepare meals.		
Stay home when children are sick.		
Shop for children's clothes.		
Vacuum rugs.		
Take children to doctor.		
Attend school functions.		
Attend parent-teacher interviews.		
Help children with homework.		
Handle finances.		
Do the dishes.		
Do the laundry.		
Clean bathrooms.		
Discipline children.		
Change beds.		
Feed pets.		
Maintain lawn.		
Maintain car.		
Put children to bed.		
Other (describe)		

RECOMMENDATIONS FOR GENDER-SENSITIVE FAMILY SOCIAL WORK

Gender-sensitive practice promotes equality between men and women. The FSW strives to help family members examine their assumptions about gender roles as a prerequisite for deciding which aspects to keep and which to discard.

Within the context of marital relationships, a gender-sensitive philosophy embraces equality in decision making and shared participation in household tasks and child care. FSWs help families to understand the connection between socially constructed gender roles and family dynamics.

Family social work that is gender-sensitive is action-oriented, not merely nonsexist. Whereas nonsexist counselors attempt to avoid reinforcing stereotypical thinking about gender roles, proactive gender-sensitive family social workers help clients to recognize how their own perceptions have been affected by internalizing these stereotypes. Clients are better helped when they have an opportunity to perceive and overcome social and political barriers.

The following guidelines will be helpful for FSWs who aim for gender-sensitive practice:

- Do not focus solely on mother-child interactions. Make every effort to include fathers in the intervention, thereby ensuring that both parents are actively involved in the lives of the children.

- Do not concentrate treatment on mothers only. Consider both parents when looking at parenting, taking histories, and changing individual behaviors. Fathers must be included in all aspects of assessment and intervention.

- Discuss gender-related issues with families. Help clients determine the division of household and child care tasks between parents (Goldenberg & Goldenberg, 1996). Explore the distribution of power within the family, and be especially alert to signs of abuse of power such as evidence of domestic violence.

- Look for the strengths of women, rather than concentrating on pathology.

- Integrate the socio-political status of gender into family work (Good, Gilbert & Scher, 1990). Do not assume that any family member should or should not do something just because of gender. Males can do laundry, just as females can work outside the home.

- Be conscious of personal biases. This involves confronting personal agendas and becoming aware of blind spots related to gender (Brock & Barnard, 1992). Families improve more when social workers are warm and actively structure interventions with families (Green & Herget, 1991).

- Realize that families take different forms and that no monolithic family structure is superior to all others. Judgments about the desirability of family structure and composition must thereby be made in terms of the effects on family members, not adherence to rigidly prescribed gender roles.

- Recognize that increasing equitability will require that one family member give up some power and privilege. The member who benefited the most from the inequity may resist relinquishing power.

- Some families may prefer adhering to traditional gender roles. In working with these families, the family social worker should not impose different beliefs on them. However, the family social worker must be certain that the entire family is satisfied with the current role division, rather than being enforced by the most powerful family member.

- Encourage family members to take pride in their contributions to family life. Women's work is as essential as men's work.

CHAPTER SUMMARY

The gender-sensitive perspective captures an attitude regarding the impact of traditional gender roles on problems experienced by families. Traditional family therapists endorse a systems view of family functioning in which members share equal responsibility for family problems, but gender-sensitive FSWs recognize unequal power distributions and strive to empower women and children who have been victimized by inequitable family power arrangements.

Family social workers seek to understand gender roles within the economic, political, and social contexts in which families exist. Gender-sensitive FSWs strive for political, economic, and social justice for women and children, whom they perceive as unequal partners in family life.

Feminist theory acknowledges the core inequality that is inherent in most spousal relationships. Sources of gender-based power include the legal system, societal norms, educational and financial resources, personality differences, life circumstances (age, location, or life stage), and emotional factors.

Gender-sensitive social workers seek to empower families by increasing their awareness of available options. Parents can be encouraged to share equally in child care and household tasks, raising their children in a nonsexist atmosphere that recognizes each individual's capabilities and contributions to family life.

12 Culturally Sensitive Practice

Family social workers must be able to work with clients from diverse ethnic and cultural backgrounds. Culture and ethnicity are related but not interchangeable concepts: "Culture refers to the culmination of values, beliefs, customs, and norms that people have learned, usually in the context of their family and community. Ethnicity relates to a client's identity, commitment, and loyalty to an ethnic group" (Jordan & Franklin, 1995, p. 169). Awareness of the historical background of different ethnic groups is important, as is knowledge of the customs and beliefs shared by members of each group. Following is a discussion of four diverse populations—African American, Hispanic American, Asian American, and Native American—followed by guidelines for assessment and intervention of families from each group. We conclude by discussing issues involved in working with children from minority groups.

CHARACTERISTICS SHARED BY PEOPLE OF COLOR

Family social workers must be careful not to stereotype people, as individual differences exist among people of similar ethnic and cultural backgrounds. Some of these differences may be related to varying levels of acculturation. Still, certain characteristics distinguish ethnic minority cultures from the dominant or majority white middle-class culture in the United States and Canada. Ho (1987) outlines six characteristics: ethnic minority reality, impact of external systems on minority cultures, biculturalism, ethnic differences in minority status, ethnicity and language, and ethnicity and social class.

1. *Ethnic minority reality:* Members of ethnic minority groups often experience poverty and racial discrimination, resulting in underutilization of mental health services.

2. *Impact of external system on minority cultures:* Ethnic minority values may conflict with those of the majority culture on issues such as exerting control over versus living in harmony with the environment, orientation to time (past, present, future), "doing" versus "being" orientation, individual autonomy versus collectivity, and the importance of nuclear versus extended family relationships.

3. *Biculturalism:* The ethnic minority person belongs to two cultures. The level of acculturation into the dominant culture is an important aspect of the assessment of families seeking mental health services.

4. *Ethnic differences in minority status:* Status of various ethnic minority groups differ. Some groups experience more discrimination than others. For instance, refugees may receive better treatment than the descendants of slaves. Skin color is another determinant of status; populations of darker skin color often experience harsher societal discrimination.

5. *Ethnicity and language:* Ethnic minority people seeking mental health services from non-bilingual helpers are at risk of being misunderstood or even misdiagnosed. Use of interpreters is fraught with problems; for instance, asking a bilingual child to interpret between the family social worker and an elderly family member can upset the hierarchical structure of the family by putting the child in a position of power.

6. *Ethnicity and social class:* Social class (level of education, income, standing in the community) is important to assess, as higher status usually leads to a higher level of well-being and greater access to resources. In some cases, however, individuals may be discriminated against by the dominant culture despite their high social-class standing, while at the same time being rejected by other members of their ethnic group because of their high level of acculturation into the mainstream culture. (List headings are from Ho, 1987, pp. 14–18; explanations have been paraphrased by the authors.)

These six factors will be discussed further as we explore the history and family styles of African, Hispanic, Asian, and Native American populations.

AFRICAN AMERICANS

Ho (1987) describes the African American family as stressing "collectivity, sharing, affiliation, deference to authority, spirituality, and respect for the elderly" (p. 188).

History

A group characterized by being uprooted from its homeland and brought to this country involuntarily, African Americans have experienced more societal discrimination than most other ethnic groups. Hill (in Jordan, Lewellen, & Vandiver, 1994) identified six survival skills utilized by African Americans in a hostile society: (1) strong kinship bonds; (2) strong education and work achievement orientation; (3) flexibility in family roles;

(4) commitment to religious values and church participation; (5) a humanistic orientation; (6) an endurance of suffering.

Beliefs About Family

Ho (in Jordan, Lewellen, & Vandiver, 1994) calls attention to the high ratio of female-headed households among African American families. One cause may be high mortality rates of African American males. Consequently, families tend toward egalitarian sharing of roles. Mothers often shoulder the economic, breadwinner burden, as well as taking responsibility for child care. The extended family network is likely to be involved in supporting the family, as is the church "family."

Children are treated in an egalitarian fashion and given responsibility based on age. The oldest child may be responsible for looking after younger sisters and brothers.

HISPANIC AMERICANS

Hispanic Americans are also called Latinos, Mexicanos, Hispanics, Spanish-speaking Americans, Spanish Americans, and Spanish-surnamed Americans; this population has a higher percentage of poor and unemployed members than the other groups discussed here (Ho, 1987).

History

Ho (1987) discusses five unifying values of the various Hispanic subgroups, though each group has distinct differences due to the melding of their Hispanic culture with that of various indigenous Indian groups. These five values are

1. *Familism:* a sense of family obligation and pride.
2. *Personalism:* a value placed on the inner qualities of the individual's uniqueness and goodness. (Machismo, a related concept, refers to the male's sense of self-assurance and calm when threatened.)
3. *Hierarchy:* a value on social class position, including a patriarchal structure.
4. *Spiritualism:* a belief in good and bad spirits that intervene in one's life.
5. *Fatalism:* a belief that one cannot master the world and that one's destiny is inevitable (Ho in Jordan & Franklin, 1995).

Beliefs About Family

Similarities across subcultures may be seen in the Hispanic American family structure. For instance, the individual's needs are viewed as secondary to those of the family (Jordan, Lewellen, & Vandiver, 1994). The family system is patriarchal and hierarchical; the father is the head of the household and the parents have authority over the children. Belief in the intervention of good or bad spirits leads families to attribute mental illness to bad spirits and to rely on help from folk healers and priests.

ASIAN AMERICANS

As with African American families, Asian American families comprise many subcultures with diverse backgrounds, beliefs, and values. Similarities that cut across groups, as outlined by Ho (1987), are identified here.

History

Asian American families share Confucian and Buddhist philosophies and ethics. They value living in harmony with nature and fostering interpersonal relationships. Buddhism encourages "harmonious living involving compassion, a respect for life, and moderation in behavior; self-discipline, patience, modesty, and friendliness, as well as selflessness" (Ho, 1987, p. 25). Confucian philosophy and ethics "specify a familial hierarchy which demands loyalty, respect, and obedience, especially to the parents" (Jordan, Lewellen, & Vandiver, 1994). Time orientation is toward the past and present, rather than toward the future. Ancestors are important to their surviving family members in that members strive to perpetuate the family's good name.

Beliefs About Family

The structure of Asian American families is hierarchical and patriarchal. Parents are influential in mate selection. Children respect and obey their parents, and wives respect and obey their husbands. The wife may have low status in the family, but educational attainment may raise her status. Families are maintained by a sense of obligation and consequently undergo shame or loss of face if family expectations are not met. Siblings have special roles and obligations according to birth order, with the eldest son obliged to provide a home for his widowed mother. The oldest son carries the highest status among the siblings; the youngest daughter may be obliged to care for her elderly parents. Children in the roles of eldest son and youngest daughter have higher rates of stress-related illness than other children, reflecting the strains involved in carrying out their familial obligations.

NATIVE AMERICANS

Acculturation varies among members of tribal groupings of Native Americans. Some live on reservations in primarily rural areas, where they remain isolated and may speak little English. At the other extreme are families living in urban areas, separated from their Indian heritage and totally acculturated into the majority culture. In between are those who try to maintain a balance between their ancestral heritage and the culture of the dominant society (Ho, 1987). The family social worker must be sensitive to each family's level of acculturation, while remaining aware of Native Americans' unique historical background.

History

Members of different tribes hold different beliefs, yet there are certain unifying concepts that distinguish Native Americans from members of other cultures (Ho, 1987). Nature is important to Native Americans, who believe that they are one part of the whole and who strive to appreciate and maintain a balance with other living things. Spiritually, Native Americans believe that all growing things and animals have spirits or souls that should be respected. The respect for nature leads the Native American to view time in terms of natural cycles or seasons.

Native Americans display a cooperative spirit when interacting with others, rather than a competitive orientation. "This concept of collaterality reflects the integrated view of the universe where all people, animals, plants, and objects in nature have their place in creating a harmonious whole" (Ho, 1987).

"Giveaway" is a traditional Native American practice of bestowing one's belongings on others to honor them or to honor deceased relatives. Native American children are taught to respect others' right to be or do as they wish, and not to meddle. The Native American believes in good triumphing over evil; therefore, people are viewed as primarily good. Religious beliefs vary among the different tribes, but a similar emphasis is placed on rituals and ceremonies. Tribal medicine people may be consulted for treatment of physical and mental problems, rather than physicians or other health professionals.

Beliefs About Family

Extended family networks (which may include non-kin namesakes) are important. These groups may or may not live together in one household, but extended family groups provide support for Native American families. Support may be in the form of modeling marital and parental roles. Traditionally, marriages were arranged by two families, with the husband joining the wife's household but retaining authority with his own kin. Spousal interactions were not intimate, with the wife having lower status than her husband, to whom she was to be supportive and submissive. Today, the level of acculturation influences marital relationships. Native Americans who are most acculturated to the majority society have the most egalitarian spousal relationships. Intermarriage is common between members of different Native American groups, and between Native Americans and members of other racial groups. Divorce and remarriage are acceptable practices in Native American society. In some tribes, polygamous relationships are accepted.

Children, who are seen as important to the renewal of tribal life, historically have held high status in Native American families. Children were disciplined and taught by extended family members in an egalitarian fashion. Corporal punishment was not used; rather, "observation and participation" (Ho, 1987) were preferred child-rearing techniques. In the extended family environment, the child was surrounded by many siblings and cousins, with the older children often caring for and teaching the younger children.

▉ YOUR ETHNIC BACKGROUND

What is your own ethnic background? List five beliefs that stem from your unique background.

GUIDELINES FOR ASSESSING MINORITY FAMILIES

Mapping techniques such as genograms, ecomaps, and time lines are particularly helpful because they emphasize assessment of the extended family. The FSW will also observe family interactions during home visits.

Assessment Issues for African American Families

Socioeconomic status, educational level, cultural identity, family structure, and reactions to racism are important variables in assessing African American families (Sue & Sue in Jordan, Lewellen, & Vandiver, 1994). An ecomap can be used to collect important information about family strengths and community resources, the quality of relationships between family members, and family members' relationships with their neighbors (Ho, 1987).

Assessment Issues for Hispanic American Families

Hispanic American families may experience discrimination, underemployment, and lack of housing or other resources, and these problems should not be overlooked in the assessment (Jordan, Lewellen, & Vandiver, 1994). Level of acculturation, or assimilation into the ways of the dominant culture, is a major issue for Hispanic families. Three levels of acculturation are commonly found among Hispanic American families: immigrant families who have just arrived, immigrant-American families, and immigrant-descent families (Padella et al. and Casas & Keefe in Jordan, Lewellen, & Vandiver, 1994).

The first group, newly arrived immigrant families, have yet to be acculturated into the new country's values and ways. Family members usually speak little or no English.

Immigrant American families, the second group, consists of parents born in the old country and children born in the new country. This may result in a clash between oldsters and youth as children are acculturated more rapidly into the new country.

The third group, immigrant-descent families, consists of all generations born in the new country. Members of this group are likely to be fully acculturated into the new country.

Assessment Issues for Asian American Families

Acculturation to the dominant society is a concern when assessing Asian American families. Barriers to service provision may include unfamiliarity with the health care system in a new country, language difficulties, and cultural traditions and values that conflict with those of the dominant culture (Jordan, Lewellen, & Vandiver, 1994). Vietnamese and Laotian families may have spent time as refugees in resettlement camps, and thus been exposed to great traumas. The family social worker should be sensitive to this possibility and assess the family's need to obtain appropriate services for stress-related illnesses.

Assessment Issues for Native American Families

Red Horse (1980) describes three types of Native American families that require different kinds of assistance. First is the traditional family governed by tribal customs and beliefs. Older members speak the native language, and the extended family network is influential. The second type is the nontraditional or bicultural family. Though the extended family network is important and the older generation may speak the native tongue, English is primarily spoken. The family interacts freely and comfortably with members of the dominant culture. The third type is the pan-traditional family. These families are seeking to reconnect with their cultural heritage. Bicultural families are most apt to seek services from mental health professionals. When traditional or pan-traditional families require help, they are likely to consult tribal community helpers or religious leaders.

In addition to considering the family type when assessing Native American families, the family social worker should be aware of their history as victims of discrimination. Historically, Native Americans were coerced into signing unfavorable treaties that stripped them of their land and way of life. In some cases, children were separated from their parents. Consequently, Native Americans have experienced poverty, unemployment, alcoholism, family disruption, and other effects of discrimination.

GUIDELINES FOR INTERVENTION WITH MINORITY FAMILIES

The International Association of Psychosocial Rehabilitation Services established a goal of developing culturally competent services. Cultural competence refers to sensitiveness and responsiveness to different cultures. Recognition of ethnic and cultural differences should include efforts to adapt treatment to fit the culture and ethnicity of the family and community context in which services are delivered. To achieve cultural competence in service provision, the IAPRS (1997) recommends:

1. Inclusion of culturally competent concepts in organizations' mission statements, policies, procedures, and practices.
2. Inclusion of cultural competence standards and indicators in organizations' research and evaluation programs.
3. Inclusion of cultural competence training programs in organizations' operations.
4. Quantity and quality of support given to staff members who belong to under-represented minority groups.
5. Increased bilingual/bicultural staff from target ethnic and cultural groups.
6. Increased number of volunteers, board, and staff from target ethnic and cultural groups.
7. Increased number of chapters, agencies, and staff who attend multicultural activities, conferences, and seminars.
8. Increased number of clients served from ethnic and cultural target groups.
9. Increased self, family, and community referrals from ethnic and cultural target groups.
10. Reduced incidence of agency dropouts, emergencies, and rehospitalizations among members of targeted ethnic and cultural groups.
11. Increased documentation of advocacy activities specifically against cultural, sexist, ethnic, and disability discrimination.
12. Increased meetings between agency representatives and cultural and ethnic community leaders.
13. Increased involvement of family, especially extended family as defined by the cultural or ethnic group, in the rehabilitation process.
14. Availability of services and brochures that are language-appropriate.
15. Agency environment reflecting the target ethnic and cultural group(s) served.
16. Increased number and type of multicultural activities that occur in the agency.
17. Increased number and type of culturally appropriate modalities, alternative approaches, and innovative methods.

Family therapy techniques for FSWs to use with minorities are those that promote bonding between the social worker and the family. In order to engage the family, the social worker may adopt the family's verbal and nonverbal communication style and relevant metaphors. Other family systems techniques that may be used include behavioral methods such as social skills training. For instance, specialized treatment packages are available to help families learn better communication, problem solving, or anger management techniques. (See Franklin & Jordan, 1998.)

Intervention with African American Families

Lewellen and Jordan (1994) found that feelings of family empowerment and satisfaction with services were related to successful family intervention. Further, trust and communication style were important variables. African Americans, in comparison to other ethnic groups, reportedly were more sensitive to such matters as insensitivity of the family worker. Members of this group reported less trust in the establishment, including mental health service providers. Lack of trust may result in guarded communications and defensive interactions with the family social worker. Specific recommendations for working with African American families include the following (Jordan, Lewellen, & Vandiver, 1994, p. 12):

1. Offer services to the extended family network or to groups of families who support each other.

2. Take into account the needs of single, female heads of households, including transportation problems, accommodation to work schedules, and babysitting needs.

3. Consider flexible hours for meetings so that extended family members may attend. Also, consider transportation and lodging needs for extended family.

4. Services should be brief and time-limited to encourage attendance of families who may distrust the mental health system.

5. Treatment focusing on psychoeducational and social skills methodology may be used, as well as direct communication with the family about treatment issues.

6. The family social worker must be willing and able to acknowledge racism and issues that may impede self-disclosure by African American family members.

7. African American family members value mutuality and egalitarianism; thus, the family social worker should provide services that respect the client family and include the family in the decision-making process.

Intervention with Hispanic American Families

Intervention issues for Hispanic American families may be identified by looking at families according to their level of acculturation:

> Group 1, newly arrived immigrant families, need concrete services such as language instruction, information, referral, and advocacy. Efforts must be made to reach out to these families as they may not access services on their own due to language and cultural barriers.
>
> Immigrant-American families may require conflict resolution, problem-solving, or anger management training due to intergenerational conflicts.
>
> Immigrant-descent families are more comfortable seeking traditional mental health services. They likely speak both Spanish and English in the home and are acculturated into the dominant culture (Padella et al. and Casas & Keefe in Jordan, Lewellen, & Vandiver, 1994, p. 13).

The family social worker may be considered as equal to a healer, priest, or physician by the Hispanic American family, depending on the family's level of acculturation. In fact, the family may have consulted a priest or folk healer first, before seeking services from an agency.

Jordan, Lewellen, and Vandiver (1994, p. 14) make the following recommendations for work with Hispanic American families:

1. Time-limited treatment which includes the family and extended family, due to the importance and insularity of the family;

2. Content sensitive to the family's level of acculturation, beliefs, hierarchy, and traditions;

3. Treatment sensitive to role confusion and conflict the newly arrived family may be experiencing; thus, techniques including communication skills, negotiation training, and role clarification may be important;

4. Treatment sensitive the family's need for education, information, and referral services;

5. Inclusion of folk healers, priests, or other nonrelative helpers.

Intervention with Asian American Families

Jordan, Lewellen, and Vandiver (1994) suggest techniques to enhance service provision to Asian American families. Because hierarchy is important to Asian American families, treatment plans should include high-status members of the family or community. The family social worker may be seen as an authority figure and can use this status to implement positive family changes. The social worker must be sure to show respect for members of the family. Services offered within the family's neighborhood are believed to increase client participation in treatment.

Clear communication between the family social worker and family members is essential. The social worker should avoid using slang, jargon, or regional expressions. Also, if an interpreter must be used, he or she should be sensitive to the family's culture and social class. Treatment should include psychoeducational techniques. The entire family may be included in the treatment, with deference shown by the family social worker to the elderly members. Other families in the community—in centers, churches, or temples—may be utilized in support/social groups for treatment of problems such as severe and persistent mental illness.

Intervention with Native American Families

Ho (1987) makes the following recommendations for treating Native American families in a sensitive manner:

1. Provision of concrete services may be necessary for Native American families experiencing difficulties due to lack of food, housing, or other necessities. Provision of necessities helps the social worker to engage with family members.

2. The family social worker's communication with the Native American family should be "open, caring, and congruent . . . (and delivered) in a simple, precise, slow, and calm" manner (Ho, 1987, p. 94).

3. To get to know the Native American family, the FSW should observe their communication patterns and styles and note how members of the extended family network interact with one another. "To do this, the family social worker needs to be attentive, talk less, observe more, and listen actively" (Ho, 1987, p. 95).

4. Mapping techniques may be used to learn about the extended family.

5. The Native American value of the collective indicates the need for mutual establishment of treatment goals.

6. Problem solving may be facilitated by "(a) social, moral, organic reframing/relabeling; (b) mobilizing and restructuring the extended family network; (c) promoting interdependence as a family restructuring technique; (d) employing role model, educator role, and advocate role; (e) restructuring taboos for problem solving; and (f) collaborative work with medicine person, paraprofessional, and therapist helper" (Ho, 1987, p. 99).

DIFFERENT BACKGROUNDS

Talk with a friend who is from an ethnic or cultural background different from your own. Identify similarities and differences in values and beliefs. What problems would you anticipate in working with a client from the same group as your friend, considering your different values and beliefs.

SPECIAL ISSUES IN WORKING WITH MINORITY CHILDREN

Gibbs, Huang, and associates (in Jordan & Franklin, 1995) discuss five special issues that are particularly relevant when assessing and treating children of color: psychosocial adjustment, relationships with family members, school adjustment and achievement, peer relationships, and adaptation to the community.

Psychosocial Adjustment

The family social worker must be sensitive to ethnic and cultural factors when doing a psychosocial assessment of a child from an ethnic minority family. The social worker must have knowledge of the family's ethnic group, including familiarity with its beliefs, customs, and values. However, the FSW must also recognize that within each ethnic group, much individual variation exists. Therefore, it is important for the social worker to learn as much as possible about each family's beliefs, customs, and patterns of interaction. Areas to be covered in the psychosocial assessment include:

1. *Physical assessment:* low-income, ethnic minority children may be experiencing physical problems due to malnutrition or lack of proper medical care such as routine checkups and vaccinations. A physical (or eye, or dental) exam may be needed.

2. *Emotional assessment:* Feelings of self-esteem, competence, and other aspects influencing children's affect may be a product of the children's ethnic background. The family social worker should verify his or her assumptions to ascertain cultural norms.

3. *Behavioral assessment:* Behavioral factors such as aggression and achievement may be culturally determined and different from the dominant culture. For instance, achievement in sports or music may be valued more highly than academic performance. Guilt or shame may be used by the family to manage aggression.

4. *Coping and defense mechanisms:* The child may learn externalizing behaviors as coping and defense mechanisms to deal with anxiety or fear. Examples are acting-out behaviors such as fighting or talking back.

Relationships with Family Members

The family's view of appropriate child behavior is a critical element for assessment. Areas to look at include:

1. *Parent-child relationship:* Ethnic minority families may differ from the dominant culture with respect to the relationship between parents and children. Variations range from hierarchical and patriarchal relationships such as those seen in some Asian American families, to the egalitarian parent-child relationships of some Native American tribes.

2. *Birth order:* Families characterized by hierarchical structures may have rigid role prescriptions for the children. For example, the youngest daughter in an Asian American family may be charged with caring for her elderly parents.

3. *Age:* Sibling relationships may be prescribed by age; for instance, older children in Native American families may provide teaching and role modeling for younger siblings and cousins.

4. *Sex:* Male and female family members may be expected to perform different roles and may hold higher or lower family status.

5. *Family expectations:* Other expectations may be imposed on family members, such as dictates about whom children should marry, or who will care for children or elderly relatives.

School Adjustment and Achievement

School is the environment in which children interact most often with others outside the family. Factors related to school performance, provide important indicators of well-being, but assessments must include attention to ethnicity. Four important indicators of school adjustment and achievement are psychological adjustment, behavioral adjustment, academic achievement, and relationships with peers.

1. *Psychological adjustment:* Ethnic minority parents and children may fear school or view it negatively if the values of the dominant culture differ drastically from those of the family.

2. *Behavioral adjustment:* Ethnic minority families may teach their children externalizing behaviors to cope with or to solve problems. Use of these types of acting-out behaviors may get children into trouble in the school setting. It is also important for FSWs to recognize that behavioral problems may reflect underlying health problems, such as attention deficit disorder, fetal alcohol syndrome, or vision problems.

3. *Academic achievement:* If a minority child's grades in school are below average, the child may be having trouble with books and tests that are not culturally sensitive. Parents who are unfamiliar with the school system may not provide appropriate support or modeling of efficient study skills.

4. *Relationships with peers:* Children may fear appearing different from their peers and thus may be excluded (or exclude themselves) from peer group activities. Peer support from children of their own ethnic group may be unavailable.

The following example illustrates some of the issues faced by children who belong to ethnic minorities:

> Sally Redmond, a seven-year-old second grader, came to the family social work agency with her parents because of problems at school. Sally told the FSW that she did not like her school and did not care if she never went back. Her teacher has reported that Sally is quiet and withdrawn at school, has no friends, and does not take part in most activities.
>
> Sally's parents, Lou and Darlene, adopted their daughter when she was two years old. Sally's birth parents were both Korean, and she was placed in a

Korean orphanage at birth. The little girl has black hair, black eyes, and dark skin, unlike Lou and Darlene who are fair-skinned blondes.

The family social worker visited with Sally on the school playground, where she also had the opportunity to observe Sally's behavior during recess. The other children ignored Sally for the most part, but when she got in the way of some boys playing football, they called her "dumb." Later, when asked about the boys, Sally said they always talk to her like that and often make fun of the way she looks. She said she feels best when playing with the African American children "because they have skin like mine."

Sally told the FSW that she wished she looked more like her (adoptive) mother and that if she did, she would have more friends. Her teacher mentioned to the FSW that Sally does not do well in school because "She does not give me eye contact when I talk."

After talking with Sally, her parents, and her teacher, the FSW began to realize that none of the adults had much knowledge about Korean culture.

Peer Relationships

Assessment of the minority child's peer interactions gives the family social worker an important indicator of the child's level of acculturation into the majority culture.

1. *Peer interactions:* Children's relationships with peers may be an indicator of their well-being. "Fitting in" with others and having a peer support group is important to the child's self-esteem and sense of belonging. Indicators include the child's report of friendships, as well as involvement in group activities.

2. *Degree of involvement:* The family social worker can assess the level of involvement by asking questions about the child's hobbies and other activities. Examples include sports or other team memberships, Girl or Boy Scouts, and clubs. Also, does the child have a close friend among his or her schoolmates?

3. *Opposite-sex relationships:* For adolescents who are beginning to think about opposite-sex relationships, assessment considerations include availability of partners. For instance, does the minority adolescent feel accepted by others at school dances and in dating relationships?

Adaptation to the Community

Indicators of community involvement are important to the assessment of the minority child's fit into the broader social environment. The family social worker can assess group and work involvements, as well as family members' reactions to the child's community activities.

1. *Group involvement:* The family social worker may need to assess groups in which the child participates, such as church, recreation centers, and clubs. Also, the level of involvement is an important indicator of the child's successful participation. For instance, how often does the child attend church, does he or she have friends there, and in what church-spon-sored activities does the child participate.

2. *Work involvement:* Adolescents may hold jobs in the community that must be assessed for their appropriateness. Concomitantly, adoles-cents may want jobs but need help in finding appropriate employment.

3. *Family members' reactions to child's community involvement:* Family members' level of acculturation may affect their reactions to the child's group and/or work activities. The family social worker may need to help families accept their children's interactions outside of the family; or they may need to help the family to allow children freedom to explore re-lationships in the community.

4. *Child's special interests or abilities:* Identifying children's special interests, and especially their special abilities, is important to the devel-opment of a successful intervention plan. The family social worker may build on the child's strengths to help promote adjustment to a culture dif-ferent from that of the family of origin. For instance, some children may excel in sports or music rather than academic endeavors. Successful per-formance in these areas may mitigate poor school performance and in-crease the child's self-esteem.

VALUES AND BELIEFS

Compare your values and beliefs to those of your parents. Identify some similarities and some differences in values and beliefs.

CHAPTER SUMMARY

In this chapter, people of color—African, Hispanic, Asian, and Native Amer-icans—were discussed with a focus on revealing their unique history and beliefs about family. Assessment should take into account the special themes and issues of each group.

Racism is a central issue when treating African American families; themes include strong kinship bonds, strong education and work achieve-ment orientation, flexibility in family roles, commitment to religious values and church participation, a humanistic orientation, and an endurance of suffering.

Hispanic families vary according to their level of acculturation into the dominant culture; five themes are familism, personalism (including *machismo*), hierarchy, spiritualism, and fatalism.

Asian American families value living in harmony with nature and with other people. Loyalty, respect for hierarchy, and obedience are dominant themes.

Native American families believe in living in harmony with the natural world. Themes include a cooperative view of the universe, and honor and respect for others.

Recommendations for treatment of ethnic minority families include techniques to engage the family members, sensitivity to communication styles and relevant metaphors, and behavioral methods including social skills training. Treatment issues unique to each group were reviewed. Special issues to consider when working with children from minority families include psychosocial adjustment, relationships with family, school adjustment and achievement, peer relationships, and adaptation to the community.

The family social worker who is knowledgeable about various cultural and ethnic backgrounds increases her or his ability to be a caring and sensitive helper. The culturally sensitive family social worker does not stereotype people but is genuinely interested in learning about their unique background.

13

Family Social Work with Children

Family social workers often intervene in situations involving child abuse and neglect, sexual abuse, suicide risk, and parent-child conflict. For each of these problems, we will present information and interventions. These problems can appear either separately or together, and a family social worker should refer the family to a specialist who has expertise in a particular area. In addition, some of these problems may coexist with the problems presented in the next chapter. After referring the family to a specialist, the FSW usually will continue to work with the family. Coordination of services and reinforcement of intervention with the specialist becomes important.

Many clients involved in family-centered programs function well and can benefit from time-limited, problem-focused family social work. Other families experience multiple problems, including overwhelming stress, poor psychological or physical health, poor coping skills, inadequate or absent social support, and lack of environmental resources. Intervention for overburdened families such as these must take the form of specialized, intensive services, and family social workers who serve these families need specific skills and knowledge.

Family social work becomes more challenging when it involves stressful or unusual circumstances. The FSW must be aware that unexpected problems may surface during family work, and problems usually have a profound impact on *all* family members. Although the problem may arise with one individual, as in substance abuse or sexual abuse, the problem affects all family members with varying degrees of severity. The FSW must recognize the signs or behaviors associated with these problems, and he or she must determine what issues are most important and urgent, then respond appropriately. Finally, tapping into other resources probably will be necessary. The social worker should enlist them as needed. Especially important is awareness of support systems within the community.

We caution family social workers to remember that the presence of a problem does not mean that the family acknowledges it, accepts it, or is ready to address it. Breaking down family resistance will often be a difficult initial task. FSWs need to recognize that not all problems can be addressed immediately, and families may make progress in small increments.

Family social workers are likely to encounter families dealing with more than one problem at a time. The problems presented in this chapter will affect the entire family unit, and the FSW must remember that the family, rather than one individual, is the client. Supporting and strengthening the family is the ultimate goal of any family intervention, but it does not supersede concern for the well-being of individual family members. Some problems cannot be addressed while the family remains together, because maintaining family integrity would place a family member at continued risk. Family violence is one such problem.

PHYSICAL ABUSE AND NEGLECT

> Children are the only people in North America whom it is legal to strike (Zigler & Hall, 1991).

Many North American families are violent (Gelles & Straus, 1988) and physical discipline of children is widely accepted in our culture. A popular argument rationalizing child abuse is that parents should be allowed to physically "discipline" children without state interference. Similarly, many parents believe in the adage of "Spare the rod and spoil the child." In reality, this biblical saying refers to the rod that shepherds used to guide their sheep, not a stick used for striking. Most Americans believe that good parenting involves some physical punishment (Gelles & Straus, 1988). Family social workers must reject these arguments and help parents learn more effective parenting skills that do not involve the use of physical force.

In addition to the parent-abuser, child-victim scenario, siblings can also be abusers and parents can be victims. However, we refer specifically here to parental abuse of children. Most definitions of child abuse include some form of physical assault or sexual abuse. Further, physical and sexual abuse are almost always accompanied by emotional maltreatment. Child abuse can also involve parental use of negative and inappropriate control strategies with a child (Wolfe, 1987). The term *maltreatment* includes both child physical abuse and neglect; they are often found together in the same family (Garbarino & Gilliam, 1987).

Neglect is more difficult to define than abuse. A range of value systems and differing parenting styles confounds identification. For the purposes of this book, neglect is defined as deprivation of basic needs (such as shelter, clothing, medical attention, education, and food) as well as severe emotional deprivation resulting from poor caring and protection. Social workers must distinguish between parents who *cannot* and those who *do not* provide basic necessities for their children. Neglect accounts for more child deaths than does physical abuse and must be taken seriously by family social workers.

A final form of abuse is emotional maltreatment. While a family social worker may witness emotional abuse, it is difficult to define and perhaps most subject to interpretations based on values and differing styles of parenting.

Family social workers must be alert to signs that child abuse or neglect may be occurring. Signs may include unexplained cuts, fractures, burns, or bruises, or an unusual number of "accidents." Children may be timid or frightened, or conversely, aggressive. Because family social workers are in clients' homes frequently, they are more likely than office-based professionals to notice signs of child abuse and neglect. In fact, it is possible that more children come into foster or residential care while receiving home-based services because of the monitoring function of working in the home.

When child abuse is identified, family social workers must grapple with complex choices related to protecting the victim versus maintaining the integrity of the family. Family social workers often define success as keeping the family together, yet abused children cannot always be protected while remaining in their families. Children's safety must come first. When working with abusive families, the family social worker may experience anxiety about child safety, particularly when the FSW is not present in the home. These anxieties are usually a red flag that there is risk, and the FSW should inform his or her supervisor.

The following example illustrates factors that may contribute to child abuse and neglect.

> The Lile family came to the attention of the family social worker, Jim Lloyd, after an elementary school teacher reported bruises on one of the children. The Liles had recently moved to the area from another state so that Mr. Lile could accept a promotion within his company.
>
> Sam and Teresa Lile had been married for one year. When they met, Teresa was raising two daughters from a previous relationship. The children's father had left Teresa when she was pregnant with their second child.
>
> At the time of the FSW's first visit, the girls were eight and six years old. The FSW learned that the older daughter, Jessie, had been diagnosed with ADHD and placed on Ritalin at the age of three. In the evening and during the weekends, Jessie was off her medication, and her behavior was disruptive.
>
> Sam was not accustomed to living with children, yet he wanted to be a father to the girls. He planned to adopt them. He believed that Jessie's behavior problems were largely due to Teresa's lenient parenting style. He tried to "tighten the reins" and used a belt when the children were "out of line." Teresa was lonely, feeling lost without family members and friends nearby. She left most of the parenting responsibilities to her new husband. Sam wanted Teresa to get a job, but she was having trouble finding work.
>
> Mr. Lloyd, the FSW, identified the following issues to be addressed:
>
> 1. Lack of knowledge regarding parenting and disciplinary techniques.
> 2. Isolation and lack of social support system.

3. Job counseling for Teresa.
4. Information about ADHD for Sam.

Factors Contributing to Child Abuse and Neglect

The causes of child abuse are not clear-cut. Because causes of abuse are varied and interrelated, the best we can do is describe some factors that accompany abuse.

Correlates of child abuse include (but are not limited to) the following overlapping conditions:

- **Isolation from family and friends.** Garbarino and Crouter (1978) view maltreatment as largely a problem of inadequate support systems and resources. Feedback is one function of social support, and abusive parents often do not receive corrective information about parenting. Parents who mistreat their children seem to have difficulty forming stable and healthy social relationships. They may also have difficulty remaining in treatment. Family social work in the home helps to break down social isolation. For families who need support but do not seek it, a home-based service seems to be more promising than agency-based services because it eliminates the need for transportation to office appointments. In the process of family work, FSWs can diminish client isolation through ongoing contact while helping families establish and nurture formal and informal support networks. Parents are more likely to abuse their children when social contact is limited and when the contact that does occur is negative or aversive (Wahler, 1980). Parents may need the FSW's help in developing social skills. Contrary to the notion that families should be independent and self-reliant, strong families are closely connected with sources of social support (Garbarino & Gilliam, 1987).

- **Negative interactions within the family.** Parents in abusive families may lack empathy and be more punitive than nonabusing parents (Kavanaugh, Youngblade, Reid, & Fagot, 1988). Abusive parents often do not know how to reward appropriate child behavior. In fact, determinants of abusive behavior can be found in the day-to-day transactions between parents and their children (Burgess & Youngblade, 1988). Such parents are poor observers of their children's behavior—they ignore "bad" behavior and fail to follow through on commands they give their children. They seem to be negative when they do have verbal interactions with their children and to display less physical affection. Children are likely to behave poorly, because rewards are applied inconsistently. This leaves the parents with little influence over their children's behavior, who then turn to harsher disciplinary measures. It is important that family social workers recognize ongoing dysfunctional patterns and that they not blame the child for provoking the abuse.

- **Inappropriate expectations of the children.** Abusive parents may lack knowledge of child development. Child maltreatment often stems from incompetence in the role of caregiver (Garbarino & Gilliam, 1987). Parents may harm their children because of ignorance and lack of parenting skills. By utilizing the developmental perspective to educate parents about children's developmental capacities and needs, family social workers can change parents' unrealistic expectations concerning their children and provide greater awareness of what to expect (Garbarino & Gilliam, 1987).

- **High rates of stress.** Child abuse has been associated with extreme stress that involves both social isolation and buildup of life crises. Abusive parents usually have fewer helpful neighbors, friends, or relatives to call upon in times of need. Strong and supportive social networks seem to offset the negative impact of stress. Low income, combined with disruptive demographic factors, is a potent generator of life crises that precipitate maltreatment (Garbarino & Crouter, 1978; Gil, 1970; Webster-Stratton, 1985). Stressors can include poverty, unemployment, low educational attainment, substance abuse, depression, anxiety, and the child's temperament. Children who are overly active, irritable when tired, or obstinate can be challenging to raise. Abusive mothers may also be clinically depressed (Webster-Stratton, 1991). Parental stress may be acute or chronic (Patterson & Dishion, 1988). Stress may also be associated with larger-than-average family sizes and single- or step-parenting (Burgess & Youngblade, 1988).

- **Lack of parenting skills.** Parents who abuse their children may have limited knowledge of child management techniques and skills. They have difficulty rewarding appropriate child behavior. Abusive parents rely excessively upon coercive and aversive methods of control and lack consistent and positive child management techniques (Denicola & Sandler, 1980). Lack of effective parenting skills seems to be part of a larger deficit of social skills (Patterson & Dishion, 1988). Lack of parenting skills has also been associated with stress and an absence of personal and social resources (Garbarino & Gilliam, 1987).

RECOGNIZING CHILD ABUSE OR NEGLECT

List some of the signals that would cue a FSW to the possibility of child abuse or neglect. Under what circumstances should the FSW report this behavior to authorities?

Intervention with Families in Which Children Are Abused or Neglected

Perhaps the most difficult situation for FSWs to face is one in which a child is being harmed. Parents who abuse their children may create feelings of anger in people who work with them. Family social workers may ask themselves, "How can I help this parent who has hurt a child, when I find this behavior so detestable?" We suggest that FSWs consider the parents' feelings apart from their behavior. Although the abusive parent's actions are not acceptable, feelings of frustration, fatigue, or helplessness propelling the actions are legitimate feelings with which the family social worker may empathize. Likewise, family social workers must accept their own negative reactions toward the parent without translating these feelings into rejection.

The FSW should consider the entire family as the client, unless the child's safety will be at risk if the family remains intact. The public child welfare agency is mandated with the responsibility of determining whether a child should be brought into foster care, although a family-centered social worker may have input into this decision. Seeing the family as the client creates a context in which the child is helped when the parent is helped. The social worker's goal is to strengthen parenting skills and help the family to function in healthier ways. Providing this kind of assistance may enable parent and child to remain together.

Unfortunately, accepting parents' feelings and recognizing their needs does not automatically result in ease of communication and productive interaction between parents and FSWs. A parent may not trust the FSW, especially if the parent was abused as a child. Family social workers need considerable support from supervisory and collegial staff when working with maltreating parents.

Families may come to the attention of a family social worker after a referral to a child welfare agency. Interventions that are home-based and where the social worker actively reaches out to families produce better results than other interventions (Cohn, 1979). Abusive families often are hard to engage and may drop out from treatment. In addition, intensive programs yield better results than less intensive programs. Intensive programs are those in which the social worker works with the family for hours or even days at a time. These programs are a departure from traditional 50-minute, weekly, office-based appointments. Families may come to treatment because of court orders; consequently the FSW must put intensive efforts into engagement and diminishing resistance before moving on to other family interventions. Special precautions must be taken to ensure the safety of the children.

FSWs should discuss concerns with parents, keeping in mind that parents will probably feel defensive and threatened. Once the social worker has established sufficient rapport and trust to interact effectively with a parent, the parent is less likely to disguise what is happening. Discussions about child maltreatment can usually be accomplished without jeopardizing the relationship. The guiding principle is to explore the abuse with an attitude of sincere concern rather than judgment. Family social workers must convey that they want to help the parents as well as protect the children. Most parents do not want to hurt their children, and if assistance is offered in a non-accusatory manner, most will accept it. However, parents must also be informed that the social worker is legally obligated to report suspected abuse. Family social workers should not mislead parents into believing that they will overlook the parents' behavior because of their relationship with the family.

Treatment needs of abusive parents center on developing effective child management skills and techniques that will alleviate their reliance upon coercive methods and impulsive responses. Abusive parents report that they benefit from learning child management skills (Coleman & Collins, 1997). For example, in one program, a parent said, "I liked learning different ideas on how to handle behaviors, such as breaking power struggles by offering choices." Other parents appreciated learning different techniques of discipline. Thus, modifying parent-child interaction styles may reduce the risk of child abuse.

During the FSW's home visits, parents can receive immediate feedback on their daily interactions with their children that are most likely to provoke abusive responses. Removal of a child from the home changes these patterns temporarily. Intervention to stop child abuse and neglect best focuses on an educational approach. The FSW can modify family functioning by supporting adaptive functioning, assisting with problem solving, and promoting behavioral change. FSWs can teach parents about the developmental stages their children are experiencing. Social workers also can teach parents positive parenting techniques, such as the use of time-out, contracting, and rewards to modify children's behavior.

CHILD SEXUAL ABUSE

Sexual abuse within the family was unacknowledged for many years. The problem receives more attention today, and there are different beliefs about what intervention best addresses the problem. Sexual abuse has been traced to family dynamics, individual psychopathology, or a combination of the two (Coleman & Collins, 1990). Sexual abuse of children within the family is a complex issue, with many possible causes and treatment options. Gender sensitivity is especially important when working with sexually abusive families, because most often the offender is male and the victim is female. In some cases, removal of the offender from the family may be the safest option, but child welfare agencies have different protocols and guidelines regarding this issue. When removal of the offender is impossible or unlikely and the victim's safety cannot be guaranteed, the next option is removal of the victim.

The offender is usually someone familiar to the child, either in a parental or sibling role. Child sexual abuse can be classified by the relationship between the offender and the child. The offender may be the child's father, mother, stepparent, parent's partner, sibling, member of the extended family (such as a grandparent, uncle, aunt, or cousin), friend, acquaintance, baby-sitter, teacher, or stranger. The offender can be the victim's age or older, male or female, and may commit the abuse alone or as part of a group. Most of the time the offender lives in the household or is a friend of the family.

The family social worker should pay close attention to family structure when working with these families. Often power is distributed unequally between the parents. The mother may be incapacitated through depression or illness, while the father may exercise tight control over family members. There may be wife abuse as well as child abuse. Often these families are isolated from most connections outside the family (Bagley & Ramsey, 1984; Briere, 1992; Browne & Finkelhor, 1986; Courtois, 1979; Everstine & Everstine, 1989; Hall & Lloyd, 1993, Meiselman, 1990).

Abuse does not inevitably lead to severe trauma, but it does affect every child (Briere, 1992). Characteristics of the abuse can affect how traumatic it is for the child. These include but are not limited to the following factors (Watchel, 1988):

- Frequency and duration of the abuse;
- The amount of force used to obtain compliance;
- Closeness of the offender to the victim;
- Age of the victim;
- The type of response to disclosure that the victim receives;
- The quality of support systems available to the victim.

Effects of sexual abuse on children are described later in this section.

Validation of Sexual Abuse Allegations

There is no ultimate test of truthfulness of a child's report of sexual abuse. Diagnoses of sexual abuse are rarely based on obvious physical signs. Rates of false allegations range from 8 percent to 28 percent and are more prevalent in cases of custody and visitation disputes (Yuille, no date).

Factors Contributing to Sexual Abuse

There are several theories concerning the causes of child sexual abuse, with each theory accompanied by a related intervention. Finkelhor (1986) identifies four predispositions for sexual abuse:

- The abuser must have the motivation to sexually abuse a child;
- The abuser must overcome internal inhibitions;
- The abuser must overcome child resistance;
- The abuser must be able to overcome environmental impediments to abusing.

FIGURE 13.1   Models for Treating Intrafamilial Sexual Abuse

Model	Reasons for the Abuse	Legal Involvement	Family Integrity	Evidence	Interventions
Child advocacy	Abuse is the sole responsibility of the abuser, stems from personal issues of the perpetrator, and may be maintained by family dysfunction.	Law is needed, but revictimization by the courts is a major concern.	Father should leave the house (permanently).	Some evidence concerning family structure. Some evidence to suggest deviant perpetrator arousal.	Individual counseling for family members and specialized offender treatment.
Multi-modal, Multi-step (Sgroi)	Many reasons: individual and family.	Legal involvement is needed.		Success is when the child is free from risk of abuse.	Group therapy, mother-daughter counseling.
Reconstructive (Giarretto)	Abuse stems from both individual and family factors.	Legal involvement is needed.	Father should leave the house (temporarily).	Variable levels of success. Mixed rates of success for programs that have been evaluated.	Starts with individual and then moves to group and family therapy.
Family systems	Abuse results from family dysfunction.	Early models considered legal involvement counter-therapeutic. Recently, family systems therapists have softened their stance.	In most cases, family can safely remain together.	Sparse evidence of effectiveness.	Family therapy can be started soon after disclosure.

Source: Adapted from Coleman, H., & Collins, D. (1990). The treatment trilogy of father-daughter incest. *Child and Adolescent Social Work Journal, 7* (40), 339–355.

Certain theories of family functioning are problematic when applied to situations involving child sexual abuse. In particular, the family systems approach has several shortcomings. Family systems theorists often blame mothers for sexual abuse, alleging that the mother encourages, colludes with, or condones the abuse. Mothers may also be faulted for failing to be adequate sexual partners to their husbands. Family systems theorists suggest that daughters may receive special privileges in the family because of the abuse (Trepper & Barrett, 1986). These explanations minimize the responsibility of the abuser, overlook the abuser's motivation, and ignore what occurs in order for the abuser to overcome internal inhibitions. In addition, family systems theory fails to acknowledge that some offenders may be sexually attracted to children.

Another common myth holds that the intrafamilial sexual offender is different from offenders who abuse children outside the family. We suggest that FSWs not assume a difference, because many offenders abuse children both within and outside the family.

The family systems perspective has been accused of minimizing the child's trauma at being sexually abused and suggesting that "sexual activity" may be less traumatic for children than the breakup of the family (Trepper & Barrett, 1986). To the contrary, children often experience acute psychological effects that resemble those observed in adults following a sexual assault (Jones & McQuiston, 1986). The following short-term effects have been associated with sexual abuse:

- Depression is a common symptom associated with child sexual abuse (Bagley & McDonald, 1984; Bagley & Ramsay, 1984).
- Fear and anxiety may be prevalent (Browne & Finkelhor, 1986). Symptoms related to anxiety can include psychomotor agitation, nightmares and night terrors, and fears and phobias (Jones & McQuiston, 1986).
- Sleep disturbances, distractibility, and hyperalertness may be evident.
- Feelings of guilt and helplessness may be expressed (Beitchman, Hood, Zucker, daCosta, & Akman, 1991; Jones & McQuiston, 1986; Sgroi, 1983).
- Behavior problems may include lying, stealing, or aggressiveness; substance abuse; school-related problems; and running away from home (Beitchman, Hood, Zucker, daCosta, & Akman, 1991; Jones & McQuiston, 1986).
- Suicidal thoughts and behaviors may occur (Beitchman, Hood, Zucker, daCosta, & Akman, 1991; Brooks, 1985).
- Children may exhibit poor social skills and difficulty trusting others (Sgroi, 1983).

For adolescents, short term-effects may include depression, poor self-esteem, and suicidal ideation (Beitchman, Zucker, Hood, DaCosta, &

Akman, 1991; Porter, Blick, & Sgroi, 1983). Teens may "act out" their trauma through running away from home or displaying "out-of-control" behavior (Jones & McQuiston, 1986). Children and adolescents who have been sexually abused have a greater risk for self-destructive behaviors including suicide attempts, aggressions towards others, self-mutilation, and drug and alcohol abuse (Caviola & Schiff, 1989).

Adolescents may show destructive sexual behaviors such as promiscuity (Beitchman, Zucker, Hood, DaCosta, & Akman, 1991; Jones & McQuiston, 1986), becoming involved indiscriminately in sexual relationships. Adolescent victims of sexual assault also are at greater risk of developing eating disorders such as anorexia nervosa (Jones & McQuiston, 1986).

Family systems theorists have difficulty explaining abuse in which the perpetrator is not the father—e.g., abuse between siblings (Loredo, 1983). Using Finkelhor's framework, mothers can be viewed as a potential environmental impediment to the abuse. That is, mothers need to monitor their children. However, this argument poses a serious dilemma to gender-sensitive family social workers. Mothers also have a life of their own and cannot be confined to the house to monitor the behavior of all family members. As Florence Rush (1980) suggested, "Why should a mother have to protect children in their own family?"

Intervention with Families in Which Children Have Been Sexually Abused

How does a family social worker intervene in families where there has been sexual abuse? Ideally, the FSW should refer the family to a specialist in the area of sexual abuse. The abuse needs to be reported to appropriate child welfare agencies, if this has not already occurred. Child welfare authorities will probably notify the police. The first responsibility of the family social worker is to protect children's safety.

To ensure the safety of the child, often the best immediate solution is for a legally mandated agency to separate the child from the offender. Removing the offender from the home is preferable but not always possible. A child who is removed from the home may be placed with relatives, in foster care, or at a treatment facility. Children who are removed from their homes have a double burden: the trauma of the assault and the added trauma of separation from home, neighborhood, friends, and family. Removing a child from the family may also suggest to the child that she or he is being punished and was responsible for the abuse. Unfortunately, such separation may be necessary to ensure the child's safety.

POSSIBLE FACTORS IN SEXUAL ABUSE

Based on Finkelhor's Four-Factor Model for sexual abuse, make a list of items that would fit under each factor. Beside each item, list two possible steps that a family social worker could take to address each factor.

Separating the offender from the child, calling the police, and filing a complaint can protect society and the child for a short time. But these actions do not protect the offender from his own impulses, leaving the victim and other children in jeopardy. Psychological treatment for the offender may be useful. Institutionalization separates the offender from potential victims, offers a thorough assessment of the offender and his situation, and allows a thoughtful decision to be made about his future, all of which will probably help protect the victim more effectively.

To formulate interventions, FSWs should review Finkelhor's four predispositions for abuse and developing a plan for addressing each one:

1. The offender's *motivation to abuse* must be dealt with as an individual issue that is probably beyond the expertise of the family social worker. Deviant sexual arousal will be an important focus of intervention, as will issues such as the offender's own history as a victim of abuse. Referral to a specialist will be necessary.

2. Addressing the offender's likelihood of *overcoming internal inhibitions* again falls under the purview of a specialist, particularly when the offender has problems with substance abuse, impulse control, or psychopathology. However, the family social worker can convey to the offender that the behavior is unacceptable and that the role of the FSW is to protect the child.

3. *Child resistance* is another point of intervention that can be targeted by the family social worker. Children can be taught about sexual abuse and shown how to be more assertive. Children can also learn to tell someone about the abuse (preferably the nonoffending parent) or another person who will act on the information. The child's relationship with a nonoffending parent can also be strengthened to create an ally for the child.

4. *Environmental impediments to abuse* can be strengthened by building into the family necessary structures and mechanisms with which to address the other three predispositions. This can involve teaching family members to respect personal privacy and personal boundaries. Social isolation of the family should also be addressed. Other siblings in the family should be told about the abuse (when they are old enough to understand) in order to break the secret, to see if they have been abused also, and to add another dimension of monitoring in the family. Family members can be taught about healthy sexuality and respect for gender. Empowerment of the nonoffending parent also is crucial.

SUICIDAL ADOLESCENTS

Suicide rates among young people have increased over the past twenty-five years. Suicide is the tenth leading cause of death in the general population but ranks third among adolescents, surpassed only by accidents and homicide (Gilliland & James, 1993). Deaths by suicide may be mislabeled to protect surviving family members from social stigma and further grief.

Despite the large number of people whose lives have been affected by the suicide or attempted suicide of a family member or friend, the topic is not widely discussed.

Factors Contributing to Suicide Risk Among Adolescents

Suicidal youths usually experience troubles in their home environment, such as family disruption through death or divorce, or family conflicts. Suicide risk appears to be heightened by early loss of a love object through death, marital separation of parents, or an ambivalent or unsatisfactory relationship (Diekstra & Moritz, 1987; Hawton, 1986). Further, a history of sexual and physical abuse predisposes a young person to suicidal behavior (Diekstra & Moritz, 1987).

Family members of suicidal youths may also have a psychiatric disturbance that depletes family resources and leaves little energy for the needs of the young person (Hawton, 1986), who may experience feelings of isolation, neglect, and rejection. Furthermore, cases of depression seem to be clustered in families.

Young people who are at risk for suicide may feel isolated from family members and also lack a cohesive peer group, due in part to family mobility (Hawton, 1986). Experiencing rejection and isolation from peers refuels feelings of earlier familial loss and rejection or neglect. Membership in a cohesive social structure such as those provided by religious organizations, sports teams, or community groups may decrease the risk of suicide.

Intervention with Families of Suicidal Adolescents

The term "suicide threat" should be avoided because it tends to be associated with manipulation. We use the term "cue" instead. Often people close to the suicidal young person perceive cues as manipulative, particularly when there are family problems or parent-child conflict. Family social workers can help family members to understand the desperation that the young person feels and become sensitive to suicide cues. Cues may be behavioral and/or emotional and can include signs of overt or hidden depression, acting-out behaviors, irritability, argumentativeness, and poor school performance (Charles & Coleman, 1990). Relatives need to see that behind the problem behaviors lie feelings of sadness, hopelessness, and desperation.

Social workers and family members need to recognize that asking pointed questions about suicidal thoughts does not make the young person decide that suicide is a viable option or reinforce maladaptive behavior, attention-seeking, or emotional blackmail (Ross, 1985). Most important, family members must learn not to ignore signs of suicidal ideation. Gestures that appear innocuous or manipulative may in fact be precursors to later suicide attempts (Charles & Matheson, 1989). If the family and the social worker do not deal with the cues directly, the behavior may escalate until there is resolution. Resolution may come in the form of a completed

FIGURE 13.2   Maladaptive Pattern of Interaction Between Parent and Suicidal Child

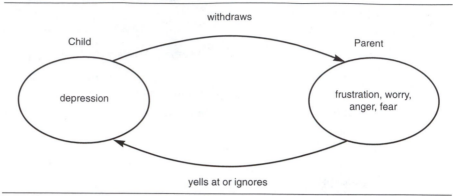

or otherwise serious attempt or amelioration of the difficulties that caused the feelings in the first place.

Figure 13.2 demonstrates how circular and repetitive patterns of suicide indicators and threats can entrench the family and the young person in maladaptive and dysfunctional patterns. Breaking the circular patterns becomes crucial. The FSW must be attuned to the signs and the family's response to the indicators.

Indicators of Suicide Risk

- Statements expressing despair or hopelessness, such as "Everybody would be better off if I were dead."
- Giving away prized possessions.
- Recent personal loss.
- History of drug and/or alcohol abuse.
- Hints of a concrete plan for suicide.
- Depression.
- Elevated mood following depression (this elevated mood may accompany a person's decision to commit suicide).

ASSESSING SUICIDE RISK IN ADOLESCENTS

List some of the signals that would alert you to the possibility that your adolescent client might be considering suicide. With a partner, role-play interviewing an adolescent at risk for suicide.

Family social workers must use methods of crisis intervention to disrupt negative circular transactions. The family needs to learn how to reach out to the suicidal young person and alter the pattern. Using the circular patterns illustrated above, the family social worker will take the following steps:

1. The social worker should use his or her assessment skills to identify possible suicidal ideation. The FSW should speak directly to the young person about the assessment. Even if the young person denies feeling suicidal, the social worker must not abandon attempts to intervene if he or she believes there is potential for suicide. The FSW should ask the young person such questions as "How is life going for you right now?" "How bad is your situation?" "Have you ever thought about killing yourself?" "How would you do it?" "What does the future look like to you?"

2. The situation must be discussed with significant others in the young person's immediate environment. These people need to understand the seriousness of the threats and also be helped to understand their role in maintaining circular interaction patterns. Once the family understands the seriousness of the situation and what they can do, they can learn how to replace avoidant or angry reactions and decrease the young person's sense of isolation and despair. Family members can be taught how to reach out to the young person in new and more appropriate ways, conveying concern and hope.

3. By reaching out to the young person, the FSW should strive to break through his or her feeling of isolation and despair, replacing them with a sense of being valued and cared for. As interactions become more positive, the youth can become engaged in addressing the issues that brought on feelings of despair.

FIGURE 13.3 Guidelines for Working with Suicidal Individuals

- Do not ignore or dismiss cues of suicide. Speaking openly about suicidal ideation will not cause the person to act upon the cues. Most people who eventually kill themselves have given prior warning about their intentions.

- Ask direct and specific questions concerning the individual's intentions. Questions should include whether the person has ever thought about suicide and how the person would go about committing suicide.

- Involve parents or significant others in the treatment plan.

- Make certain that a seriously suicidal individual is not left alone. Arrange for family members and friends to remain with the person.

- Ask children who have hinted at suicide to talk about their plan.

- Do not think that because a depression is lifting the suicide danger is over. An elevated mood following depression may accompany a decision to commit suicide.

- Be aware that signs of suicidal ideation encompass more than depression. Suicidal persons may show anger or behavior problems.

- Locate a crisis service in your community and get the suicidal individual connected with it.

4. The social worker should refer the suicidal person to a crisis counselor rather than attempt to handle the situation alone. Being responsible for the behavior of a suicidal young person is usually too much of a burden for a family social worker to bear.

5. The FSW should establish a contract with the suicidal young person to keep him or her safe until the crisis is averted.

If, despite all preventive measures, a young person commits suicide, the social worker will face the overwhelming burden of the survivors. Parents and siblings may suffer feelings of guilt and responsibility for the completed suicide. In addition, the FSW may react similarly to the suicide and should receive support. Social workers should also be aware that the suicide of a young person can have a ripple effect on the peer group, and thus interventions with schools and other social networks may be needed.

BEHAVIOR PROBLEMS AND PARENT-CHILD CONFLICT

Parent-child conflict is often encountered by family social workers. Between one-third and one-half of all family social work referrals for children and adolescents may involve behavioral problems (Kazdin, 1991). Parent-child conflict may be symptomatic of a child with behavior problems or indicative of general family distress and poor parenting skills. Behavior problems take different forms depending on the age of the child and situational and personality factors but can include noncompliant behavior, temper tantrums, aggression, argumentativeness, refusing to obey curfews, running away from home, engaging in criminal behavior, or abusing alcohol and other drugs. Parents of acting-out children often feel alone and exhausted.

Generally, intervention in families with parent-child conflict involves a five-phase process (Forgatch, 1991):

1. *Tracking behavior.* Parents should pay close attention to child behaviors. In particular, they should learn to distinguish between compliant and noncompliant child behaviors. The parents need to respond appropriately to desirable behaviors and avoid reinforcing problematic behaviors.

2. *Positive reinforcement.* When the child behaves acceptably, the parents should respond with praise or rewards such as increased privileges.

3. *Teaching appropriate discipline.* If the child's behavior is not appropriate, the parents can apply a consequence such as time-out or loss of privileges.

4. *Monitoring children.* Parents should be taught to monitor their children's whereabouts, companions, and activities.

5. *Problem solving.* Problem-solving strategies are discussed in Chapter 8. Use of problem-solving skills can help parents find solutions for their current difficulties and prevent the occurrence of future problems.

Parent-child conflict is often associated with children's behavior problems. Severity of conflict depends on the issues and personalities involved. In conflictual situations, parents are often desperate and children may be angry, rebellious, or sad.

Baynard and Baynard (1983) outline a three-step program to assist families who are experiencing parent-child conflict.

1. Have each parent make a list of the child's behaviors that are causing conflict. If there are two parents, they should make separate lists and then combine them.

2. Ask parents to cut the lists apart and separate the items into piles: one for the child, one for the parent(s), and one for items that overlap. Into the child's pile go the behaviors that will not affect the future life of the parents, even though they may have consequences for the child. Into the parent's pile go the behaviors that could have consequences for the parents. Items for the child's pile could include watching too much television, dressing sloppily, and fighting with siblings. Items for the parent's pile could include criminal activities by the child such as theft, vandalism, or assault. Items from the overlapping pile should be sorted and moved to either the child's pile or the parent's pile. In sorting through the child's problematic behaviors, parents need to consider which ones they can control and which ones they cannot.

3. Help parents learn not to take responsibility for items in the child's pile. Parents must convey to their children a sense of trust that children can make the right decisions.

CHAPTER SUMMARY

We have outlined major problems family social workers may encounter: child abuse and neglect, sexual abuse, suicide risk, and parent-child conflict. Social workers need to be aware that more than one problem may exist in the same family, making intervention complex and challenging.

Physical abuse and neglect are potentially life-threatening issues. FSWs need to be alert to signs of neglect and abuse as well as family conditions in which these problems are likely to occur. Ultimately, ensuring child safety takes precedence over keeping the family together. Family social workers can help alleviate stress for parents as well as teaching them more effective child management skills.

There are many theories about the causes of child sexual abuse. We do know that sexual abuse perpetrators are usually familiar to the child. Family social workers must recognize that sexually abused children may show many emotional and behavioral problems that need to be addressed. Further, all family members have needs and concerns that also must be addressed if the sexual abuse is to stop.

Suicidal gestures and suicide attempts create tremendous stress in families. Suicide rates among teenagers are increasing, and family social workers must be able to recognize the signs of pending trouble and reach out to prevent a completed suicide. In particular, the social worker can help the family learn ways of reaching out to the young person and helping him or her to feel hopeful and nurtured.

Finally, behavior problems and parent-child conflict can create a continual stream of family disruption and unpleasantness for everyone. Parents will benefit from learning appropriate child management techniques. The younger the child is when parents learn these techniques, the more effective the techniques can be.

Family social workers are encouraged to learn more about the problems that families face. Consultation with specialists and background reading specific to the issues are strongly encouraged.

14 Special Situations in Family Social Work

Two major problems that families face are domestic violence and substance abuse. Both problems may occur in the same family or in conjunction with other difficulties. As with other problems of this severity, the family social worker should refer clients to professionals who specialize in these areas. At the same time, the FSW needs to help design the intervention, coordinate services with the specialist, and reinforce the treatment plan during home visits. Often the intervention process is complicated by the fact that clients are involved in family social work because the court system requires it, not because they have decided to seek help for their problems.

ABUSIVE RELATIONSHIPS

Straus and Gelles (1988), in their study of domestic violence in America, found that one in six couples had experienced an incident of physical assault during the previous year. Although most of the incidents were minor, a substantial number were serious assaults. At least three percent of women in the United States were severely assaulted during the same period. Severe assault is defined as acts that have a high probability of causing an injury, such as kicking, biting, punching, hitting with an object, choking, beating up, and threatening to use (or using) a knife or gun (Straus & Gelles, 1988). An equal incidence of female-to-male assault has been reported; however, many of the latter assaults may have been acts of retaliation or self-defense (Gelles & Straus, 1988; Straus, 1993).

Children are not just bystanders when their mothers are abused (Wolfe, Jaffe, Wilson, & Zak, 1988). They may show a range of behavioral problems in response to witnessing violence in their homes. Male children are more likely to manifest problems immediately, but the effects on female children may appear years later. The negative impact of family violence upon children is an important consideration for family social workers.

Factors Contributing to Domestic Violence

Just as family social workers may see or suspect child abuse in a family, they may also suspect other kinds of family violence. While men can be the victims in spouse abuse, we focus on women because men often hurt their partners more severely. Men usually are physically stronger than women. Spouse abuse is often referred to as wife battering. Because the behavior occurs in private, domestic violence may go unrecognized. Few incidents are reported to the police, and because it is mostly female victims who have come forward, we know little about perpetrators (Dutton, 1991).

Traditionally, domestic violence was analyzed through a family-systems lens. That is, it was widely believed that abuse resulted from circular causality, homeostasis, and related family dynamics. There are several problems with explaining abusive relationships from a family systems perspective (Bograd, 1992; Dell, 1989; Myers-Avis, 1992). For example, traditional descriptions of the precursors to an assault often implied that the victim was "nagging" or otherwise provoking an assault. Clearly, these depictions are sexist and harmful. Today, few therapists recommend seeing partners conjointly when domestic abuse is occurring, at least until victim safety can be guaranteed.

Physical abuse is a way for the batterer to establish and maintain control in an interpersonal relationship (Dutton, 1991; Gilliland & James, 1993). Usually the perpetrator does not suffer from mental illness, nor does the victim have a "masochistic" personality. Obviously interpersonal violence is influenced by factors that include, but are not limited to, individual dynamics, family dynamics, and beliefs shared by peer and cultural groups.

Walker (1984) identified a cycle of violence within battering relationships (see Figure 14.1). The pattern is predictable and repetitive, and as the cycle is repeated, the phases get shorter and shorter. The cycle consists of four phases that increase in severity over time. The social worker has the best opportunity for intervention shortly after a battering incident has occurred and before the reconciliation phase begins.

FIGURE 14.1   The "Cycle of Violence" in an Abusive Relationship

1. The first phase is characterized by calmness, often described as a "honeymoon period."
2. Tension slowly starts to build in the relationship.
3. A battering episode occurs. Often the perpetrator causes the victim to feel responsible for the beating because of some alleged transgression.
4. The abuser usually feels remorse and asks forgiveness. Often the victim forgives the abuser and a period of calm in the relationship starts again.

Many battered women who stay in abusive relationships lack the economic resources to survive on their own. They tolerate abuse as long as it does not become too severe or involve the children. Often these women are strongly committed to making the relationship last. However, increased employment opportunities for women have provided the resources for women to remove themselves from violent relationships (Gelles, 1987). Battered women often lack education or work experience that would allow independent support of themselves and their children. They may therefore feel that the alternative to staying with abusive partners is poverty and loneliness. Some may remain in abusive relationships because they believe that all relationships are abusive. Others may fear the consequences of leaving, particularly if they have tried to leave in the past and have suffered repercussions from vengeful husbands or boyfriends. This fear may be real. Finally, women often see themselves (and are perceived by society) as being primarily responsible for the well-being of family relationships, and hence view the failure of the relationships as their fault. They may feel too ashamed and guilty to seek help or to leave.

There are several reasons why a battered woman may remain in an abusive relationship (Gelles & Straus, 1988):

- Poor self-concept;
- Belief that the partner will change;
- Concern for children;
- Fear of coping alone;
- Fear of stigmatization;
- Problems in developing a career.

Social isolation, combined with economic dependence, can create a sense of powerlessness and leave a woman feeling that she has no ability to free herself from a violent situation. Victims of abuse may have strong beliefs about marriage and commitment, often based on cultural or religious teachings, and may therefore be reluctant to end the marriage. Finally, there are women who out of love, dependence, fear, or desperation, cling to the hope that things will change. Dutton (1991) sums up the trap of the battered woman:

> When self-blame, dependency, depression and powerlessness are coupled with economic dependency, criminal-justice system apathy, and the belief that she cannot escape, the net effect is to produce a victim who is psychologically ill-equipped for either self-defense or escape (p. 212).

Intervention in Families Suffering from Domestic Violence

Before trying to intervene, the FSW needs to understand abusive situations and look for ways to protect victims of family violence. Clearly, a family social worker cannot impose his or her own solution. The victim must make her own decision about what to do, and then the FSW can help her follow through on her plans. Unfortunately, few abused women seek help; when they do seek help, they are likely to turn first to relative, friends, and neighbors rather than to an agency (Gelles & Straus, 1988). The family social worker may talk to an abused woman about the violence, but pushing a premature solution may undermine the worker-client relationship and rule out the possibility of finding a solution later, when the time is right.

To assist women who live with violent men, family social workers must be able to recognize signs of abuse. A woman probably will not disclose abusive behavior except in the context of a long-standing, trusting relationship with the social worker. The FSW must be sensitive to the following clues suggesting violence in the home:

- Physical signs of violence, including bruises, cuts, burns, scratches, and blackened eyes;
- Frequent physical complaints and illnesses on the part of the victim;
- Children with physical injuries and illnesses, behavioral problems, and emotional disturbances;
- Anxiety, fearfulness, apprehension, and depression;
- Self-destructive behavior, including suicidal ideation and self-deprecation;
- Insomnia and nightmares.

The above indicators are not absolute proof of abuse, but they should alert the family social worker to the possibility that something is wrong. When social workers see evidence that arouses suspicion, they are obliged to pursue the subject with their clients, albeit carefully.

Family social workers should be aware that homicide may result immediately after the victim has tried to leave an abusive relationship. In addition, homicides occur with greater frequency in families in which previous disturbances have been reported to the police, perhaps because the assaults are more severe. Nevertheless, the safety of the woman and children must be of utmost concern to the family social worker. Police recognize that intervening in domestic disputes can be extremely hazardous, and most police officers have received special training to deal with such situations. Family social workers should take steps to protect themselves when violence in a home escalates. Family social workers who have had the opportunity to learn about domestic violence as part of their professional education and to share their thoughts and experiences with colleagues and supervisors will be better equipped to handle situations involving abuse.

When a woman admits to a family social worker that she is in a battering relationship, the most important thing the social worker can do is to believe her and start intervention immediately (Walker, 1984). Once safety is assured, a multiplicity of issues can be addressed. Ensuring safety may entail moving the woman and her children to another location. Most

FIGURE 14.2   **Checklist for Working with a Battered Woman**

- Ensure safety by connecting the woman and children to an emergency shelter.
- Listen and support the woman's story.
- Be aware that it is difficult for most battered women to leave an abusive relationship.
- Determine whether medical attention is necessary.
- Acknowledge the woman's ambivalence.
- Help the battered woman examine her alternatives.
- Help the woman access community resources to enable independent living.
- Become familiar with resources available in the community.
- Work with the woman to find ways of diminishing her social isolation.

communities have emergency shelters for battered women and their children. Shelters offer battered women immediate refuge and protection but unfortunately are not likely to be used (Gelles & Straus, 1988). Most communities have crisis telephone lines. Women who have admitted that they are in an abusive relationship often start there. Figure 14.2 provides a checklist for FSWs who are working with victims of domestic violence.

In the process of deciding to leave, many abused women vacillate between staying and leaving. The social worker must be patient with the woman's ambivalence, keeping in mind that abused women are often dependent on their abusers and have low self-esteem. They may also be depressed and move through stages of mourning.

Family social workers need to examine their personal reactions to abuse and to be aware that they bring their own orientation toward family violence into the helping relationship. Self-examination prepares social workers for their own reactions when confronted with the possibility of spouse abuse, thereby enabling them to express their reactions in a way that will be helpful to their clients.

INTERVIEWING A BATTERED WIFE

With another student, role-play a social worker interviewing a woman who shows signs of having been beaten by her husband. Take turns playing the social worker and the battered wife.

The social worker must make it clear that she or he is willing to talk about the abuse. As a part of the trusting relationship that the FSW and client have established, the client needs to know that the FSW is aware of the potential for violence in people's lives (not just in this particular situation) and is open to addressing it. This approach is very different from confronting a client with one's suspicions.

If an abused woman discloses to a FSW that she is being harmed, the social worker should respond by validating her disclosure and encouraging the client to talk about the situation. After the client has talked about the abuse, the FSW may address several factors if the client is willing. These include her safety, resources available to her, and coping strategies. Victims of domestic violence may be unaware of available resources, such as emergency shelters, police, and agencies that specialize in assisting victims of domestic violence.

To help the abused woman, the FSW will need to obtain information about the type, severity, frequency, and context of the violent episodes. For example, is the woman in imminent danger of severe harm? If so, precautions must be taken to protect her safety and that of her children. If the violence is predictable, is there any way to avoid it? What resources are available to help the client? These may include police, shelters, legal assistance, counseling, and sources of financial relief. What plans can the client make for escaping violence when she senses an episode is imminent? How can she deal with violence once it has begun? These are all practical avenues to explore and can be very helpful, perhaps lifesaving, in emergencies.

Often, a battered woman has become isolated physically, emotionally, economically, and socially. The ongoing presence of a family social worker can help diminish that isolation.

In addition to linking a battered woman to community agencies for practical relief, the FSW may be able to help the client join a support group for battered women. Most battered women are unaware that other women have similar problems (Bolton & Bolton, 1987; Gelles & Straus, 1988). Learning that others have experienced the same things, have had the same feelings, and have dealt with the same realties can decrease a woman's feelings of isolation. By hearing about other women's experiences and sharing her own, a woman may also be better able to recognize alternatives to her situation. Learning that they are not alone also tends to help battered women become less self-critical and decreases their perception of themselves as being mentally unstable. Battered women often feel relieved to discover that their reactions are "normal" under the circumstances and that others have also felt afraid, helpless, angry, guilty, ashamed, and responsible for the violence.

Another way to help is to engage the abused woman in active problem solving on her own behalf. Helping her discover what she really wants, helping her identify her options and resources, and then discussing the consequences of various choices can help the client become aware of the strengths and options that she does possess. This problem-solving approach is particularly suitable for battered women because people under extreme stress tend to have difficulty thinking through their concerns and often have lost hope. Increasing an individual's sense of self-control through successful problem solving is an obvious goal for effective family social work.

Possibly the most important concept for an abused woman to accept is the fact that she does not deserve to be abused, no matter what the circumstances. It is critical that victims do not blame themselves for the brutality they suffer. Popular stereotypes and myths, though changing, have perpetuated the belief that women provoke violence and even enjoy it. Battered women often agree with these ideas, which increase their sense of shame and make it more difficult to seek help. Family social workers can do much to correct these misconceptions.

A battered woman who receives outside support is better able to access help and make changes within her family (Giles-Sims, 1983). Family social workers can provide some of the support abused clients require to eventually leave their abusive partners.

If the FSW is working with a woman who does not want to talk about the abuse she is receiving, the social worker initially should express concern and offer to listen when she is ready. The FSW may need to repeat this message many times. If the client does not respond to this approach, the social worker must not insist on pursuing the subject; doing so could alienate the client. Family social workers have found that most abused women eventually want to talk about abusive incidents.

If FSWs feel that they are in danger when visiting a violent household, they should leave quickly and notify the police. When threats to the family social worker's personal safety are serious, home visits should be terminated until the danger abates. Every family social work agency should establish clear policies and procedures for handling dangerous situations, and these should be covered in each social worker's training. If family social work is stopped, the agency should strive to maintain contact with the abused spouse, perhaps by having the FSW meet with her in another, safer environment, or attempt to reach her by telephone. It is critical for FSWs to leave the lines of communication open and offer the abused woman ongoing support.

It is not the role of the FSW to tell a battered woman what she should do. The woman will bear the consequences of whatever action she chooses to take (or not to take). Another reason to refrain from giving direct advice is that only the battered woman knows how she feels. In spite of the most sincere and skillful efforts at understanding, the FSW cannot experience the client's actual feelings. Finally, making decisions for the woman may reinforce the client's sense of powerlessness and inability to control her own life.

When working with families troubled by violence, family social workers must not allow themselves to harbor unrealistic expectations about what they can accomplish. With violent families, as with other stressful client situations, social workers should appraise their own knowledge and skills and also consult supervisors and colleagues for the information and emotional support they need to make decisions. Further, in dealing with violence, family social workers must be well informed about existing community resources and understand how to help families access them.

Abusive relationships may remain hidden from public view. The following example illustrates characteristics of an abusive relationship.

Lilly Foster spoke with the FSW, Tonya Lovett, about her situation. Lilly contacted the FSW after learning that she was pregnant. Her husband, Phil, whom Lilly described as physically and verbally abusive to her, was out of town. Lilly said that she would be "in trouble" if Phil learned that she had contacted outsiders for help. Lilly said she was concerned for the safety of their unborn child. She feared that Phil would harm the child.

Lilly reported having been married to Phil for three years. She said this was the second marriage for both, and that she was committed to "making this one work." Lilly described the courtship before her marriage as "perfect." She said Phil had seemed to be her "knight in shining armor." He didn't want Lilly to have to work, so he encouraged her to quit her job and stay home. Phil said he would always take care of Lilly, whom he called "his beautiful princess." However, in the first months after they were married, Phil became very possessive and controlling towards Lilly. He didn't want her to leave the house without telling him where she was going. He also became jealous of Lilly and imagined that she was having affairs with other men. Lilly said this accusation was ridiculous, because she rarely left home without Phil. Phil eventually wouldn't allow Lilly to go out without him, though Phil reportedly stopped in a local bar for drinks with his office buddies most days after work. Lilly said that Phil usually came home after having several drinks and that drinking made him more abusive.

The first time Lilly went out on her own against his wishes, Phil became so angry he hit her numerous times, blackening her eye and bruising her face, arms, and legs. This occurred after the couple had been married for six months. Phil was very apologetic afterward, but the beatings increased as time passed. Lilly reported that Phil was most likely to hit her if he felt jealous or if Lilly argued with him. Phil traveled as part of his job, and when he left on these trips he took Lilly's car keys, her wedding rings, and anything else of value that she might sell to obtain money. Lilly never was given any cash; Phil accompanied her wherever she went and paid for groceries and other purchases. Lilly reported that Phil gradually kept her away from her family and friends and that she had become isolated.

Mrs. Lovett, the FSW, realized that Lilly had no social support or financial resources. The FSW believed that Lilly had sought help only because of her concern for the safety of the baby she was expecting, and that Lilly greatly feared the wrath of her husband if he were to find out she had asked for help. Mrs. Lovett began to intervene immediately by connecting Lilly to an emergency shelter where experts in family violence could listen to her story and support her. As a resident of the shelter, Lilly would receive medical and financial help and counseling to examine her alternatives.

SUBSTANCE ABUSE

Substance abuse can exist in families regardless of the age, gender, culture, educational attainment, or occupational status of family members. In addition, within some client groups, polydrug use (use of more than one substance) may also be prevalent.

Until recently, interventions with addicted individuals have paid scant attention to the family or community context (Nichols & Schwartz, 1998).

Although many therapists still prefer an individual approach, some addiction specialists have begun to use a family systems approach in working with substance abusers. Family systems theorists propose that drug abuse causes family dysfunction and conflict. Some also assert that family dysfunction causes substance abuse. Substance abuse can also mask underlying family problems such as sexual abuse or family violence.

Families of substance abusers share common characteristics, particularly family functioning that revolves around the addict's behavior. All areas of family life adapt to the addiction. It is common for family members to deny that addiction is the problem and also feel shame about it. The substance abuse is not discussed among family members or with anyone outside the family. All families have family secrets, but families of substance abusers seem to have more of them. These secrets are the source of much emotional pain for all family members.

Further, family members may inadvertently support the continuation of substance abuse because chemical dependency maintains the status quo. Family members become accustomed to living with inconsistency, insecurity, and fear concerning the routine parts of daily life.

Mealtimes change from day to day, and family members cannot rely upon one another. In addition, family relationships are not very cohesive, an important issue because family cohesiveness can delay or reduce the use of substances by children. Besides diminishing the likelihood of addiction, strong family bonds can also promote children's self-esteem and positive attitudes towards school.

Open expression of feelings is often difficult in these families, especially feelings of sadness, love, and tenderness. Family members may not feel close yet they worry about each other. They may also use family conflict to mask feelings of vulnerability, and such conflict may occur between parent and child or between partners. Anger and hatred may lurk beneath the surface. More typically, the family social worker will observe guilt and blame among family members. In families of substance abusers, parents speak to each other less but children speak with one another more. In addition, daily chores take considerably longer to complete in families troubled by substance abuse. Parents are disengaged emotionally from their children, and family members avoid conflict and confrontation (Aponte & VanDeusen, 1981).

When one partner in a marriage is a substance abuser, the other partner may blame and resent the spouse. Moreover, the entire family may resist treatment. Thus, getting the partner of a substance abuser into treatment may be difficult. The partner may be reluctant to examine his or her own behavior and attitudes in relation to the substance abuse. The family social worker should recognize patterns of blame, avoidance, and resistance.

Substance abuse infiltrates all parts of family life. The erratic and unpredictable behavior of the addict creates a predictable response from family members. Family structures evolve through a process in which family members' behaviors adjust to avoid stress and conflict associated with substance abuse. Eventually, the family adapts to the addict's dysfunctional behaviors to achieve homeostasis, and at the same time homeostasis increases the likelihood that substance abuse will continue because the system organizes to keep the addiction going.

Chemical dependency is debilitating to families especially in the area of effective parenting. It may also accompany violent behavior in families. While some suggest that substance abuse *causes* family violence, it is more probable that it impairs judgment and self-control and gives an excuse for the behavior. For example, one of the authors was working with a family in which the daughter had been sexually abused repeatedly by her stepfather. When the stepfather was confronted about his behavior, his defense was, "But I had too much to drink." The social worker's response was, "I am really glad you told me that. You have two problems to work with: the sexual abuse of your daughter *and* your drinking!" Other FSWs have had clients who reported, "He does hit me and the kids, but only when he has been drinking. When he is sober, he is a great guy." Unfortunately, this excuse can hide a potentially dangerous and dysfunctional family style.

Family members use many defense mechanisms, and both the family and the addict often *deny* and *minimize* the addiction. Often the wall of denial can be impenetrable. Additionally, family members may believe that substance abuse is not a family problem but is the exclusive responsibility of the addicted family member. The father mentioned above was more willing to admit to his sexually abusive behavior than he was to admit that he had a substance abuse problem. Family social workers must realize that substance abusers typically deny being addicted and have learned to camouflage the problem. Until people admit having a problem, they will not accept help. Social workers often must make extraordinary efforts to get clients into treatment and to prevent them from dropping out prematurely (Aponte & VanDeusen, 1981).

If attempts to get clients into treatment fail and if the children are endangered because of the addiction, further action will be necessary. The FSW will need to notify child welfare authorities, particularly if the children are being neglected, abused, or placed at risk through nonsupervision. Children of substance abusers often do not get their physical or emotional needs met, and parenting is inconsistent. Further, children of addicts are more likely to be delinquent, depressed, or suicidal (Wegscheider, 1981).

Interventions with Children of Substance Abusers

Children of substance abusers face an increased risk of chemical dependency. Nevertheless, children are remarkably resilient, and having a substance-abusing parent does not necessarily doom children to enter a life of addiction. Between 70 and 92 percent of children of substance abusers do not become chemically dependent (Bernard, 1992). Unfortunately, children of substance abusers may become preoccupied with how to bring predictability into their lives (Gilliland & James, 1993).

Children of substance abusers show distress in various ways. Besides assuming characteristic roles discussed later, a child may develop problem behaviors in response to the parent's addiction. While the behaviors described may stem from reasons not directly related to chemical dependency, the role of substance abuse should be considered. All these problems argue strongly in favor of working with every family member and thereby improving the lives of future generations.

The following behaviors may indicate that children are being affected by a parent's addiction:

- Lateness for school or frequent school absenteeism.
- Concern expressed by the child about arriving home late from school or other activities.
- Children wearing improper clothing, having poor hygiene, being ill frequently, or being fatigued most of the time.
- Immature behavior such as bed-wetting, daytime soiling, and thumb sucking.
- Avoidance of arguments and conflict.
- Fear that peers will have contact with his or her parents.
- Temper outbursts, agitation, or aggression.
- Exaggerated concern with achievement or the need to please authority figures (Northwest Indian Child Welfare, 1984).

Even when children of addicts do not become substance abusers themselves, they can experience difficulties related to their parent's substance abuse. Children of substance abusers may face the following problems (Northwest Indian Child Welfare, 1984):

- *Fetal alcohol syndrome.* Fetal alcohol syndrome (FAS) results from maternal consumption of alcohol during pregnancy. Symptoms can include physical deformity or mental retardation. Children with FAS often require specialized medical attention. [Children with fetal alcohol effects (FAE) show some of the problems associated with FAS.]
- *Bonding difficulties.* Children of substance abusers often lack healthy attachment to caretakers because of caretaker unavailability, both physically and emotionally. Infants may be diagnosed with failure to thrive, and older children may have difficulty forming healthy social attachments.
- *Health problems.* Children of substance abusers tend to suffer more frequent illnesses than other children because of lack of proper nutrition, hygiene, and medical attention.
- *Educational problems.* Because basic survival consumes a lot of energy, children may have little energy available for learning. Social factors may also interfere with learning, including school

absenteeism, tardiness, and missing after-school activities because of worry about getting home on time. Children of substance abusers may be reluctant to have their teachers meet parents. In addition, substance-abusing parents are unlikely to help children with school-related problems. These children can be unpopular at school because of their relationship difficulties and because they are dirty or badly dressed. They may also alienate peers by being aggressive, having temper tantrums, or reverting to infantile behavior. Negative social experiences at school can damage children's self-esteem and make them more vulnerable to substance abuse.

- *Social problems.* Children of substance abusers often show many problems with their social functioning. They may be isolated and because of peer rejection, may not have adequate opportunities to interact with other children or develop good social skills. Children of substance abusers are more likely than other children to become substance abusers themselves. Children of substance abusers face an increased risk of physical, sexual, or psychological abuse, dropping out of school, unwed pregnancy, delinquency, mental health problems, and attempted suicide (Johnson, 1990–1991).

In addition to suffering from personal problems, children of substance abusers often assume distinctive roles (Maisto, Galizio, & Connors, 1995). These roles include the following (Bean-Bayog & Stimmel, 1987; Northwest Indian Child Welfare Institute, 1984):

- The *responsible one* (the family hero) is frequently the oldest child. This child is likely to be a high achiever but feel inadequate. "Parentification" of the child may be reinforced by alcoholic parents who praise the child for achieving high levels of mastery and self-control. This behavior response seems to be related to the alcoholic's issue of dealing with a lack of willpower.

- The *scapegoat* (the acting-out child) is often at the center of family chaos, distracting family members' attention from the substance abuser. The child may act angry and defiant, but is actually hurting inside.

- The *lost child* (the adjuster) relinquishes personal needs and accommodates to situations by suppressing these needs. The child does not question the family system but is often lonely or quiet. These children are often middle children who, because of their lack of presenting problems, may be overlooked by social workers.

- The *placater* (the leveler) is a sensitive child who copes by trying to make everyone feel better, solving disputes, carrying messages, and blaming himself for problems. These children are "pleasers" who appear very polite. Many placaters grow up to be professional helpers.

- The *family mascot* (the distracter), often the youngest child, provides comic relief for the family. The child behaves immaturely and is seen as the baby of the family, in need of protection. This child may feel fearful and anxious and may also be hyperactive.

These roles are also seen in families with other types of difficulties as well as addiction. The roles interfere with "normal" childhood behavior and may continue long past childhood, creating difficulties in later life.

Intervention in Families with Substance Abusers

If a family social worker suspects that a client has a problem with substance abuse, he or she should carry out the following tasks:

- Identify and assess the problem;
- Openly discuss the addition with the family;
- Provide support while the family changes;
- Connect the family with specialized professional services;
- Provide case coordination and management after specialized treatment begins.

Social work with families of substance abusers often involves trying to alter family dynamics so that members no longer camouflage or collude with the substance abuse (Aponte & VanDeusen, 1981). Although family intervention often involves interviews with all family members, its aims may also be accomplished with one person or a family subsystem such as the couple (Bowen, 1973). A family approach to addictions is useful because it assists the entire family by changing family structure and dynamics to help members refuse to facilitate the addiction. A family approach looks at *circular causality* because the behavior of each person in the family affects everyone else. In alcoholism, where negative stereotypes and attitudes are prevalent, family social workers can convey a nonjudgmental attitude toward the family. Connecting family members with Alcoholics Anonymous and Al-Anon can also help them alleviate their feelings of blame and guilt.

When assessment of the family occurs in the home, the FSW can observe daily routines and determine how substance abuse affects mealtimes, homework, and bedtimes. The social worker can also assess the family's resources, such as competencies of each member and support from relatives. Families need to learn about the effects of substance abuse and to become aware that the problems they are experiencing are related to the addiction.

In working with families of substance abusers, the FSW should validate family and individual strengths and guide the family toward problem solving. Obtaining a comprehensive assessment of the family helps the FSW to understand effects of the addiction on individual family members and identify behaviors that perpetuate the addiction.

Engaging the family must precede all other interventions. The family must accept help in order to work toward change. The social worker usually must overcome the family's initial resistance. Getting past denial is a pressing task for the FSW, because denial prevents effective intervention. Confrontation should be used skillfully (Gilliland & James, 1993). In addition, family routines, individual differences, interaction, behaviors, coping patterns, and disciplinary procedures should be analyzed. Observation of family interactions at different times of the day may be necessary to obtain a comprehensive picture of family functioning. Conflicts and problems should be noted. Contact with schools, addiction specialists, doctors, and church leaders should be made during the assessment phase. It may be necessary to provide concrete assistance, such as ensuring that the family has sufficient financial resources to survive while the addicted family member is receiving inpatient treatment.

Because families often will acknowledge the severity of the problem only during periods of severe chaos and disorganization, social workers should not expect the family to readily volunteer information about the problem. FSWs should instead rely on indirect cues. Gradually, as alcoholism progresses through stages, the spouse and the older children are likely to acknowledge the problem and refuse to camouflage it.

Roles of the Family Social Worker

Addiction requires treatment by specialists. Nevertheless, family social workers can play several crucial roles while assisting families of substance abusers: nurturer, teacher, coordinator, and advocate. By carrying out these roles, FSWs can help to reduce family dysfunction and improve family communication.

Nurturer A strong worker-family relationship is important for successful family work. Intense and frequent contact with the family helps the FSW to develop a helping relationship.

Families in crisis depend on the FSW to stimulate hope, which will give them the courage to make the necessary changes. Unfortunately, families referred for service usually are people who have trouble developing relationships. Because of negative life experiences, these families have developed a mistrust of authority, institutions, and helping professionals. A close relationship with the FSW can encourage families to use appropriate services.

Teacher The family social worker is a teacher and trainer who can help family members learn a variety of skills: home management and life skills, communication and relationship skills, parenting and child management skills, assertiveness skills and self-advocacy, the skills of problem solving, utilization of community resources, and finally, constructive coping.

The social worker can teach skills by explaining, modeling, role-play, coaching, and encouraging. He or she can help the family to work out a budget, find housing, plan nutritious meals, or divide housekeeping tasks.

Teaching practical skills is often necessary because families of substance abusers may have difficulty performing routine tasks. It is important to find out what the family does well and what they want to learn, using the helping relationship as the vehicle that facilitates that learning.

Coordinator Family social work requires frequent family contact, and the FSW should be aware of coordination needs and problems. The goals of service coordination are to develop joint treatment plans whenever possible, to spell out the roles and functions of all involved agencies and team members, and assure that the efforts of all agencies are directed toward common goals. The methods and techniques used should not conflict with each other or confuse family members. The social worker will need to monitor services provided by other helpers and determine when the efforts of various agencies are at cross-purposes. It may be necessary to act as the family's advocate when services are not forthcoming, but the FSW should support the efforts of other agencies. In addition, each service provider will need accurate information about the family and about other services that are being provided.

The social worker should assist family members to develop their own support network that will remain in place after the intensive work is done. Sources of alternative support can be as varied as the circumstances of family members and can include community organizations, religious organizations, cultural groups and activities, parenting classes, and groups who share special interests (athletics, culture, karate, gardening). Resolution of strained relationships between the client family and members of the extended family may be necessary before the involvement of extended family can be constructive.

INTERVENTIONS WITH A SUBSTANCE ABUSER

> If you discovered your client had a problem with substance abuse but was denying it, what would you do? List some family systems interventions you could employ to help the client acknowledge the problem. Keep in mind the different roles of the family social worker.

Advocate The family social worker often intervenes or fights for the family but should also teach the family how to advocate for themselves. Immediate intervention on behalf of the family or one of its members generates hope, validates the social worker's credibility, and shows caring and commitment. However, before acting on the client's behalf, the FSW should ask the following questions: Could my client accomplish this without my support? Could we attempt it jointly? Does she or he merely need the impetus to begin? Does she or he need a sounding board to evaluate options and plan strategies? By advocating and teaching self-advocacy, the FSW empowers family members to help themselves.

WORKING WITH INVOLUNTARY CLIENTS

Clients often enter family work reluctantly. Some are visibly resistant. Clients who are experiencing problems such as sexual abuse, family violence, or substance abuse often show strong resistance at the onset of family social work. Resistance by clients is not surprising, because many people enter family social work feeling anxious, frightened, or ashamed. In addition, parents often feel like failures when a problem attracts agency attention.

Families may also be resistant to the actions of a particular agency because of past experience or because of what the agency represents to them. Some families may have been involved with other agencies without seeing any change in their problems. Clients may be concerned about possible breaches of confidentiality or anticipated lack of agency understanding of their situation. As a result, they may choose to be minimally compliant, doing only enough work to get by. Most involuntary clients are resistant clients, but not all resistant clients are involuntary.

Involuntary clients typically receive services from an agency without asking for them. They may not be motivated to engage in family social work, and they may refuse to work toward the goals that the FSW or agency has identified. They often arrive at an agency because they have been forced to receive help by public officials. In this light, assessment of involuntary clients should be done carefully because of the possibility that the problems are dangerous, illegal, or both.

Willingness to become involved in family work varies from one family to another. Even voluntary clients fall along a continuum of motivation for services. At one extreme end of the continuum are clients who are legally mandated to receive service and who do not believe they have a problem. Somewhere in the middle are those who believe they have a problem but do not want to enter treatment to make the necessary changes. The ideal clients recognize they have a problem and want to change their circumstances to eliminate the problem.

Family members often show varying degrees of reluctance toward acknowledging a problem and engaging in the necessary work to produce change. An especially complex situation occurs when there is some form of victimization within the family and the perpetrator does not want to change.

Involuntary clients are often mandated to receive agency intervention because of problems involving child welfare, mental health, or criminal justice. An overarching issue often is substance abuse. For all these categories of problems, laws exist to force clients into treatment against their will. When clients enter treatment against their will, they are likely to be resistant.

Even when there is no legal mandate forcing clients into treatment, some clients become involved because of pressure from family members or friends. For example, the spouse of a substance abuser may threaten to leave unless the person goes into treatment. Children usually have little leverage to force the family into work unless the child's behavior becomes so problematic that it is difficult to ignore, as when a child becomes suicidal or runs away from home. When some family members are resistant to family work, they are likely to hamper the progress of the rest of the family.

In another common scenario, some family members agree that there is a problem, but they believe that the problem belongs to someone else in the family. This is a very common stance among families in which teenagers are "acting out." The challenge for the social worker is to help all family members understand their roles in the development of the problem.

Clients usually look for one of two outcomes from family social work. Some just want to eliminate the pain created by the problem, and in the process they want to be "nurtured." These clients may be satisfied once the initial stress has been alleviated, and they may avoid making difficult or lasting changes. Other clients want to change their lives in concrete ways. They are willing to work hard to achieve needed changes in their lives. These are the most rewarding clients for family social workers.

Involuntary or otherwise resistant families usually benefit from a clear contract stating the expected outcomes of their actions. The FSW's task is to convey that despite the involuntary nature of their involvement in the work, some choices remain, and every choice is associated with an anticipated outcome. For example, those who are ordered into work for reasons of abuse but refuse to become involved may find that the FSW has written a letter to the court or that their children have been placed in foster care. Ultimately, the social worker can empathize with clients' anger and fears about family social work and discuss how the involuntary nature of the work affects everyone.

Families need to know that participating in family social work is their choice. When families understand that there are certain issues over which they have control, their resistance may decrease. The FSW should emphasize that freedom from unwanted agency intervention will occur when the conditions of the court order or contracted work are met. The contract should contain some recognition of client self-determination and state the conditions under which the family will become free from agency and legal intrusion.

Work with involuntary clients should begin by focusing on specific, concrete changes. Clients should be informed that some conditions of the work are not negotiable, and they need to understand the specific conditions for termination.

As uncomfortable as it may be, family social workers must clearly describe the conditions linked to involuntary family social work. For example, if the social worker is required to prepare a court report, families should know about this at the outset. Clients must know what is expected of them as well as what is negotiable. When clients do not want to work, the family social worker can point out that the family has a right not to participate but that nonparticipation involves some consequences. In summary, the family social worker must discuss the nature of the problem, his or her role, nonnegotiable requirements, procedures mandated by the referral source, negotiable requirements, and choices available to the clients (Hepworth & Larson, 1993).

Family social workers should keep in mind that motivation is the flip side of resistance. Motivation is present when families have a sincere desire to change something in their lives. Resentment and negativity undermine motivation. When clients feel blamed by the social worker and agency for their problems, without any concomitant understanding or empathy, they may view the FSW as a threat. Family social workers must be prepared to face clients' feelings of hostility and anger and to respond openly to the negative feelings. Arguing usually accomplishes little and can escalate clients' hostility and resentment. Since resistance to work may be part of a family's general style of dealing with outsiders, empathic responses by the family social worker can provide an example of appropriate behavior. We suggest not confronting client perceptions until trust and acceptance have developed. Direct confrontation about responsibility for problems during the assessment phase is likely to produce defensiveness rather than lead to change (Ivanoff, Blythe, & Tripodi, 1994).

By recommending that FSWs not confront client perceptions early in the work, we are not saying that FSWs should collude with client dysfunction. The single most important skill for working with family resistance is being able to identify when it may be counterproductive to push an issue with the family (Brock & Barnard, 1992). Appropriate work with resistant clients entails looking for windows of opportunity to induce change. Sometimes clients may block the development of a working contract by insisting on pushing through their own definition of the problem. Social workers may be able to find a common ground somewhere between the FSW's and the client's definitions of the problem. Once the initial barriers are broken, many FSWs discover that clients gradually drop their defensiveness in defining the problem. Social workers need to remember that defensiveness serves a protective function for clients, and this protective stance can be dropped only after clients feel safe. Overcoming resistance usually involves finding out about the FSW and evaluating him or her (Lum, 1994).

Work with involuntary clients can be just as effective as work with voluntary clients (Ivanoff, Blythe, & Tripodi, 1994, p. 57). The most positive results seem to be related to the quality of worker-client interaction. One last word of advice is in order: a wise worker must be able to recognize the difference between a resistant family and an ineffectual intervention.

CHAPTER SUMMARY

Two serious problems that affect families are domestic abuse and substance abuse. A cycle of violence keeps women trapped in abusive relationships. Other reasons for remaining in the home include lack of financial and social resources to leave. Women may also feel powerless to make major changes in their lives. Family social workers should be able to recognize signs of abuse. Safety of family members is the primary concern for family social workers. In addition, family social workers must be willing to discuss the issue openly and to recommend community resources to assist battered women and their children. The battered woman, however, must be the one to make decisions about what actions to take about the abusive relationship.

Another problem that a family social worker is likely to encounter is substance abuse. Substance abuse affects every member of a family. These families may experience disrupted daily routines, have trouble expressing feelings, and assume rigid family roles that interfere with individual functioning. Children often experience problems in many areas of their lives. Substance abuse is particularly difficult to treat because abusers often deny having a problem. Family social workers should encourage open communication among family members and allow them to discuss their concerns about the substance abuse. Social workers should be prepared to discuss how the substance abuse is affecting the family.

When clients are involved in family social work involuntarily, the FSW must provide clients with a clear definition of the requirements and anticipated outcomes of the intervention, as well as consequences of noncompliance. The FSW should be prepared to acknowledge and discuss clients' feelings of hostility and resistance. Early confrontation of clients' perceptions is not advisable; resistant clients are likely to drop their defensive posture only after they have begun to engage with the FSW. An important aspect of working with involuntary clients is being alert for windows of opportunity to induce change.

References

Alexander, J., Holtzworth-Munroe, A., & Jameson, P. (1994). The process and outcome of marital and family therapy: Research review and evaluation. In A. Bergin & S. Garfield (Eds.), *Handbook of psychotherapy and behavior change* (4th ed.) (pp. 595–630). Toronto: Wiley.

Alexander, J., & Parsons, B. (1973). Short-term behavioral intervention with delinquent families: Impact on family process and recidivism. *Journal of Abnormal Psychology, 81*(3), 219–225.

Alexander, J., & Parsons, B. (1982). *Functional family therapy.* Monterey, CA: Brooks/Cole.

Aponte, H., & VanDeusen, J. (1981). Structural family therapy. In A. S. Gurman & D. P. Kniskern (Eds.), *Handbook of family therapy.* New York: Brunner/Mazel.

Armstrong, L. (1987). *Kiss daddy goodnight: Ten years later.* New York: Pocket Books.

Arnold, J., Levine, A., & Patterson, G. (1975). Changes in sibling behavior following family intervention. *Journal of Consulting and Clinical Psychology, 43*(5), 683–688.

Bagley, C., & MacDonald, J. (1984). Adult mental health sequels of child sexual abuse, physical abuse and neglect in maternally separated children. *Canadian Journal of Community Mental Health, 3,* 15–26.

Bagley, C., & Ramsey, R. (1984). Sexual abuse in childhood: Psychosocial outcomes and implications for social work practice. *The Journal of Social Work and Human Sexuality, 4,* 33–47.

Bandler, R., Grinder, J., & Satir, V. (1976). *Changing with families.* Palo Alto, CA: Science and Behavior Books.

Barker, R. (1981). *Basic family therapy.* Baltimore: University Park Press.

Barker, R. (1995). *The social worker dictionary* (3rd ed.). Washington, DC: NASW.

Baum, C., & Forehand, R. (1981). Long-term follow-up assessment of parent training by use of multiple outcome measures. *Behavior Therapy, 12,* 643–652.

Baynard, R., & Baynard, J. (1983). *How to deal with your acting-up teenager.* New York: M. Evans & Company.

Bean-Bayog, M., & Stimmel, B. (Eds.). (1987). *Children of alcoholics.* New York: Haworth Press.

Beavers, W. (1981). A systems model of family for family therapists. *Journal of Marriage and Family Therapy, 7,* 299–307.

Becvar, D., & Becvar, R. (1993). *Family therapy: A systemic integration* (2nd ed.). Boston: Allyn & Bacon.

Becvar, D., & Becvar, R. (1996). *Family therapy: A systemic integration* (3rd ed.). Boston: Allyn & Bacon.

Beitchman, J., Hood, J., Zucker, K., daCosta, G., & Akman, D. (1991). *The short- and long-term effects of child sexual abuse on the child.* Ottawa: National Clearinghouse on Family Violence.

Bernard, D. (1992). The dark side of family preservation. *Affilia, 7*(2), 156–159.

Berry, M. (1997). *The family at risk.* Columbia, SC: University of South Carolina Press.

Beutler, L., Machado, P., & Allstetter Neufelt, A. (1994). Therapist variables. In A. Bergin & S. Garfield (Eds.), *Handbook of psychotherapy and behavior change* (4th ed.) (pp. 229–269). Toronto: Wiley.

Blum, H., Boyle, M., & Offord, D. (1988). Single-parent families: Child psychiatric disorder and school performance. *Journal of the American Academy of Child and Adolescent Psychiatry, 27,* 214–219.

Bodin, A. (1981). The interactional view: Family therapy approaches of the Mental Research Institute. In A. S. Gurman & D. P. Kniskern (Eds.), *Handbook of family therapy* (pp. 267–309). New York: Brunner/Mazel.

Bograd, M. (1992). Changes to family therapists' thinking. *Journal of Marital and Family Therapy, 18,* 243–253.

Bolton, F., & Bolton, S. (1987). *Working with violent families: A guide for clinical and legal practitioners.* Beverly Hills, CA: Sage Publications.

Bowen, M. (1973). Alcoholism and the family system. *Family: Journal of the Center for Family Learning,* pp. 20–25.

Bowlby, J. (1969). *Attachment.* New York: Basic Books.

Braverman, L. (1991). The dilemma of homework: A feminist response to Gottman, Napier, and Pittman. *Journal of Marital and Family Therapy, 17,* 25–28.

Breunlin, D. (1988). Oscillation theory and family development. In C. Falicov (Ed.), *Family transitions: Continuity and change over the life cycle.* New York: Guilford Press.

Briere, J. (1992). *Child abuse trauma: Theory and treatment of the lasting effects.* Newbury Park, CA: Sage Publications.

Brock, G., & Barnard, C. (1992). *Procedures in marriage and family therapy.* Boston: Allyn & Bacon.

Brooks, B. (1985). Sexually abused children and adolescent identity development. *American Journal of Psychotherapy, 39,* 401–410.

Browne, A., & Finkelhor, D. (1986). Impact of child sexual abuse: A review of the research. *Psychological Bulletin, 99,* 66–77.

Burden, D. (1986). Single parents and the work setting: The impact of multiple job and homelife responsibilities. *Family Relations, 35,* 37–43.

Burgess, R., & Youngblade, L. (1988). Social incompetence and the intergenerational transmission of abusive parenting practices. In G. Hotaling, D. Finkelhor, J. Kirkpatrick, & M. Straus (Eds.), *Family abuse and its consequences* (pp. 38–60). Newbury Park, CA: Sage Publications.

Caplan, P., & Hall-McCorquodale, I. (1985). Mother-blaming in major clinical journals. *American Journal of Orthopsychiatry, 55,* 345–353.

Caplan, P., & Hall-McCorquodale, I. (1991). The scapegoating of mothers: A call for change. In J. Veevers (Ed.), *Continuity and change in marriage and the family* (pp. 295–302). Toronto: Holt, Rinehart & Winston of Canada.

Carter, B. (1992). Stonewalling feminism. *The Family Therapy Network, 16*(1), 64–69.

Carter, B., & McGoldrick, M. (Eds.). (1988). *The changing family life cycle: A framework for family therapy* (2nd ed.). New York: Gardner Press.

Caviola, A., & Schiff, M. (1989). Self-esteem in abused chemically dependent adolescents. *Child Abuse and Neglect, 13,* 327–334.

Charles, G., & Coleman, H. (1990). Child and youth suicide. *Canadian Home Economics Journal, 40*(2), 72–75.

Charles, G., & Matheson, J. (1991). Suicide prevention and intervention with young people in foster care in Canada. *Child Welfare, 70*(2), 185.

Cherlin, A. (1983). Family policy: The conservative challenge to the progressive response. *Journal of Family Issues, 4*(3), 417–438.

Cohn, A. (1979). Effective treatment of child abuse and neglect. *Social Casework, 6*(24), 513–519.

Coleman, H. (1995). *A longitudinal study of a family preservation program.* Unpublished doctoral dissertation. Graduate School of Social Work, Salt Lake City, Utah.

Coleman, H., & Collins, D. (1990). The treatment trilogy of father-daughter incest. *Child and Adolescent Social Work Journal, 7*(40), 339–355.

Coleman, H., & Collins, D. (1997). The voice of parents: A qualitative study of a family-centered, home-based program. *The Child and Youth Care Forum (Special Edition on Research in the Field of Child and Youth Care), 26*(4), 261–278.

Collins, D. (1989). Child care workers and family therapists: Getting connected. *Journal of Child and Youth Care, 4*(3), 23–31.

Collins, D., Thomlison, B., & Grinnell, R. (1992). *The social work practicum: An access guide.* Itasca, IL: F. E. Peacock.

Coontz, S. (1996). The way we weren't: The myth and reality of the "Traditional Family." *National Forum, 76*(4), 45–48.

Courtois, C. A. (1979). The incest experience and its aftermath. *Victimology, 4,* 337–347.

Crichton, M. (1995). *The lost world.* New York: Ballantine.

Curtner-Smith, M. E. (1995). Assessing children's visitation needs with divorced noncustodial fathers. *Families in Society, 76*(6), 341–348.

Davis, K. (1996). *Families: A handbook of concepts and techniques for the helping professional.* Pacific Grove, CA: Brooks/Cole.

Davis, L., & Proctor, E. (1989). *Race, gender, and class.* Englewood Cliffs, NJ: Prentice Hall.

Dell, P. (1989). Violence and the systemic view: The problem of power. *Family Process, 23,* 1–14.

Denicola, J., & Sandler, J. (1980). Training abusive parents in child management and self-control skills. *Behavior Therapy, 11,* 263–270.

Diekstra, R., & Moritz, B. (1987). Suicidal behavior among adolescents: An overview. In R. Diekstra (Ed.), *Suicide in adolescence* (pp. 7–24). Boston: Martinus Nijhoff Publishers.

Dutton, D. (1991). Interventions into the problem of wife assault: Therapeutic, policy, and research implications. In J. Veevers (Ed.), *Continuity and change in marriage and the family* (pp. 203–215). Toronto: Holt, Rinehart & Winston of Canada.

Duvall, E. (1957). *Family transitions*. Philadelphia: Lippincott.

Dye Holten, J. (1990). When do we stop mother-blaming? *Journal of Feminist Family Therapy, 2*(1), 53–60.

Efron, D., & Rowe, B. (1987). *Strategic parenting manual*. London, Ontario: J.S.S.T.

Egan, G. (1994). *The skilled helper*. Pacific Grove, CA: Brooks/Cole.

Eichler, M. (1988). *Nonsexist research methods: A practical guide*. Boston: Allen & Unwin.

Eichler, M. (1997). *Family shifts: Families, policies, and gender equality*. Toronto: Oxford University Press.

Epstein, N., Baldwin, D., & Bishop, S. (1983). The McMaster family assessment device. *Journal of Marital and Family Therapy, 9*, 171–180.

Epstein, N., Bishop, D., & Levin, S. (1978). The McMaster model of family functioning. *Journal of Marriage and Family Counseling, 4*, 19–31.

Everstine, D., & Everstine, L. (1989). *Sexual trauma in children and adolescents: Dynamics and treatment*. New York: Brunner/Mazel.

Ewing, C. (1978). *Crisis intervention in psychotherapy*. New York: Oxford University Press.

Finkelhor, D. (1986). Sexual abuse: Beyond the family systems approach. In T. Trepper & M. Barrett (Eds.), *Treating incest: A multiple systems perspective* (pp. 53–66). New York: Haworth Press.

Fischer, J., & Corcoran, J. (1994). *Measures for clinical practice*. New York: Free Press.

Forehand, R., Sturgis, E., McMahon, R., Aguar, D., Green, K., Wells, K., & Breiner, J. (1979). Parent behavioral training to modify child noncompliance: Treatment generalization across time and from home to school. *Behavior Modification, 3*(1), 3–25.

Forgatch, M. (1991). The clinical science vortex: A developing theory of antisocial behavior. In D. Pepler & K. Rubin (Eds.), *The development and treatment of child aggression* (pp. 291–315). Hillsdale, NJ: Lawrence Erlbaum Associates.

Foster, S., Prinz, R., & O'Leary, D. (1983). Impact of problem-solving communication training and generalization procedures on family conflict. *Child and Family Behavior Therapy, 5*(1), 1–23.

Franklin, C., & Jordan, C. (1999). *Brief family practice: Innovations and integrations*. Pacific Grove, CA: Brooks/Cole.

Fraser, M., Pecora, P., & Haapala, D. (Eds.) (1991). *Families in crisis*. New York: Aldine de Gruyter.

Furstenberg, E. (1980). Reflections on marriage. *Journal of Family Issues, 1*, 443–453.

Gabor, P., & Collins, D. (1985–86). Family work in child care. *Journal of Child Care, 2*(5), 15–27.

Gambrill, E. (1983). *Casework: A competency-based approach*. Englewood Cliffs, NJ: Prentice-Hall.

Garbarino, J. (1982). *Children and families in their social environment*. New York: Aldine de Gruyter.

Garbarino, J., & Crouter, A. (1978). Defining the community context of parent-child relations: The correlates of child maltreatment. *Child Development, 49*, 604–616.

Garbarino, J., & Gilliam, G. (1987). *Understanding abusive families*. Lexington, MA: Lexington Books.

Gavin, K., & Bramble, B. (1996). *Family communication: Cohesion and change*. New York: HarperCollins.

Geismar, L., & Ayres, B. (1959). A method for evaluating the social functioning of families under treatment. *Social Work, 4*(1), 102–108.

Geismar, L., & Krisberg, J. (1996). The Family Life Improvement Project: An experiment in preventive intervention. *Social Casework, 47*, 563–570.

Gelles, R. (1987). *Family violence*. Newbury Park, CA: Sage Publications.

Gelles, R. (1989). Child abuse and violence in single-parent families: Parent absence and economic deprivation. *American Journal of Orthopsychiatry, 59*(4), 492–503.

Gelles, R., & Straus, M. (1988). *Intimate violence: The causes and consequences of abuse in the American family*. New York: Simon & Schuster.

Gil, D. (1970). *Violence against children: Physical child abuse in the United States*. Cambridge, MA: Harvard University Press.

Giles-Sims, J. (1983). *Wife-beating: A systems theory approach*. New York: Guilford Press.

Gilliland, B., & James, R. (1993). *Crisis intervention strategies*. Pacific Grove, CA: Brooks/Cole.

Giovanonni, J. (1982). Mistreated children. In S. Yelaja (Ed.), *Ethical issues in social work*. Springfield, IL: Charles C. Thomas.

Gladow, N., & Ray, M. (1986). The impact of informal support systems on the well-being of low-income single-parent families. *Family Relations, 35*, 57–62.

Glick, P. (1989). The family life cycle and social change. *Family Relations, 38*, 123–129.

Goldenberg, H., & Goldenberg, I. (1994). *Counseling today's families*. Pacific Grove, CA: Brooks/Cole.

Goldenberg, I., & Goldenberg, H. (1996). *Family therapy: An overview* (4th ed.). Pacific Grove, CA: Brooks/Cole.

Goldner, V. (1985a). Feminism and family therapy. *Family Process, 24*(1), 31–47.

Goldner, V. (1985b). Warning: Family therapy may be hazardous to your health. *The Family Therapy Networker, 9*(6), 18–23.

Goldner, V. (1988). Generation and hierarchy: Normative and covert hierarchies. *Family Process, 27*(1), 17–31.

Goldstein, H. (1981). Home-based services and the worker. In M. Bryce & J. Lloyd (Eds.), *Treating families in the home: An alternative to placement*. Springfield, IL: Charles C. Thomas.

Good, G., Gilbert, L., & Scher, M. (1990). Gender-aware therapy: A synthesis of feminist therapy and knowledge about gender. *Journal of Counseling and Development, 68*, 227–234.

Goodrich, T., Rampage, C., Ellman, B., & Halstead, K. (1988). *Feminist family therapy: A casebook*. New York: W. W. Norton.

Gordon, L. (1985). Child abuse, gender, and the myth of family independence: A historical critique. *Child Welfare, 64*(3), 213–224.

Gordon, S., & Davidson, N. (1981). Behavioral parent training. In A. S. Gurman & D. P. Kniskern (Eds.), *Handbook of family therapy* (pp. 517–553). New York: Brunner/Mazel.

Green, R., & Herget, M. (1991). Outcomes of systemic/strategic team consultation: III. The importance of therapist warmth and active structuring. *Family Process, 30*, 321–336.

Grunwald, B., & McAbee, H. (1985). *Guiding the family: Practical counseling techniques.* Muncie, IN: Accelerated Development.

Gurman, A. S., & Kniskern, D. P. (1981). Family therapy outcome research: Knowns and unknowns. In A. S. Gurman & D. P. Kniskern (Eds.), *Handbook of family therapy* (pp. 742–776). New York: Brunner/Mazel.

Gurman, A. S., & Kniskern, D. P. (Eds.). (1981). *Handbook of family therapy.* New York: Brunner/Mazel.

Hackney, H., & Cormier, L. (1996). *The professional counselor: A process guide to helping* (3rd ed.). Toronto: Allyn & Bacon.

Haley, J. (1976). *Problem-solving therapy.* New York: Harper & Row.

Hall, L., & Lloyd, S. (1993). *Surviving child sexual abuse: Handbook for helping women challenge their past* (2nd ed.). Bristol, PA: Palmer Press.

Hanson, S. (1986). Healthy single-parent families. *Family Relations, 35,* 125–132.

Hartman, A., & Laird, J. (1983). *Family-centered social work practice.* New York: Free Press.

Hawton, K. (1986). *Suicide and attempted suicide among children and adolescents.* London: Sage Publications.

Helton, L., & Jackson, M. (1997). *Social work practice with families: A diversity model.* Boston: Allyn & Bacon.

Hepworth, D., & Larsen, J. (1993). *Direct social work practice: Theory and skills.* Homewood, IL: Dorsey Press.

Hetherington, E., Cox, M., & Cox, R. (1978). Play and social interaction in children following divorce. *Journal of Social Issues, 35,* 26–49.

Hill, R. (1986). Life-cycle stages for types of single-parent families: A family development theory. *Family Relations, 35,* 19–29.

Ho, M. K. (1987). *Family therapy with ethnic minorities.* Newbury Park, CA: Sage Publications.

Holman, A. (1983). *Family assessment: Tools for understanding and intervention.* Newbury Park, CA: Sage Publications.

Horne, A. M., & Passmore, J. L. (1991). *Family counseling and therapy* (2nd ed.). Itasca, IL: F. E. Peacock.

Hudson, W. (1982). *The clinical measurement package: A field manual.* Chicago: Dorsey Press.

Hunter College Women's Studies Collective. (1995). *Women's realities, women's choices* (2nd ed.). New York: Oxford University Press.

International Association of Psychosocial Rehabilitation Services. (1997). PSR standards and indicators for multicultural psychiatric rehabilitation services. *PSR Connection,* Issue 4, p. 7.

Isaacs, C. (1982). Treatment of child abuse: A review of the behavioral interventions. *Journal of Applied Behavior Analysis, 15,* 273–294.

Ivonoff, A., Blythe, B., & Tripodi, T. (1994). *Involuntary clients in social work practice.* New York: Aldine de Gruyter.

Jackson, D. (1972). Family rules: Marital quid pro quo. In G. Erickson & T. Hogan (Eds.), *Family therapy: An introduction to theory and technique* (pp. 76–85). Monterey, CA: Brooks/Cole.

Johnson, D., & Johnson, F. (1994). *Joining together* (5th ed.). Boston: Allyn & Bacon.

Johnson, H. (1986). Emerging concerns in family therapy. *Social Work, 31*(4), 299–306.

Johnson, J. (1990–91). Preventive interventions for children at risk: Introduction. *The International Journal of the Addictions, 25*(4A), 429–434.

Jones, D., & McQuiston, M. (1986). *Interviewing the sexually abused child.* Denver: C. Henry Kempe National Center for the Prevention and Treatment of Child Abuse and Neglect.

Jordan, C., & Franklin, C. (1995). *Clinical assessment for social workers: Quantitative and qualitative methods.* Chicago: Lyceum.

Jordan, C., Lewellen, A., & Vandiver, V. (1994). A social work perspective of psychosocial rehabilitation: Psychoeducational models for minority families. *International Journal of Mental Health, 23*(4), 27–43.

Kadushin, A., & Kadushin, G. (1997). *The social work interview* (4th ed.). New York: Columbia University Press.

Kaplan, L. (1986). *Working with the multiproblem family.* Lexington, MA: Lexington Books.

Kaslow, N., & Celano, M. (1995). The family therapies. In A. Gurman & S. Messer (Eds.), *Essential psychotherapies: Theory and practice* (pp. 343–402). New York: Guilford Press.

Kavanaugh, K., Youngblade, L., Reid, J., & Fagot, B. (1988). Interactions between children and abusive versus controlling parents. *Journal of Clinical Child Psychology, 17*(2), 137–142.

Kazdin, A. (1991). Effectiveness of psychotherapy with children and adolescents. *Journal of Consulting and Clinical Psychology, 59,* 785–798.

Kilpatrick, A., & Holland, T. (1995). *Working with families: An integrative model by level of functioning.* Boston: Allyn & Bacon.

Kinney, J., Haapala, D., & Booth, C. (1991). *Keeping families together: The Homebuilders Model.* New York: Aldine de Gruyter.

Klein, N., Alexander, J., & Parsons, B. (1977). Impact of family systems intervention on recidivism and sibling delinquency: A model of primary prevention and program evaluation. *Journal of Consulting and Clinical Psychology, 45*(3), 469–474.

Kohlert, N., & Pecora, P. (1991). Therapist perceptions of organizational support and job satisfaction. In M. Fraser, P. Pecora, & D. Haapala (Eds.), *Families in crisis* (pp. 109–129). New York: Aldine de Gruyter.

Lambert, M., & Bergin, A. (1994). The effectiveness of psychotherapy. In A. Bergin & S. Garfield (Eds.), *Handbook of psychotherapy and behavior change* (4th ed.) (pp. 143–189). Toronto: Wiley.

Langsley, D., Pittman, F., Machotka, P., & Flomenhaft, K. (1968). Family crisis therapy: Results and implications. *Family Process, 7*(2), 145–158.

Ledbetter Hancock, B., & Pelton, L. (1989). Home visits: History and functions. *Social Casework, 70*(1), 21.

LeMasters, E. (1957). Parenthood as crisis. *Marriage and Family Living, 19,* 325–355.

Lewellen, A., & Jordan, C. (1994). Family empowerment and service satisfaction: An exploratory study of families who care for a mentally ill member. Unpublished manuscript. The University of Texas at Arlington.

Lewis, J. (1988). The transition to parenthood: 1. The rating of prenatal marital competence. *Family Process, 27*(2), 149–166.

Loredo, C. (1983). Sibling incest. In S. Sgroi (Ed.), *Handbook of clinical intervention in child sexual abuse* (pp. 148–176). Toronto: Lexington Books.

Lum, D. (1992). *Social work practice with people of color: A process-stage approach.* Pacific Grove, CA: Brooks/Cole.

Mackie, M. (1991). *Gender relations in Canada.* Toronto: Harcourt Brace Canada.

Maisto, S., Galizio, M., & Connors, G. (1995). *Drug use and abuse.* Toronto: Harcourt.

Maluccio, A., & Marlow, W. (1975). The case for the contract. In B. Compton and B. Galaway (Eds.), *Social work processes*. Homewood, IL: Dorsey.

Maslow, A. (1967). *Toward a psychology of being*. New York: Van Nostrand Reinhold.

Masson, J. (1994). *Against therapy*. Monroe, ME: Common Courage Press.

McGoldrick, M. (1988). Ethnicity and the family life cycle. In B. Carter & M. McGoldrick (Eds.), *The changing family life cycle: A framework for family therapy* (pp. 69–90). New York: Gardner Press.

McGoldrick, M., & Gerson, R. (1985). *Genograms in family assessment*. New York: Norton.

McGoldrick, M., & Giordano, J. (1996). Overview: Ethnicity and family therapy. In M. McGoldrick, J. Giordano, & J. Pearce (Eds.), *Ethnicity and family therapy* (pp. 1–30). New York: Guilford Press.

McGoldrick, M., Giordano, J., & Pearce, J. (Eds.). (1996). *Ethnicity and family therapy*. New York: Guilford Press.

McNeece, A., & DiNitto, D. (1994). *Chemical dependency: A systems approach*. Englewood Cliffs, NJ: Prentice-Hall.

Meiselman, K. (1980). *Resolving the trauma of incest: Reintegration therapy with survivors*. San Francisco: Jossey-Bass.

Miller, S., Hubble, S., & Duncan, B. (1995). No more bells and whistles. *The Networker, 19*(2), 53–63.

Minuchin, S. (1974). *Families and family therapy*. Cambridge, MA: Harvard University Press.

Munson, C. (1993). *Clinical social work supervision*. New York: Haworth Press.

Myers-Avis, J. (1992). Where are all the family therapists? Abuse and violence within families and family therapy's response. *Journal of Marital and Family Therapy, 18*, 225–232.

Nelson, S. (1987). *Incest: Act and myth*. London, England: Redwood Burn, Ltd.

Nichols, M., & Schwartz, R. (1995). *Family therapy: Concepts and methods* (3rd ed.). Boston: Allyn & Bacon.

Nichols, M., & Schwartz, R. (1998). *Family therapy: Concepts and methods* (4th ed.). Boston: Allyn & Bacon.

Northwest Indian Child Welfare Institute. (1984). *Cross-cultural skills in Indian child welfare*. Portland, OR: Northwest Indian Child Welfare Institute.

Okun, B. (1996). *Understanding diverse families*. New York: Guilford Press.

Olson, D. (1986). Circumplex model VII: Validation studies and FACES III. *Family Process, 26*, 337–351.

Patterson, G., DeBaryshe, B., & Ramsey, E. (1989). A developmental perspective on antisocial behavior. *American Psychologist, 44*, 329–335.

Patterson, G., & Dishion, T. (1988). Multilevel family process models: Traits, interaction, and relationships. In R. Hinde & J. Stevenson-Hinde (Eds.), *Relationships within families* (pp. 283–310). Oxford: Clarendon Press.

Patterson, G., & Fleischman, M. (1979). Maintenance of treatment effects: Some considerations concerning family systems and follow-up data. *Behavior Therapy, 10*, 168–185.

Peterson, L. (1989). Latchkey children's preparation for self-care: Overestimated, underrehearsed, and unsafe. *Journal of Clinical Child Psychology, 18*, 2–7.

Petro, N., & Travis, N. (1985). The adolescent phase of the family life cycle. In M. Mirkin & S. Koman (Eds.), *Handbook of adolescent and family therapy*. New York: Gardner Press.

Pett, M. (1982). Predictors of satisfactory social adjustment of divorced parents. *Journal of Divorce, 5*(4), 25–39.

Pimento, B. (1985). *Native families in jeopardy: The child welfare system in Canada.* Toronto: Centre for Women's Studies in Education, Occasional Papers, No. 11.

Pleck, E. (1987). *Domestic tyranny: The making of social policy against family violence from colonial times to the present.* New York: Oxford University Press.

Pogrebin, L. (1980). *Growing up free.* New York: McGraw-Hill.

Pollack, W. (1998). *Real boys: Rescuing our sons from the myths of boyhood.* New York: Random House.

Porter, F., Blick, L., & Sgroi, S. (1983). Treatment of the sexually abused child. In S. Sgroi (Ed.), *Handbook of clinical intervention in child sexual abuse* (pp. 109–145). Toronto: Lexington Books.

Powers, G. (1990). Design and procedures for evaluating crisis. In A. Roberts (Ed.), *Crisis intervention handbook: Assessment, treatment, and research* (pp. 303–325). Belmont, CA: Wadsworth.

Red Horse, J. (1980). Family structure and value orientation in American Indians. *Social Casework, 61,* 462–467.

Richmond, M. (1917). *Social diagnosis.* New York: Russell Sage Foundation.

Ross, C. (1985). Teaching the facts of life and death: Suicide prevention in schools. In M. Peck (Ed.), *Youth suicide* (pp. 147–169). New York: Springer.

Rothery, M. (1993). The ecological perspective and work with vulnerable families. In M. Rodway & B. Trute (Eds.), *Ecological family practice: One family, many resources* (pp. 21–50). Queenston, Ontario: Edwin Mellen.

Rush, F. (1980). *The best-kept secret: Sexual abuse of children.* Englewood Cliffs, NJ: Prentice-Hall.

Sanders, J., & James, J. (1983). The modification of parent behavior: A review of generalization and maintenance. *Behavior Modification, 7*(1), 3–27.

Sandler, J., VanDercar, C., & Milhoan, M. (1978). Training child abusers in the use of positive reinforcement practices. *Behavior Research and Therapy, 16,* 169–175.

Satir, V. (1967). *Conjoint family therapy.* Palo Alto, CA: Science and Behavior Books.

Satir, V., & Baldwin, M. (1983). *Satir step by step: A guide to creating change in families.* Palo Alto, CA: Science and Behavior Books.

Sgroi, S. (Ed.). (1983). *Handbook of clinical intervention in child sexual abuse.* Toronto: Lexington Books.

Sheafor, B., Horejsi, C., & Horejsi, G. (1997). *Techniques and guidelines for social work practice* (4th ed.). Toronto: Allyn & Bacon.

Shulman, L. (1992). *The skills of helping individuals, families, and groups* (3rd ed.). Itasca, IL: F. E. Peacock.

Smith, S. (1984). Significant research findings in the etiology of child abuse. *Social Casework, 65*(6), 337–346.

Spanier, G., Lewis, R. & Cole, E. (1975). Marital adjustment over the family life cycle: The issue of curvilinearity. *Journal of Marriage and the Family, 37,* 263–275.

Steffen, J., & Karoly, P. (1980). Toward a psychology of therapeutic persistence. In P. Karoly & J. Steffen (Eds.), *Improving the long-term effects of psychotherapy: Models of durable outcome* (pp. 3–24). New York: Gardner Press.

Steinhauer, P. (1991). Assessing for parenting capacity. In J. Veevers (Ed.), *Continuity and change in marriage and family* (pp. 283–294). Toronto: Holt, Rinehart & Winston.

Stokes, T., & Baer, D. (1977). An implicit technology of generalization. *Journal of Applied Behavior Analysis, 10*(2), 349–367.

Straus, M. (1993). Physical assault by wives. In R. Gelles & D. Loseke (Eds.), *Current controversies on family violence* (pp. 67–87). Newbury Park, CA: Sage Publications.

Straus, M., & Gelles, M. (1988). How violent are American families? Estimates from the National Family Violence Resurvey and other studies. In G. Hotaling, D. Finkelhor, J. Kirkpatrick, & M. Straus (Eds.), *Family abuse and its consequences* (pp. 14–37). Newbury Park, CA: Sage Publications.

Sue, D., & Sue, D. (1990). *Counseling the culturally different: Theory and practice.* New York: Wiley.

Sutton, C., & Broken Nose, M. A. (1996). American Indian families: An overview. In M. McGoldrick, J. Giordano, & J. Pearce (Eds.), *Ethnicity and family therapy* (pp. 31–44). New York: Guilford Press.

Thompson, C., & Rudolph, L. (1992). *Counseling children* (3rd ed.). Pacific Grove, CA: Brooks/Cole.

Tomm, K. (1987a). Interventive interviewing: I. Strategizing as a fourth guideline for the therapist. *Family Process, 26,* 3–13.

Tomm, K. (1987b). Interventive interviewing: II. Reflexive questioning as a means to enable self-healing. *Family Process, 26,* 167–183.

Tomm, K. (1987c). Interventive interviewing: III. Intending to ask lineal, circular, strategic, or reflexive questions? *Family Process, 27,* 1–15.

Tomm, K., & Wright, L. (1979). Training in family therapy: Perceptual, conceptual, and executive skills. *Family Process, 18,* 227–250.

Trepper, T., & Barrett, M. (Eds.). (1986). *Treating incest: A multiple systems perspective.* New York: Haworth Press.

Truax, C., & Carkhoff, R. (1967). *Toward effective counseling and psychotherapy: Training and practice.* New York: Aldine de Gruyter.

Tuzlak, A., & Hillock, D. (1991). Single mothers and their children after divorce: A study of those "who make it." In J. Veevers (Ed.), *Continuity and change in marriage and the family* (pp. 303–313). Toronto: Holt, Rinehart & Winston of Canada.

Visher, W., & Visher, J. (1982). Stepfamilies in the 1980s. In J. Hansen & L. Messinger (Eds.), *Therapy with remarriage families* (pp. 105–119). Rockville, MD: Aspen Systems Corporation.

Wahler, R. (1980). The insular mother: Her problems in parent-child treatment. *Journal of Applied Behavior Analysis, 13,* 207–219.

Walker, L. (1984). *The battered woman syndrome.* New York: Springer.

Wallerstein, J. (1983). Children of divorce: The psychological tasks of the child. *American Journal of Orthopsychiatry, 53,* 230–243.

Wallerstein, J. (1985). The overburdened child: Some long-term consequences of divorce. *Social Work, 30,* 12–22.

Wallerstein, J., & Kelly, J. (1980). *Surviving the breakup: How children and parents cope with divorce.* New York: Basic Books.

Watchel, A. (1988). *The impact of child sexual abuse in developmental perspective: A model and literature review.* Ottawa: National Clearinghouse on Family Violence.

Watzlawick, P., Beavin, J., & Jackson, D. (1967). *Pragmatics of human communication*. New York: W. W. Norton.

Watzlawick, P., Weakland, J., & Fisch, R. (1974). *Change: Principles of problem formation and problem resolution*. New York: W. W. Norton.

Weakland, J., & Fry, W. (1974). Letters of mothers of schizophrenics. In D. Jackson (Ed.), *Communication, family, and marriage* (pp. 122–150). Palo Alto, CA: Science and Behavior Books.

Webster-Stratton, C. (1985). Comparisons of abusive and nonabusive families with conduct disordered children. *American Journal of Orthopsychiatry*, *55*(1), 59–69.

Webster-Stratton, C., & Hammond, M. (1990). Predictors of outcome in parent training for families with conduct-problem children. *Behavior Therapy*, *21*, 319–337.

Wegscheider, S. (1981). *Another chance: Hope and health for the alcoholic family*. Palo Alto, CA: Science and Behavior Books.

White, M. (1986). Negative explanation, restraint, and double description: A template for family therapy. *Family Process*, *25*, 160–184.

White, M. (1989). *The externalizing of the problem and the reauthoring of the lives and relationships*. Adelaide, Australia: Dulwich Centre Publishers.

Wilcoxon, A. (1991). Grandparents and grandchildren: An often-neglected relationship between significant others. In J. Veevers (Ed.), *Continuity and change in marriage and the family* (pp. 342–345). Toronto: Holt, Rinehart & Winston of Canada.

Wilson, G. (1995). Behavior therapy. In R. Corsini & D. Wedding (Eds.), *Current psychotherapies* (pp. 197–228). Itasca, IL: F. E. Peacock.

Wolfe, D. (1987). *Child abuse: Implications for child development and psychopathology*. Newbury Park, CA: Sage Publications.

Wolfe, D., Jaffe, P., Wilson, S., & Zak, L. (1988). A multivariate investigation of children's adjustment to family violence. In G. Hotaling, D. Finkelhor, J. Kirkpatrick, & M. Straus (Eds.), *Family abuse and its consequences* (pp. 228–243). Newbury Park, CA: Sage Publications.

Wolfe, D., Sandler, J., & Kaufman, K. (1981). A competency-based parent-training program for child abusers. *Journal of Consulting and Clinical Psychology*, *49*(5), 633–640.

Wood, K., & Geismar, L. (1986). *Families at risk: Treating the multiproblem family*. New York: Human Sciences Press.

Worden, M. (1994). *Family therapy basics*. Pacific Grove, CA: Brooks/Cole.

Wright, L., & Leahey, M. (1994). *Nurses and families: A guide to family assessment and intervention*. Philadelphia: F. A. Davis.

Yuille, J. (no date). *Training programs and procedures for interviewing and assessing sexually abused children: A review and annotated bibliography*. Ottawa: Health and Welfare Canada.

Zigler, E., & Hall, N. (1991). Child abuse in America: Past, present, and future. In D. Cicchetti & V. Carlson (Eds.), *Child maltreatment: Theory and research on the causes and consequences of child abuse and neglect* (pp. 38–75). Cambridge, MA: Harvard University Press.

Zurvain, S., & Grief, G. (1989). Normative and child-maltreating AFDC mothers. *Social Casework*, *7*(2), 76–84.

Name Index

Aguar, D., 13
Akman, D., 238, 239
Alexander, J., 14, 103, 105, 164
Allstetter Neufelt, A., 114
Aponte, H., 255, 256, 259
Armstrong, L., 205
Arnold, J., 14
Ayres, B., 16, 51, 102

Baer, D., 174
Bagley, C., 236, 238
Baldwin, D., 129
Baldwin, M., 32, 150, 151, 157, 158
Bandler, R., 109, 133, 140, 188
Barker, R., 120, 188, 193
Barnard, C., 29, 42, 48, 54, 82, 103, 105, 122, 147, 148, 150, 151, 152, 153, 158, 189, 206, 211, 264
Barrett, M., 202, 238
Baum, C., 14, 15, 164
Baynard, J., 245
Baynard, R., 245
Bean-Bayog, M., 258
Beavers, W., 129
Beavin, J., 43, 155
Becvar, D., 62, 63, 150, 178
Becvar, R., 62, 63, 150, 178
Beitchman, J., 238, 239
Bergin, A., 114
Bernard, D., 256
Berry, M., 17, 18
Bertalanffy, Von, 41
Beutler, L., 101, 114
Bishop, D., 52
Bishop, S., 129

Blick, L., 239
Blum, H., 77
Blythe, B., 264
Bodin, A., 155
Bograd, M., 248
Bolton, F., 75, 77, 252
Bolton, S., 75, 77, 252
Booth, C., 12, 90, 95, 141, 152, 156, 168, 182, 187
Bowen, M., 259
Bowlby, J., 202
Boyle, M., 77
Bramble, B., 21, 23
Braverman, L., 209
Breiner, J., 13
Breunlin, D., 63
Briere, J., 236
Brock, G., 29, 42, 48, 54, 82, 103, 105, 122, 147, 148, 150, 151, 152, 153, 158, 189, 206, 211, 264
Broken Nose, M. A., 48
Brooks, B., 238
Browne, A., 236, 238
Burden, D., 75, 77
Burgess, R., 232, 233

Caplan, P., 202
Carkhoff, R., 115, 119
Carter, B., 61, 62, 77, 201, 209
Caviola, A., 239
Celano, M., 27
Charles, G., 241
Cherlin, A., 204
Chess, Betty, 192
Cohn, A., 234
Cole, E., 66

Coleman, H., 11, 13, 93, 94, 114, 131, 168, 182, 188, 196, 207, 235, 241
Collins, D., 11, 13, 93, 94, 97, 114, 121, 131, 168, 182, 188, 196, 207, 235
Coontz, S., 21, 22
Corcoran, J., 52, 53, 54
Cormier, L., 118
Courtois, C. A., 236
Cox, M., 75
Cox, R., 75
Crichton, M., 40, 43
Crouter, A., 232, 233
Curtner-Smith, M. E., 64

daCosta, G., 238, 239
Davidson, N., 163, 171, 172, 173
Davis, K., 176, 177
Davis, L., 110
DeBaryshe, B., 12, 16, 164
Dell, P., 248
Denicola, J., 164, 165, 233
Diekstra, R., 241
Dishion, T., 233
Duncan, B., 93, 94, 114
Dutton, D., 248, 249
Duvall, E., 61, 62
Dye Holten, J., 205

Efron, D., 3
Egan, G., 131, 141
Eichler, M., 24, 54, 63, 74, 76, 77, 202, 208
Ellman, B., 203
Epstein, N., 52, 129
Everstine, D., 236

Subject Index